# Obligations to Future Generations

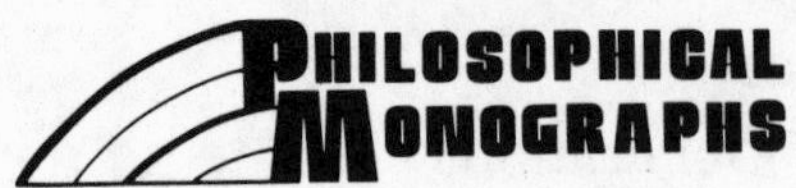
PHILOSOPHICAL
MONOGRAPHS

# Obligations to Future Generations

*Edited by*
*R. I. SIKORA and BRIAN BARRY*



*Philosophical Monographs*
Second Annual Series

Temple University Press
Philadelphia

**Library of Congress Cataloging in Publication Data**

Main entry under title:

Obligations to future generations.

(Philosophical monographs)
1. Social ethics. 2. Ethics. 3. Human ecology–Moral and religious aspects. I. Sikora, Richard I., 1927- II. Barry, Brian M. III. Series: Philosophical monographs (Philadelphia, 1978- )
HM216.015 170 78-5495
ISBN 0-87722-132-4
ISBN 0-87722-128-6 pbk.

Temple University Press, Philadelphia 19122

Published 1978
Printed in the United States of America
ISSN: 0363-8243

# Contents

# Introduction

Until the development of nuclear weapons it seemed obvious to almost everyone that mankind had an almost unlimited future. The question of whether there could be an obligation to make sacrifices to ensure the continued existence of the human race didn't arise because no one thought that any such sacrifice would ever be necessary. However, that the human race will unquestionably survive no longer seems obvious or perhaps even probable. Now it seems clear that any number of events could occur which would be a threat to human survival. Suppose there is a conflict between two countries, one of which has nuclear weapons and the other not; this could lead to a major war in which all mankind could be destroyed. If the side with nuclear capability, for instance, were losing using only conventional arms there would be an almost irresistible temptation to avert defeat by using its nuclear weapons even if doing so meant a risk of killing everyone alive. But one would be far more likely to accept such a risk if the question of the prevention of future generations is taken to be morally irrelevant than if one thought that their prevention would be morally wrong. Large population increases are also a threat to mankind's survival. Paradoxically, increasing the world's population may decrease the number of people who exist in the future because the more people there are the more potentially lethal pollution there will be, the more danger of conflict over limited resources there is likely to be, etc., so that the more people there are, the greater the threat to the existence of future generations will be. The question then of whether or not it is wrong to prevent the existence of future generations is not an idle academic issue but bears directly on very real contemporary problems.

In the last analysis, the central question seems to be whether and to what degree it can be morally incumbent on us to make sacrifices to bring happy people into the world or to avoid preventing them from being brought into the world. The papers in the first part of this collection all deal with this question in one way or another. The first papers answer it negatively; the others answer it affirmatively, being grouped roughly in terms of how strong an affirmative stand they take.

Thomas Schwartz holds not merely that it is in no way wrong *per se* to prevent the existence of happy people but that it is permissible to use resources in such a way that there will be a much less happy world population in the future than there would have been otherwise. His central premises are: (1) that to do something morally wrong, some *particular person* must be less well off than he would have been otherwise; and (2) (following Derek Parfit) that if we deplete our resources rather than conserving them, *different particular people* will be born so that no one (or almost no one) will be worse off through our having squandered our resources. Many philosophers would regard his conclusion as so obviously untenable that rather than accept it they would reject (1). Another consequence that follows from these two premises is that a prospective mother (in a case where the wrong time of conception could result in having a deformed child, for instance) would have no obligation whatsoever (aside from whatever effect her action would have on other people) to choose a time of conception that would lead to her having a happy baby rather than another baby who would have a life barely worth living.

Mary Warren also holds that we have no moral obligation to create happy people (although she doesn't take Schwartz's extreme view on the consumption of natural resources). She attempts to reconcile the view that there is an obligation *not* to make unhappy possible people actual with the view that there is no obligation to make *happy* possible persons actual. She distinguishes possible persons who will never exist from those who will exist at some time in the future (and who consequently already exist in the timeless sense) and argues that our moral concern should be confined to those people who exist in the timeless sense and whose welfare we can influence. She thinks that: (1) this principle allows us to be concerned with the welfare of possible *un-*

*happy* people while (2) allowing us not to be concerned with the welfare of possible *happy* people. William Anglin argues that she is mistaken in (1)–that you can't move a possible unhappy person into the category of timeless person to get an obligation regarding him, and then move him out again because his existence would be wretched. Either a person exists in the timeless sense or he does not.

Jan Narveson, like Warren, holds that it is wrong to increase the total utility by adding population at the expense of those who would otherwise exist. But unlike Warren, he sees that this principle is not adequate taken by itself. He adds that if you are going to conceive a child and if one time of conception will result in a happier child being born than another time, you have an obligation to choose the time when the happier child would be born; but he modifies Parfit's principle drastically by holding that you have this obligation only if other things are equal. Unless other people would benefit by the prospective mother's having the happier child, she only has an obligation to choose the time of conception which would result in the happier child being born if doing so requires no sacrifice whatever from her. He supposes that this complex principle can be derived from the view that utilitarianism applies to everyone who exists in the timeless sense.

Jonathan Bennett agrees with Narveson that we have no obligation to prevent the extinction of mankind (except insofar as this would affect actual persons) but he would be willing to make sacrifices, and even to fight, for the preservation of mankind because of his strong interest in the completion of certain human projects. In order to avoid commitments which might have counterintuitive consequences he makes no appeal to principles or even to an interest in the completion of projects with certain general characteristics. His justification for being prepared to fight for the preservation of mankind lies rather in the fact that he has an intense interest in the completion of certain specific projects of the species of which he is a member. Like Bernard Williams, he thinks that an individual is entitled to assign far more importance to the projects with which he is concerned than utilitarianism would allow, but unlike Williams, he stresses the specificity of certain of these projects.

Robert Scott defends a position somewhere between the view that population policies should maximize the *average* happiness level and the view that they should maximize the *total* happiness level (classical utilitarianism). His principle is designed to avoid the key objection to a simple compromise between these views—that it is wrong to assign any negative value at all to adding happy people who will lower the average solely by having a lower happiness average than those who already exist. He deviates from these two views in that he counts the interests of future people less heavily than those of people who already exist. While this enables him to avoid some counterintuitive consequences of the other two theories, that the interests of *all* future persons (including those whose existence is inevitable) should be discounted is hard to accept. L. W. Sumner attacks average utilitarianism on the grounds that it is incompatible with timeless utilitarianism, and he defends classical utilitarianism on the grounds that it can be derived from timeless utilitarianism.

R. I. Sikora argues (1) (in contrast with Warren, Narveson and Sumner) that timeless utilitarianism is incomplete with respect to the question of whether we have an obligation to add happy people to the world; (2) that the most plausible of the views that we have no obligation to make sacrifices to add happy people as well as the views that we *do* have such obligations imply what Parfit calls the repugnant conclusion, and (3) that our moral intuitions on the question of when it is permissible *per se* to add to the world large groups of people some of whom will have wretched lives strongly suggest that classical utilitarianism is correct on matters of population size, and that, despite objections by Bennett, these intuitions are totally incompatible with the view that there is no obligation whatsoever to add happy people to the world. He puts forward a meta-ethical theory which makes our obligations a function of what we would choose if we were epistemically rational, contending that it provides a better support than other meta-ethical theories for the claim that we have a *prima facie* obligation to add happy people; and that regardless of what "obligation" means, once it is admitted that you would do a thing if you were epistemically rational, the case for doing it is unassailable.

One of the most encouraging things about the debate as to whether it is or is not in any way wrong *per se* to prevent the existence of happy people is that it has become clear that the question is not, as J. J. C. Smart and many others once supposed, beyond the scope of rational considerations. It turns out that both positions commit one to all sorts of consequences in the rest of one's ethical system, and that frequently one's intuitions on these consequences are stronger than those on the original issue. There is fortunately far more agreement on the possible consequences than there has been on the original question, and in fact—what seems almost never to occur in philosophy—some philosophers have been led to change their minds. This gives us some reason to hope that there will be increasing agreement, though there will always be room for self-serving rationalizations or for a person with systematically atypical intuitions.

The remaining three papers lay less emphasis on the questions involving the existence, size and composition of future generations that are discussed in the rest of the volume. They are primarily addressed to the question what, if anything, we owe future generations, assuming that they will exist. Mary Williams's paper attacks the common notion that the interests of future people should be subject to discounting at some standard rate and puts forward an ingenious argument in favor of using renewable resources at a rate that is compatible with maintaining the maximum sustainable yield. Gregory Kavka proposes that, whatever we owe contemporaries to whom we are bound by no special obligations ("strangers"), we also owe those who are to come in the future. The latter part of his paper introduces some population questions and he concludes that among the things we may owe future generations are better contraception and the end of traditional pronatalist norms. The paper by Brian Barry also brings together the problems of intergenerational and international relations, developing an attack on the notion that justice or injustice cannot be predicated of relationships where the "circumstances of justice" do not apply. After a detailed examination of David Hume's presentation of the doctrine he turns to its revival by John Rawls and suggests that Rawls's theory is an uneasy amalgam of a Humean structure, in which the doctrine of the circumstances of justice plays an essential role, and a Kantian one with which the doctrine cannot be accommodated. He concludes with a proposal of his own.

# *Part I*: Should Intrinsic Value Be Placed on the Preservation of Mankind?

# Obligations to Posterity

*THOMAS SCHWARTZ*

You've heard it said that we owe certain things to posterity, remote as well as near. These things include an adequate supply of natural resources, a clean environment, a healthy and varied gene pool, a rich cultural heritage and a limit on population size.

I disagree: Whatever we may owe ourselves or our near posterity, *we've no obligation extending indefinitely or even terribly far into the future to provide any widespread, continuing benefits to our descendants*. The contrary claim rests on an identifiable fallacy.

Both this fallacy and my own position are most easily illustrated in the case of population control. I begin, then, by arguing that we've no obligation to our distant descendants severely to limit population growth—to adopt, let us say, a *severely restrictive* population policy in preference to a more or less *laissez-faire* policy—even granting that uncontrolled procreation would beget a drop in the quality of human life.

### *1. The Case of the Disappearing Beneficiaries*

The claim that we owe it to our distant descendants to restrict population growth rests on something like this assumption:

> It is reasonable to expect that the (severely) restrictive population policy would somehow benefit our distant descendants, while the (more or less) laissez-faire policy

> would somehow harm them, or at least deprive them of some significant benefit they would otherwise have enjoyed.

I will argue that this assumption is false if interpreted so as to be relevant to the moral assessment of population policies.

The assumption can be interpreted two ways:

> *Way 1.* If the laissez-faire policy were adopted, it is likely that at least some of our distant descendants would lack some significant benefits which those same descendants would have enjoyed under the restrictive policy.

*Objection*: Suppose the laissez-faire policy has been adopted. Consider those of our distant descendants whose lives will have been significantly affected thereby. Let *X* be any one of them. Then it is quite certain that *X* would *not have existed* under the restrictive policy and hence will not lack any benefit he would have enjoyed under the restrictive policy.

For *X* to be one of those possible individuals, say *Y*, who would have existed under the restrictive policy, it is not enough that *Y* would have had *X*'s name, else I'd be identical to all the Thomas Schwartzes in the world. Nor is it sufficient that *Y* would have had *X*'s ancestry, else my son and daughter would be identical. What *would* insure that *Y* would have been the same person as *X*—that *X* would have been *Y*, had the restrictive policy been adopted?

That's notoriously controversial. Happily, we've no need to enter the controversy. For it is quite certain that no one born under the restrictive policy would have been the same person as *X*, by *any* plausible criterion of personal identity.

The restrictive population policy would have brought about a future world different from the future world of the adopted laissez-faire policy, and *X* is one of those significantly affected by the choice of the laissez-faire policy. So the circumstances of *X*'s life would not have been fully replicated under the restrictive policy. *X*'s parents might not have existed under the restrictive policy. Had they both existed, they might not have met. Had they met, they might not have mated. Had they mated, they might not have procreated. Even had they procreated, their offspring, *Y*, would have been conceived under conditions at least a little different from those of *X*'s conception.

But that makes it virtually impossible for *Y* to have developed from the *same pair of gametes* as *X*, hence virtually impossible for *Y* to have had the *same genotype* as *X*. After all, trivial circumstantial differences could easily have determined whether intercourse, ejaculation or conception occurred at any given time. And the most minute circumstantial differences would have affected *which particular spermatazoon fertilized the ovum* and *what particular pattern of meiosis was involved in the production of either gamete*. Let the circumstances surrounding *Y*'s conception be as similar to those surrounding *X*'s conception as one can realistically suppose, given my assumption about *X* and *Y*. Still, *Y* would have been no more likely than *X*'s non-twin sibling to have had *X*'s genotype.

The combination of a different genotype and a different environment insure all manner of further difference: *Y* would not have been composed of the *same matter* as *X*, and he would not have *looked the same* as *X*. He would not have had the *same beliefs or attitudes* as *X*, and he would not have had the *same capacities*, the *same character* or the *same personality* as *X*. As a result, *Y* would not have had the *same psyche* as *X*–by any sensible standard of sameness of psyche. Neither would *Y* have fulfilled the *same social roles and relationships* as *X*.

In sum, *Y* would have differed from *X* in origin (different gametes), in content (different matter, different mind) and in basic design (different genotype), and he would have been shaped by a different environment to perform different functions. We have no more reason to identify *Y* with *X* than we have to identify siblings raised apart with each other.

To put the point another way: Let the *controlled population* comprise those possible future people who would be born under the restrictive population policy and significantly affected by the choice of that policy. Let the *uncontrolled population* comprise those possible future people who would be born under the laissez-faire policy and significantly affected by the choice of that policy. These two possible populations will quickly start to diverge and eventually diverge completely (I have, in effect, argued), so that no member of either will belong to the other.

Lest one think that the rate of divergence will taper off, precluding complete divergence, or that complete divergence won't occur within the remotely foreseeable future, it is worth noting that once the two possible populations begin to diverge, the rate of divergence will increase exponentially.

To see why, let us divide the future, somewhat arbitrarily, into generations 1, 2, 3, etc. Let $p(i)$ be the probability that a randomly selected member of the uncontrolled population born in the $i$th generation also would belong to the controlled population. Such a person won't belong to the controlled population unless both his parents belong. But the probability that his mother belongs is $p(i-1)$, and similarly for his father. Therefore, if membership by his mother in the controlled population and membership by his father in the controlled population are independent events, then the probability that *both* his parents belong to the controlled population is $p(i-1)^2$, so that:

$$(*) \quad p(i) \leqslant p(i-1)^2.$$

To be sure, membership by his mother in the controlled population and membership by his father in the controlled population might not be completely independent events. As I've argued, though, if $X$ belongs to the uncontrolled population, it is extremely unlikely that $X$ also belongs to the controlled population, *even if* both $X$'s parents belong, circumstances being sufficiently different to preclude conception involving the very gametes from which $X$ sprang. So $(*)$ still is eminently plausible. If anything, $p(i)$ is *far less* than $p(i-1)^2$.

But according to $(*)$, as soon as the two possible populations diverge a little, they will continue to diverge at an exponentially increasing rate: As soon as $p(i)$ is even a little less than 1, $p(i)$ will rapidly approach zero. For example, if $p(i) = .8$, $(*)$ implies that $p(i+6) \leqslant .0000005$. This means that even if, after several generations, there still are fully 8 chances in 10 that a member of the uncontrolled population also belongs to the controlled population, the chances of this happening six generations later are at most one in two million. And if, as I've suggested, $p(i)$ really is a lot *less* than $p(i-1)^2$, then it shouldn't take even six additional generations for complete divergence to obtain.

*Way 2.* Although none of our distant descendants would exist under both the restrictive and the laissez-faire population policies, the society that comprises our distant de-

> scendants—the *future society*, for short—would itself exist under both policies. One and the same *society* can have different *individual members* under different circumstances, actual and hypothetical. And while no *individual member* of the future society would be better off under the restrictive policy than *he* would be under the laissez-faire policy, the *future society itself* would be better off. Its standard of living would be higher, its civilization superior.

*Objection*: Let us concede that one and the same future society would exist under both the restrictive and the laissez-faire policies, although it had none of the same members under the two policies. Still, this "society" would not be better off under the restrictive policy *in any morally relevant sense*. The fact that one policy would in some sense be better than another for something called a society, although in no sense better for any *person*, constitutes no *moral* ground for prescribing the former policy.

Some of those now alive may feel an urge to insure that the future society will be an appealing one in which to live, with an admirable civilization. And if sufficiently many people are minded this way, that fact may constitute some sort of justification for some sort of restrictive population policy. But such a policy would be no favor to our *distant descendants*. *They* could not reproach us for having adopted a laissez-faire policy instead. The beneficiaries of the restrictive policy would be *ourselves*—those of us, anyway, who get their kicks from the prospect of a flourishing future society.

## 2. *The Fallacy*

The claim that we owe it to our distant descendants to restrict population growth owes its appeal to a special fallacy of ambiguity—the Fallacy of Beneficiary-Conflation, to give it a name.

Consider the assumption that our distant descendants would be better off under the restrictive population policy than under the laissez-faire policy. To contend that this provides some support for the position that we owe it to our distant descendants to adopt the restrictive policy is to contend that a certain proposition of the form:

(B) D's would be better off under R than under L.

provides some support for the corresponding proposition of this form:

(O) We owe it to D's to adopt R in preference to L (supposing both are feasible options).

Here, "D's" can be construed as "all the D's," "some of the D's," "a large number of D's," "the set of D's" or whatnot. And "better off" admits of innumerable constructions.

But however these questions of interpretation be decided, another ambiguity remains. (B) can be interpreted two ways:

(B1) Those who are *in fact* D's would be better off under R than those *very same individuals* would be under L.

(B2) Those who would be D's if R were adopted would be better off under R than those who would be D's would be under L if L were adopted.

Surely only (B1) would, if plausible, provide any support for (O). But in the population case, only (B2) has any plausibility. So, in the population case, the use of (B) to support (O) rests on an ambiguity: (B) would, if plausible, provide some support for (O), but under a different interpretation from that which renders (B) plausible. In general, when (B) owes its plausibility to (B1) rather than (B2), one cannot use (B) to support (O).

Here is another way to look at what is basically the same error:

Statements to the effect that we owe such and such benefits to our distant descendants apparently are applications of the following principle, or some watered down version of it:

(ODD) We owe it to our distant descendants to bequeath to them the means for the best possible life.

There are two ways to interpret (ODD), a weak and a strong way:

(WODD) We owe it to our distant descendants to insure that the distant future population, *however it be constituted*, has the means for the best life of which *it* is capable.

(SODD) We owe it to our distant descendants *both* to insure that the distant future population, however it be constituted,

> has the means for the best life of which it is capable, *and* to insure that the distant future population *is so constituted* as to be capable of enjoying the best life of which *any possible* distant future population is capable.

Where (WODD) just enjoins us to protect and improve the *circumstances* of the distant future population—the non-human resources available to our distant descendants, that is—(SODD) enjoins us, in addition, to protect and improve the *composition* of the distant future population.

We may wish to water down these principles by adding various qualifications, by eliminating or weakening the superlative, or by stipulating that the alleged obligation is defeasible. But there will remain this important difference between the two principles: Only (SODD) tells us to do anything about the composition of the future population. As a result, only (SODD) can prescribe the restrictive population policy.

Depending on whether and how it is watered down, (SODD) might also prescribe questionable policies of selective breeding, infanticide or sterilization. If not, then even (SODD), once watered, might be too weak to prescribe the restrictive population policy.

If it is strong enough (properly qualified) to prescribe the restrictive population policy, then (SODD) is *too* strong.

To see why, imagine a choice between a (severely) restrictive population policy, leading to a distant future population R, and a (more or less) laissez-faire policy, leading to a distant future population L. Suppose R and L have no members in common—an eminently realistic assumption, we now know. And suppose R would enjoy a better life under the restrictive policy (measured any way you like) than L would enjoy under the laissez-faire policy (else there'd be no semblance of a case for the restrictive policy).

Then (WODD) allows us to adopt either policy, while (SODD) requires us to adopt the restrictive policy. According to (SODD), we owe it to our distant descendants to adopt the restrictive policy.

But suppose we *in fact* adopt the laissez-faire policy instead. Then L comprises our distant descendants. So if (SODD) is true, we've wronged the members of L (some of them, anyway), hence denied them some benefit they would have enjoyed (or could reasonably be expected to have enjoyed) under the restrictive policy. But we've done no such thing, since no member of L would even have existed under the restrictive policy. Consequently, (SODD) is not generally true.

### 3. *The General Argument*

Let P be any policy designed to provide some significant, widespread, continuing benefits to posterity, near and remote. P might be a long-range policy designed to limit population growth, to keep man's natural environment clean, to conserve natural resources, to maintain and possibly to improve the gene pools of certain species, to foster the arts and basic sciences, or to do any number of other things. I contend that we do not owe it to our distant descendants to adopt P.

With P interpreted as a restrictive population policy, I have argued:

> (1) Were P not adopted, our distant descendants significantly affected by P's non-adoption would be people who would not have existed had P been adopted.

This remains true when P is taken to be any other long-range policy designed to provide significant, widespread, continuing benefits to our descendants, close and distant.

The argument is the same as in the population case: Compare the world as it would be were P adopted–the *plus-P world*, let us call it–with the world as it would be were P *not* adopted–the *minus-P world*. Because P would have a widespread, continuing impact, human procreation would generally take place under somewhat different conditions in the two worlds. So if *X* is any significantly affected future denizen of the minus-P world, the conditions of *X*'s conception are not fully replicated in the plus-P world. Even if *X*'s parents met, mated and procreated in the plus-P world (a big "if"), this would occur in an environment sufficiently different from that of the minus-P world to insure that their offspring developed out of a pair of gametes different from *X*'s, hence that their offspring had a genotype different from *X*'s. That plus a somewhat different environment would result in further differences–different matter, different appearance, different personality, different capacities, different character, different beliefs, different attitudes, different social roles. And once the affected populations of the two worlds begin to diverge, their divergence will accelerate exponentially.

So much for proposition (1). Here is how we get from (1) to my conclusion that we don't owe it to our distant descendants to adopt P:

(2) If *A* has an obligation to *B* to do something, then *A*'s not doing it would wrong *B*. [premise]

(3) If *A*'s not doing something would wrong *B*, then, were *A* not to do that thing, *B* would lack some significant benefit he would have enjoyed (or could reasonably be expected to have enjoyed) had *A* done it. [premise]

(4) Were *A* not to do something, and were *B* not significantly affected thereby, then *B* would not lack any significant benefit he would have enjoyed (or could reasonably be expected to have enjoyed) had *A* done that thing. [premise]

(5) Were P not adopted, none of our distant descendants *not* significantly affected thereby would lack any significant benefit he would have enjoyed (or could reasonably be expected to have enjoyed) had P been adopted. [from (4)]

(6) Were P not adopted, none of our distant descendants significantly *affected* thereby would lack any significant benefit he would have enjoyed (or could reasonably be expected to have enjoyed) had P been adopted. [from (1)]

(7) Were P not adopted, none of our distant descendants would lack any significant benefit he would have enjoyed (or could reasonably be expected to have enjoyed) had P been adopted. [from (5) and (6)]

(8) Our not adopting P would not wrong any of our distant descendants. [from (3) and (7)]

(9) Therefore, we have no obligation to any of our distant descendants to adopt P. [from (2) and (8)]

### 4. *On What We Owe to Whom*

Could there be other grounds for adopting P?

I don't see how we can be *morally required* to adopt P unless we owe it to *someone* to adopt P–unless our *not* adopting P would, in some broad sense, *wrong* someone. True, something can be morally *permissible* without being morally *required*. But if (as is likely) P involves some coercive intervention by the state (taxation, for example), I don't see how P can even be morally permissible unless we owe it to someone to adopt P (or at least to pursue some objective toward which P is one of several optional means).

Might we owe it to ourselves or our near posterity to adopt P?

P would provide significant, widespread, continuing benefits to our distant descendants. So if the benefits we and our near posterity would get from P are similar to those our distant descendants would get from P, then it is likely that some *less costly* policy would provide just us and our near posterity with the same benefits. And so long as such an alternative policy is available, I don't see how we can owe it to ourselves or our near posterity to adopt the more costly P instead.

I suggest that we might owe it *to each other* to adopt P, not because we'd get from P certain benefits similar to those our distant descendants would get, but for this reason:

Many of us want mankind to prosper and to continue to prosper on into the distant future. Among those who feel this way, each would rather that everyone contribute to this goal than that no one contribute. But apart from moral considerations, each would rather that everyone *else* contribute and *he not* contribute than that *everyone* contribute. It's like taxes: Each of us prefers everyone paying to no one paying. But apart from moral considerations and fear of punishment, each prefers everyone but himself paying to everyone paying. In the case at hand: Many of us want our remote posterity to live in a clean, commodious, well-stocked world. Of those who feel this way, each would rather that everyone (himself included) bear a reasonable share of the cost of achieving these shared goals than that the goals not be achieved. But apart from moral considerations, each *most* prefers that everyone *else* bear the cost and he bear none of it.

Other things equal, however, it would be *unfair* for one who shares these goals not to bear a fair share of the cost of achieving them—just as it would be unfair for a citizen not to pay his taxes, for someone who likes clean public roads to throw trash out his car window, or for a member of a tug-of-war team to feign pulling. In general:

> Other things equal, if every member of some group would rather that all members help achieve a certain shared objec-

> tive than that none (or almost none) help, then it would be unfair to the others for one member not to help while the others (most of them, anyway) helped.

There are exceptions to this principle: The objective in question might be intrinsically illicit (lynching a Negro); its achievement might impose significant, undeserved external costs on someone (consumers, in the case of monopoly pricing); or a member of the group in question might merit an exemption (an elderly, infirm passenger in a stalled car that is being pushed by the other, more robust passengers). Still, there often is an obligation to observe the principle—to pull one's weight, to co-operate, not to be a free rider, not to take unfair advantage of one's fellows. One owes this obligation, when it exists, to those others who are helping to achieve the objective at issue.

So those who would like our distant descendants to enjoy a clean, commodious, well-stocked world just may owe it to their like-minded contemporaries to contribute to these goals.

# Do Potential People Have Moral Rights?

*MARY WARREN*

By a potential person I shall mean an entity which is not now a person but which is capable of developing into a person, given certain biologically and/or technologically possible conditions. This is admittedly a narrower sense than some would attach to the term "potential." After all, people of the twenty-fifth century, if such there will be, are in some sense potential people now, even though the specific biological entities from which they will develop, i.e., the particular gametes or concepti, do not yet exist. For there do exist, in the reproductive capacities of people now living and in the earth's resources, conditions adequate eventually to produce these future people, provided of course that various possible catastrophes are avoided. Indeed, in *some* sense of "potential" there have been countless billions of potential people from the beginning of time. But I am concerned not with such remote potentialities but with presently existing entities which are capable of developing into people. The question I want to ask is whether or not the fact that an entity is a potential person is, in itself, grounds for ascribing moral rights to that entity, in particular the right to be permitted or enabled to become a person.

It is worth noting that potential people need not be genetically human, though all those which we know of at present obviously are. If a serum were invented which would cause kitten embryos to develop into intelligent, self-aware, language-using beings, as in Michael Tooley's example,[1] then kitten embryos would have become potential people. True, the actualization of that potentiality would be dependent upon technological intervention in a way in which that of a normal human fetus is not; but it would not be a less genuine potentiality for that reason, any more than a human fetus which will survive only if its mother is given a drug to prevent miscarriage is not therefore a potential person. Potential personhood is the capacity to become a person, regardless of whether or not that capacity is likely to be realized. On the other hand, when I speak of *merely* potential people, I shall mean those which, though they have that capacity, will in fact never become people.

Now the concept of a person is fuzzy enough that it is notoriously difficult to say just when in the development of a human organism it becomes a person. I believe that a human being does not become a person until sometime after its birth,[2] but I will not need to assume here that this claim is true. If human beings become people sometime after conception but before birth, as many people believe, then my question is relevant to the moral status of abortion before but not after that time. The question is surely relevant to the moral status of abortion at *some* stages of pregnancy, since it is clear that a person is not present from the moment of conception; for the very least one must be able to say of a person is that it is a sentient being, which a conceptus in the first few weeks of its existence is not.

Almost as difficult as the question of when a potential person becomes a person is that of when it becomes appropriate to speak of there being even a potential person. There is at least a potential person from conception onward, but what about before conception? Is a male or female gamete a potential person? By itself, I think not, though it might be if we were able to reproduce parthenogenetically. But I see no reason why a viable sexually mixed *pair* of gametes should not be considered a potential person. For as R. M. Hare points out, it does not seem to make a crucial conceptual difference that before conception the genetic material capable of becoming a person is in two locations, whereas afterwards it is in one.[3]

Hare has recently argued, in effect, that potential people do have a prima facie right to be permitted to become people, although he prefers to express this claim by saying that it is morally wrong, other things being equal, to prevent potential people from becoming actual.[4] He follows Tooley, and I will follow him, in calling this claim the potentiality principle. Because he believes that gametes are already potential people, and that fetuses are still only potential people, Hare concludes that the truth of the potentiality principle means that not just abortion, but contraception, and even the decision not to procreate at all, are all prima facie immoral (p. 212).

This sounds like a rather drastic conclusion; but Hare goes on to explain that it is less sweeping in its practical moral consequences than one might suppose, since the prima facie obligation to permit potential people to become actual can be overridden in any of a large number of ways. For example, he would accept as reasons adequate to justify abortion, that the pregnancy endangers the woman's health or fertility, that the abortion would permit the occurrence of another pregnancy with a better chance of resulting in a normal child, or that the parents already have as many children as they can adequately care for (p. 218). Hence, although the potentiality principle would imply that abortion, contraception and total abstinence are all "prima facie and in general wrong in default of sufficient countervailing reasons" (p. 221), it would not prevent them from being justified in a wide range of circumstances.

Consequently, one might suppose that in practice Hare's position in support of the potentiality principle is not strikingly different from the theoretically opposing position, that potential people as such have no moral rights, but that there are good independent reasons for having children and trying to avoid having abortions. And one might wonder why, if the right of a potential person to be permitted to become a person is so easily overridden, it matters whether or not there is such a right. I shall argue not only that the potentiality principle is false but that this fact has important moral consequences. It means, among other things, that in most cases no moral justification at all is required for the decision to remain celibate, use contraceptives, or to have an abortion. This conclusion makes a difference to the way we ought to treat women seeking abortions, men or women seeking contraceptives or sterilization, and people who choose to remain permanently childless. Furthermore, the failure of the potentiality principle has an important bearing upon our long-term population policies and upon the moral status of the practice of raising animals for slaughter. Properly understood, however, it does not in any way lessen our moral obligations to future generations of human beings, whose rights, I shall argue, do not depend upon their present existence as potential people.

The argument which originally persuaded me that the potentiality principle is false is an intuitive one, and runs as follows. Imagine that you are approached by alien scientists, who propose to create billions of replicas of you, that is billions of new people with your genetic code, by separating the cells of your body and using each to clone a new individual. Being moral, the aliens first ask your permission for this operation, assuring you that all these new people will be given the chance to lead reasonably happy lives on some distant planet where they will not contribute to the earth's overpopulation problems. My intuition is that you would have absolutely no moral obligation to agree to such a proposal at the cost of your own life; and indeed I think that you would not be obligated to agree even if they were to promise eventually to reconstitute you as good as new. Hence I think that any right to life which a potential person as such might have is at least billions of times as weak as that of an actual person.[5]

Unfortunately, arguments of this sort, which appeal to our intuitions regarding unusual or bizarre situations, are never conclusive. Proponents of the potentiality principle may well have intuitions different from my own, and even if they do not the case is still not closed, since our intuitions about such cases, while they may serve to clarify (the consequences of) our existing moral convictions, cannot establish what our moral convictions *ought* to be. The potentiality principle, like any specific moral claim, must ultimately be defended or refuted on the basis of some overall conception of the nature of morality.

In what follows I will try to explain why the potentiality principle cannot be true. In part 1, I will examine Hare's argument for the principle, which is based on his interpretation of the Golden Rule, but which I will argue rests upon a confusion. In parts 2 and 3 I will consider whether it is possible to argue for the potentiality principle in some way which does not involve this confusion, and present a very brief sketch of the type of moral theory which rules out such an argument. And in part 4 I will explore a few of the moral consequences of the failure of the potentiality principle and warn against one apparent consequence which in fact does not follow.

## *1. The Argument from the Golden Rule*

Hare argues that we can derive a proof of the potentiality principle—that it is wrong, other things being equal, to prevent a potential person from becoming an actual person—from a natural extension of one version of the Golden Rule, i.e., that we should do to others as we wish them to do to us. "It is," he says, "a logical extension of this form of argument to say that we should do to others what *we are glad was* done to us" (p. 212). As it happens, most of us are glad that the pregnancy which resulted in our own birth was not terminated by abortion. We are also, presumably, glad that our parents met, copulated, and conceived us in the first place. Hence, he concludes, it is a consequence of this extended Golden Rule that we have a prima facie obligation not to terminate any pregnancy which would otherwise result in the birth of a person who will be like us in being glad she or he was not aborted, and also a duty not to use contraceptives or to refrain entirely from procreating (p. 212).

I would argue, however, that even if we accept the Golden Rule as a sound moral principle, we cannot extend it to establish that we have even a very weak obligation to treat potential people in the way in which we are glad that the ones which eventually became ourselves were treated. For the extended Golden Rule, which prescribes that we behave toward others in ways in which we are glad that others once behaved toward us, is either irrelevant to the treatment of potential people, or–if it is so interpreted as to include them–incoherent.

As it stands, the principle that, other things being equal, we should treat others as we are glad that we were treated appears to be irrelevant to the treatment of potential people. For personal pronouns like "we" refer to people; we are essentially people if we are essentially anything at all. Therefore, if fetuses and gametes are not people, then we were never fetuses or gametes, though one might say that we emerged from them. The fetus which later *became* you was not *you*, because you did not exist at that time. It was not you for the same reason that your dead body will not, or that your living body with the cognitive and perceptual centers of the brain permanently destroyed would not, be you; namely, that you are a particular *person*, not just a particular human organism regardless of its stage of development or degeneration. So if it had been aborted nothing whatever would have been done to *you*, since you would never have existed. You cannot coherently be glad that you were not aborted, since in order for there to be a you at all, you cannot possibly have been aborted (during the relevant interval). And therefore the Golden Rule as Hare extends it does not proscribe abortion, much less contraception or celibacy.

But perhaps this is a problem which could be solved by a little rewording. Mightn't Hare just as well have extended the Golden Rule to cover what you are glad was done to *the potential person from which you emerged*? If the first extension is logical, mightn't this one be equally acceptable? I think not, at least not if the duties, obligations and wrongs associated with this principle are meant to be duties or obligations toward or wrongs done to potential people. For potential people, as such, are not the sort of entity toward which it is possible to have moral obligations. The very notion of acting wrongly toward a merely potential person, that is one which will never become a person, is incoherent. For who is it that is being wronged when a potential person is prevented from becoming a person? Absolutely no one. To maintain otherwise is grotesquely to misunderstand what a merely potential person is.

Merely potential people, or rather the people they might have become, are not, just as possible worlds are not, things which exist, as it were, alongside the actual world in a super-space which includes not only the actual but the possible. Or at any rate we have absolutely no reason to think that they are. They are just things which might have existed, that is, which at some time were empirically possible, but which in fact do not, never did, and never will exist. And what does not exist and never will cannot be harmed or wronged or have its rights violated.

Why is this? Because harming someone, behaving wrongly toward someone, and violating someone's rights are all extensional rather than intentional concepts. I can think about Pegasus, but I can't catch him, beat him, be unfair to him, or violate his rights. Mythical entities, which never did, do not now and never will exist, have no rights to be violated; and we have no duties or obligations toward such entities, simply because such entities cannot be acted upon in any way whatever, other than illusorily, through the intentional medium of thought.

Now Hare maintains that this sort of objection, i.e., any attempt to show that for one conceptual reason or another (he mentions the individuation problem) merely potential people cannot be the victims of moral wrongdoing, cannot be correct, because,

> It would be strange if there were an act whose very performance made it impossible for it to be wrong. But if the objection were correct, the act of aborting a possible person would be such an act;

by preventing the existence of the object of the wrongdoing, it would remove its wrongness. This seems too easy a way of avoiding wrongdoing. (p. 219)

It is clear that the language in this passage is prejudicial, since if abortion is not prima facie wrong then it is inappropriate to speak of *removing* the wrongness. But more importantly, I think that there is a simple but fatal confusion behind the notion that one can act wrongly toward a merely potential person. Why does it tend to seem "too easy" to say that to abort a potential person cannot be to act wrongly toward someone *because it prevents the very existence of the person supposedly wronged*? I suggest it is because we tend to make an error not unlike the one which Bishop Berkeley made when he argued that it is impossible to conceive of an object existing without being conceived by anyone, since to (try to) conceive of such an object is still to conceive of an object which is conceived of by someone, namely you.[6]

The error is that of illegitimately smuggling ourselves, the conceivers, into our conceptions of states of affairs which by definition exclude us. Berkeley's Hylas could not imagine a state of affairs consisting of there being an object of which no one conceives, because he could not imagine *himself* as not being part of the picture. He tried to conceive of an unconceived object, but succeeded only in conceiving of himself conceiving of an object, which then of course was not unconceived at all. Similarly, I think that when we try to imagine the state of affairs consisting of our never having existed at all, what we in fact tend to imagine is rather that we, the existing people that we are, are suddenly to have our very existence snatched away from us, as in the science fiction plot in which a time traveler "eliminates" someone by seeing to it that that person's parents never meet each other.

I will leave it to the reader to decide whether or not this science fiction scenario represents a logically possible occurrence. If it does, then no doubt this sort of total eradication of an actual person's past, present and future existence would be a terrible thing to inflict upon someone. But obviously nothing of the sort occurs in a normal case of abortion, which takes place without benefit of meddling time travelers. In the ordinary case nothing is inflicted upon anyone since there is no one for anything to be inflicted upon. If we find this hard to accept, it is because when we try to imagine our own non-existence our imaginations tend to falter. The same thing often happens when we try to imagine what it would be like to be dead. We tend to think that it would be like being shut up in a dark and silent room, with nothing there but ourselves, even though the reality of death is just the opposite: everything will go on much as before *except* ourselves.

Once this persistent confusion is eliminated, it becomes clear that it is neither meaningful nor coherent to claim, as Hare does, that God or our fathers would have done less than their moral best by us if they had not caused us to exist (p. 221). If a wrong is done when a potential person is prevented from becoming a person, it isn't done to the person who might have been, since that person is a purely mythical being. And it isn't done to the merely potential person, i.e., the non-sentient stuff which might have developed into a person, either, since non-sentient stuff cannot be wronged any more than nonexistent people can. Hence the Golden Rule cannot be extended to prove that we have duties toward merely potential people.

### 2. *The Quantity of Happiness Problem*

However, we cannot yet conclude that it is not prima facie wrong to prevent a potential person which would otherwise have become a happy person from doing so. For it might be argued that even though no one's rights are violated when a potential happy person is aborted, or never conceived, the action is still prima facie wrong because it constitutes a failure to produce a certain quantity of happiness which it is in the agent's capacity to produce, or at least not prevent. Certainly on any moral theory which counts happiness *per se* as a moral good, or which makes maximizing the *total quantity* of happiness a duty, we would have to say that, other things being equal, it is morally better to create a person who turns out to be happy than not to.

Another way to illustrate this possible defense of the potentiality principle is to consider the following question: Which world would God deserve more credit for creating, one containing fifty happy people, or one containing fifty million people who are no more and no less happy? Many people would be inclined to say that God would deserve more moral credit for creating the more populous world, even though in creating the less populous world (s)he would not have violated anyone's rights.

I think that the claim that, other things being equal, it is better to create happy people than to create no one, can be refuted. Creating happiness for people is morally good, but creating people for happiness is morally neutral. Granted, it is wrong to create people one knows will be unhappy, and worse than creating no one. But creating people one knows will be happy is not necessarily right; its moral status must be determined on the basis of the predictable effects which the existence of these new people will have on *other* people. To explain why I think that this is so will require an examination of some basic convictions about the nature of morality. Any extensive defense of these convictions would be beyond the scope of this paper. But at least we will be able to see that the rejection of the potentiality principle is required by a certain view of the proper function of morality, and one which has a good deal of plausibility.

### 3. *Sentience as the Basis of Moral Rights*

The view to which I refer is simply that morality is or ought to be a system designed to promote the interests of sentient beings. Which sentient beings? Ideally, all there are and all there ever will be. Sentience is the ultimate source of all moral rights; a being which has experiences and which prefers experiences of some sorts to those of other sorts, has on that basis alone a prima facie right that those preferences be respected by beings which have the intelligence to comprehend this fact. On the other hand, a being which lacks the capacity to have experiences, and/or to prefer some experiences to others, cannot coherently be said to have moral rights, because it has no interests to be respected.

It should not, but perhaps it does, need to be pointed out that there is a difference between sentient beings and things which are only potentially capable of sentience. Francis Wade's is one of the most recent attempts to break down this distinction. Wade argues that a human fetus is in one significant sense already a personal being, already possessed of the capacities, including sentience, which are definitive of personhood, because, ". . . its whole natural thrust is to become a functioning person."[7] But however true this may be it is still one thing to be sentient now and quite another to be the sort of thing which may become sentient at a later time.

It is also crucial to distinguish between a purely potential capacity for sentience and a present but temporarily inoperative capacity, as in the case of a person who is asleep or unconscious. Some might argue that this distinction is untenable, that to whatever degree a fetus is merely potentially sentient, so too a person who is not conscious at the moment is only potentially sentient. Wade points out, correctly, that,

> The potentiality of the fetus . . . is an active natural potentiality or tendency, which is a guarantee of the future as far as the agent is concerned.[8]

And, it might be argued, this is as much as can be said about a person in a state of unconsciousness, however certain his or her eventual awakening may be. But it is a mistake to speak of an unconscious person as merely a potential sentient being. Such a person is an actual, developed sentient being who is in a temporary state of quiescence, just as an automobile which is out of gasoline is not a *potential* automobile but an actual one which just isn't operating at the moment.

Thus, Tristram Engelhardt's remarks on the difference between the potential sentience of a fetus and that of an unconscious person, while correct, do not go far enough. He says,

> . . . the potentiality of the sleeping person is concrete and real in the sense of being based upon the past development of a full-blown human person.[9]

But for this very reason it is more accurate to say that an unconscious person is not merely a being which is *potentially* capable of sentience, but one which has an actual and present capacity for sentience, even though this capacity is not and perhaps cannot be exercised at present.

My claim, then, is that sentience is a necessary and sufficient condition for the possession of moral rights. It does not follow from this that all sentient beings deserve to have their interests given equal weight in moral considerations. All *people* have equal moral rights, but it is only people who have *full* moral rights. We needn't value the lives of the bugs that bite us as highly as our own. Nevertheless, any degree of sentience entitles its bearer to some moral consideration. For instance, I would argue that the mere capacity to feel pain, which is one form or aspect of sentience, endows its possessor with the prima facie right not to have pain inflicted upon it. And to the extent that people have rights that other organisms do not, it is because their sentience is, so to speak, of a higher order; that is, they not only have experiences but know that they have them, think about them, use them in the formulation of theories, and so on. Needless to say, most human moral systems are designed to promote the interests of only a small sub-set of sentient beings; but this only shows that we have a long way to go in becoming completely moral.

That actions are right or wrong insofar as they promote or interfere with the interests of (at least certain) sentient beings is an insight which has been elaborated and defended in various teleological and contractualist moral theories. For instance, it is very much in the spirit of utilitarianism to say that the good is what promotes the interests of sentient beings. Most of the things identified as intrinsic moral goods by the different forms of utilitarianism, e.g., happiness, pleasure, the avoidance of unnecessary pain, and the satisfaction of rational and informed desires, are things which are usually, though not always, in the interest of the being which experiences them.

But utilitarians have often risked losing sight of this central insight by speaking loosely of "maximizing happiness" as the goal of morality, as though the point were to increase the number of "units" of happiness, without regard for how thinly or unevenly they might be distributed. This is a mistake. Maximizing the extent to which people's interests are promoted does not mean—though in some cases it may be achieved by—increasing the number of people who exist and have interests to be promoted. Rather, the prima facie aim of morality should be to maximize the extent to which each *actual*—present or future—person's interests are promoted. This means maximizing not just the *average* extent of interest-promotion, although that matters, but also the *equality* of the consideration given to each person. Each person's interests must be given prima facie equal weight; but it is only people and other sentient beings, that is those who do or will exist, who can possibly have interests to be weighed. For it is only they who care, or will care, or have reason for caring, what does or does not happen.

Morality, then, should be concerned with how happy each individual is or will be, not with how many individuals exist and are happy. (Being happy is not always quite the same thing as having what is in your interest, but it will do as an approximation for present purposes.)

This means, for example, that other things being equal it is better to have one child who is very happy than two who are 51% as happy, even though in the latter case one might say that a greater quantity of happiness had been produced. It also means that a decision to have or not have a child must be evaluated on the basis of its predictable effects upon people, and possibly other sentient beings, which do or will exist, given the outcome of the decision.

This is why failing to have a child, even when you could have had a happy one, is neither right nor wrong, so long as it is considered apart from its effects upon people other than the merely potential child. But the same cannot be said of *having* a child, since in this case the action results in the existence of a new person whose interests must be taken into account. Having a child under conditions which should enable one to predict that it will be very unhappy is morally objectionable, not because it violates the rights of a presently existing potential person, but because it results in the frustration of the interests of an actual person in the future. There is all the difference in the world between so acting as to cause needless misery to real but future people and refraining from bringing people into existence. In the first instance one creates unhappiness and frustration, thus violating the moral rights of real sentient beings who are no less worthy of our consideration just because they do not exist *yet*. In the second instance, no one is harmed, no one's interests are disregarded, and hence no moral wrong is done.

## 4. *Consequences*

If I am right about this, then the use of contraceptives or abstinence to avoid parenthood are, insofar as they affect merely potential people, without moral significance. And the same is true of abortion, provided that unborn humans are only *potential* people. We have absolutely no obligation to potential children to have them. However, once we do decide to have children then we are obligated to begin taking their interests into account, and this process may even lead to a reversal of that decision.

If this were more widely recognized it might prevent a good deal of suffering from unwarranted guilt feelings. Women who have abortions and people who perform or arrange for them often suffer from the persistent suspicion that they are wronging the potential people whose development they are bringing to an end. And people who deliberately remain childless often feel or are made to feel that this is a selfish decision on their part. Such feelings are misguided. It may be that at one time having children could have reasonably been regarded as a service to society as a whole; but *that* reason for having them is gone, probably forever, and indeed the reverse is probably the case now. Not only do we not have a duty to reproduce ourselves, we may even have a prima facie duty not to.

Another consequence of the failure of the potentiality principle is that we have no obligation to try to maximize the total number of human beings, a fact which makes a tremendous difference to what our long-term population policies ought to be. Granted, the earth is finite and hence we will be forced to limit population growth at *some* point even if we do recognize such a prima facie obligation. However, if we believe that potential people have a right to life, even a very slight one, then we cannot avoid advocating a greater population expansion than we could otherwise justify. For if potential people have *no* right to life then it is clear that the expansion ought to be—or to have been—halted or reversed as soon as it becomes the case that continued growth will have an overall negative impact upon people who do or will exist.

On the other hand, if potential people do have a right to life then we are morally obligated to tolerate some overall negative impact upon actual people in order to reach a just compromise between their rights and those of potential people. But this would be a serious moral error. If we populate the world to the point that our descendants will lead less satisfactory lives than they otherwise could have, then we *will* have done less than our best by them.

Furthermore, if we ever become capable of colonizing the habitable planets of other stars then our attitude toward the potentiality principle will make a difference as to whether or not we make a point of doing so, and at what cost. If we believe that potential people have a right to life then we must conclude that we have a prima facie obligation to cover every humanly habitable planet with human inhabitants, as many as can be fitted in without undue crowding. Nor will we, in all probability, consider ourselves obligated to colonize only those planets which have no natives who object to our doing so. For the rights of natives will have to be weighed against those of the potential human beings who could live happily on their planet, and once again some compromise will have to be made.

This too would be an error. The decision whether to increase the total number of human beings by expanding into a new environment should be made on the basis of its effects upon all the sentient beings whose interests are involved. But the fact that the people thereby brought into existence will be happy cannot justify bringing them into existence at the expense of even a small overall negative effect upon the rest. To maintain otherwise is to condemn ourselves, our descendants, and all the sentient beings whose living space they will crowd, to a progressive erosion of the quality of life for the dubious purpose of creating more and more people who will be less and less happy.

There is one more consequence which seems worth noting. Peter Singer has recently pointed out that the moral status of the practice of raising other animals for slaughter is dubious at best.[10] For animals are sentient beings capable of pleasure and pain, and arguably even of thought and desire. They at least seem to all outward appearances to enjoy life, if given a chance, and to fear death and prefer to avoid it, just as we do. These seem to be powerful reasons for not killing them, except when there are sound countervailing reasons. Having no other way to nourish ourselves adequately is or would be one such sound reason. But just liking the taste of meat or the feel of a fur coat is not, since we can learn to enjoy other foods, and artificial furs, just as much.

Now one defense of the practice of raising animals for slaughter is that if we did not then we would raise far fewer of many domestic breeds. Whole species might be reduced to small fractions of their present numbers, or even become extinct. Should we respect the interests of individual animals at the cost of virtually eliminating entire species? If the potentiality principle were true, then it could be argued that it is better to bring into being creatures which will be reasonably happy for some period of time, however short, than not to bring them into being at all; that, for instance, raising chickens and wringing their necks is really better, for the chickens, than not raising them at all. But this, as I have argued, is nonsense. It is incoherent to claim that animals, any more than humans, are better off with short lives than with no lives.

Finally, there is one apparent consequence of the failure of the potentiality principle which we have already touched upon, but which needs further elaboration. To say that merely potential people are not the sort of things which can possibly have moral rights is by no means to imply that we have no obligations toward people of future generations, or that they (will) have no rights which can be violated by things which we do now. We have many obligations toward the people who will exist after us, not least of which is the obligation not to overpopulate their world. If the human race were suddenly and deliberately to stop reproducing altogether no wrong would have been done to merely potential people, who cannot be wronged, or to people of future generations, since there would not be any. (Of course wrong would probably be done to those young or soon-to-be-born people who would be condemned to an old age devoid of younger companions; but that is another matter.) If, however, there are going to be people after us, then I think that morality requires that we respect their interests, insofar as this is possible, just as we should if they were our contemporaries.

This claim is in no way inconsistent with the claim that potential people *as such* have no moral rights. For there is a clear and crucial difference between actual but future people, i.e., those who don't yet but will exist, and present but merely potential people, i.e., things which could but won't become people in the future. The difference is that the former but not the latter will be sentient beings, with interests and desires, susceptible to pleasure and pain, and therefore possessed of moral rights. Our obligations to the people of future generations is in no way based upon the present existence of identifiable objects from which they will develop, or even on the present existence of conditions sufficient to guarantee their existence. For no reasonable person would maintain that these obligations would be eliminated if people were to cease developing from potential people and instead spring into existence fully formed and without biological parents. It would be just as objectionable to act deliberately so as to lower the quality of life for such spontaneously generated people as to do so for future people generated in the normal way.

Furthermore, if future generations owed their claim to moral consideration on the part of people in the present to the present existence of potential people from which they will develop, then only the *next* generation would have such a claim, since the genetic material from which more remote generations will spring is not yet in existence. But it would be wrong to confine our consideration for the people of the future to those who will be born within the next third of a century or so, as wrong as it is to respect the rights of only some subclass of existing people. People have moral rights not because of such accidental properties as age, race, sex, or the historical period in which they exist, but because they are sentient, self-aware beings with needs and desires. If we are to protect the interests of all such beings then we cannot allow the unfortunate ambiguity in the phrase "potential people" to blind us to the morally relevant differences between the real people of the future, whose lives will be affected by what we do now, and the potential people of the present, which are not now, though they may later become, beings with moral rights.

## *Notes*

1. Michael Tooley, "Abortion and Infanticide," *The Rights and Wrongs of Abortion*, Princeton University Press, 1974, p. 75.

2. See my "On the Moral and Legal Status of Abortion," *The Monist*, Vol. 57, January 1973, pp. 43-62, for a defense of this view.

3. R. M. Hare, "Abortion and the Golden Rule," *Philosophy and Public Affairs*, Vol. 4, No. 3, Spring 1975, p. 212. All further page references not otherwise identified are to this article.

4. Hare objects to the use of the term "moral right" on the grounds that no philosopher has yet produced "a theory of rights which links the concept firmly to those of 'right', 'wrong', and 'ought'–concepts whose logic is even now a little better understood" (p. 213). I see no *especial* difficulty, however, in analyzing talk about rights, or translating it into talk about right and wrong and what we ought to do. As a rough first approximation it might be suggested that someone has a prima facie right to something if and only if other things being equal it would be wrong for anyone else to deprive that person of that thing. Insofar as one can't sensibly say that someone has been *deprived* of something unless that thing is something which the person wants or has reason to want, it is clear that rights and desires are closely connected, though the nature of the connection is difficult to state precisely. (See Tooley, pp. 60-64, for an exploration of this connection.)

5. Tooley uses the kitten example to present another intuitive argument against the potentiality principle. He argues that the "possibility of transforming kittens into persons will not make it any more wrong to kill newborn kittens than it is now" (*op. cit.*, p. 76), and that therefore potential personhood does not entail a right to life.

6. George Berkeley, "Three Dialogues Between Hylas and Philonous," *The Works of George Berkeley*, Vol. 2, edited by T. E. Jessop. Thomas Nelson and Sons, London, 1964, p. 200.

7. Francis C. Wade, "Potentiality in the Abortion Discussion," *The Review of Metaphysics*, Vol. 39, No. 2, December 1975, p. 255.

8. *Ibid.*, p. 245. (Wade is here using "agent" to mean anything which causes a change in itself or in something else, not necessarily a *conscious* agent.)

9. H. Tristram Engelhardt, "The Ontology of Abortion," *Ethics*, Vol. 84, No. 3, April 1974, p. 220.

10. Peter Singer, "Animal Liberation," *The New York Review of Books*, April 1974; reprinted in *Moral Problems*, edited by James Rachels. Harper and Row, 1975, pp. 163-177.

# In Defense of the Potentiality Principle

WILLIAM ANGLIN

This paper is a reply to the argument Mary Anne Warren gives against the potentiality principle in her paper "Do Potential People Have Moral Rights?"[1] I attack the premiss of Warren's argument and find it open to two interpretations. On the first interpretation, her argument is invalid; on the second interpretation, it begs the question.

The potentiality principle is intended to apply to those cases in which a moral agent has an opportunity either to terminate or to initiate a causal process which leads to the existence of actual people. According to this principle, an agent is morally obligated, in making his or her decision, to take into account the possible happiness or unhappiness of those people whose existence is contingent upon that decision. For example, if a woman knows that any children she might have would lead unhappy lives then she ought, other things being equal, not to have children, whereas, if she knows that any children she might have would lead happy lives then she ought, other things being equal, to have children. As another example, suppose that a moral agent called Alice is deliberating about whether she should have one or two children. Suppose also that, no matter how she chooses, it will make no net difference to the happiness of anyone other than the two children. If the one child would enjoy a net 100 units of happiness whereas the two children would each enjoy a net 51 units of happiness then, according to the potentiality principle, Alice ought to have the two children. In spite of the fact that the first child is going to exist on either alternative whereas the second child may or may not exist, the possible happiness of the second child is taken into account along with the assured happiness of the first.

Warren's argument against the potentiality principle rests on the premiss that "morality is or ought to be a system designed to promote the interests of sentient beings." Suppose that, as in the above example, a moral agent called Alice is deliberating about whether she should have one or two children. I think Warren would want to count Alice's first (and possibly only) child among the "sentient beings." For no matter how Alice chooses, there will be a first child. However, let $m$ be the number of additional children Alice will have. The question then is whether Warren means to include as "sentient beings" these $m$ children–even if $m$ turns out to be equal to 1 rather than 0. It seems that she does mean to include them because she writes:

> Maximizing the extent to which people's interests are promoted does not mean–though in some cases it may be achieved by–increasing the number of people who exist and have interests to be promoted. Rather, the prima facie aim of morality should be to maximize the extent to which each *actual*–present or future–person's interests are promoted.

Suppose then that Warren's premiss is meant to be interpreted in such a way that the $m$ additional people who actually will exist are included as "sentient beings." How, on this interpretation, are we led to conclude that the potentiality principle is false? It seems that Warren would have us reason as follows:

> Suppose Alice has a choice between bringing into existence "one child who is very happy" or "two who are 51% as happy." If Warren's premiss is right then it is better for Alice to bring the one child into existence rather than the two. But the potentiality principle would dictate that (other things being equal) Alice ought to bring the two children into existence. Hence, if the premiss is right the potentiality principle is wrong.

In response to this argument, we raise the question: how is the premiss supposed to imply that it is better that Alice bring the one child into existence? We do not know whether Alice will produce one or two children. Alice herself has not yet decided, much less done, anything about it. For all anyone knows, *m* equals 1. If *m* equals 1, however, then the two children are both "sentient beings" to whom Alice should extend moral concern. Since there is an obligation to promote their interests, there is *a fortiori* an obligation to bring them into existence. For how can Alice promote their interests if she does not bring them into existence? Thus if *m* equals 1, it is not better for Alice to have one child rather than two. Of course, it may be that *m* equals 0; in *that* case, Warren is right that it is better (on her premiss) that Alice bring the one child into existence–but only in *that* case. I think we can also see from this that Warren's premiss puts things backwards. For it is not as if we should first look and see how many people will exist and then, under some obligation to do so, bring that number of people into existence. The number *m* is not *given to* the moral agent: it is *decided by* the moral agent. That is, the term "sentient beings," insofar as it includes the *m* additional people, has no fixed meaning for the moral agent except that meaning which, without the help of Warren's premiss, the agent fixes to it. In order that Warren's premiss have a meaning which is of some use to a given moral agent and in order also that Warren's argument against the potentiality principle be construed as valid, we must interpret her premiss in such a way that "sentient beings" does not refer to the *m* additional people whose actual existence is contingent upon which decision the moral agent makes. We must interpret her premiss to mean that "morality is or ought to be a system designed to promote the interests of a *given* population of sentient beings, including the few billion people who exist now (at the time at which the moral agent is deliberating) and also the *k* people who are going to exist regardless of what the moral agent decides but not including the *m* additional people who will come into existence as a result of the moral agent's decision." If this interpretation of Warren's premiss seems a little strained, at least it has the advantage of making her argument against the potentiality principle valid. For suppose once again that Alice is deliberating about whether she should have a second child. In such a case, precisely, this additional child is not part of a *given* population. Thus granted Warren's premiss as interpreted here, it follows that Alice has no prima facie obligation to bring a second child into existence. But the potentiality principle may well dictate otherwise. Hence, the potentiality principle is false.

Let us assume then, for the benefit of Warren's argument, that the *m* additional people are not to be reckoned among the "sentient beings." In that case, is Warren's premiss true? We shall show first that it is false and second that it begs the question.

Consider the difficulty which arises from the symmetry between being obligated (other things being equal) to bring happy people into the world and being obligated (other things being equal) not to bring unhappy people into the world.[2] For it seems that to rule out any obligation to bring happy people into existence, Warren's premiss must also rule out any obligation not to bring unhappy people into existence. Suppose, for example, that Alice is deliberating about producing an additional person whose existence would result in no net happiness difference to any member of the given population but who would himself (herself) be very unhappy. Since this person is not a member of the given population, it seems to follow on Warren's premiss that there is no obligation not to bring him into existence. This hypothetical person is not something whose interests should be promoted. Warren is quite aware of this point and, having anticipated that it might be raised against her premiss, has replied to it as follows:

> Having a child under conditions which should enable one to predict that it will be very unhappy is morally objectionable, not because it violates the rights of a presently existing potential person, but because it results in the frustration of the interests of an actual person in the future. There is all the difference in the world between so acting as to cause needless misery to real but future people and refraining from bringing people into existence. In the first instance one creates unhappiness and frustration, thus violating the rights of real sentient beings who are no less worthy of our consideration just because they do not exist *yet*. In the second instance, no one is harmed, no one's interests are disregarded and hence no moral wrong is done.

There are a number of ways in which Warren's response can be understood. First, we may take her to be saying that the action is morally objectionable simply because the consequences are bad. This cannot be the right interpretation because 1) this would leave her open to the retort that it is morally obligatory to have a happy child simply because the consequences are morally good, and because 2) according to her premiss, the fact that the action results in the suffering of someone who is not a member of the given population is irrelevant. Second, we may take her simply to be repeating Jan Narveson's point[3] that if a happy person is not brought into existence then he will never be around to complain but if an unhappy person is brought into existence then he will be around to complain. This will not help Warren because 1) there is Timothy Sprigge's reply[4] that if an unhappy person is not brought into existence he will never be around to be grateful but if a happy person is brought into existence then he will be around to be grateful (in other words, just as a nonexistent happy person cannot be wronged, so a nonexistent unhappy person cannot be righted), and 2) if the unhappy person is not a member of the given population then he does not count among those entities whose interests ought to be promoted and thus his complaints are irrelevant. Third, we may take Warren to be saying that, given a decision to bring a person into existence, that person henceforth becomes a member of the given population and therefore has interests that ought to be promoted. This interpretation has support from the text. Warren says, "we have absolutely no obligation to our potential children to have them. However, once we do decide to have children then we are obligated to begin taking their interests into account, and this process may even lead to a reversal of that decision." Since it is in an unhappy person's interests not to exist, then, given the decision to bring about his existence, it is therefore obligatory to reverse that decision. This third interpretation of her reply seems to be the sort of thing Warren *has* to say if our second interpretation of her premiss is the right one. For if the unhappy person never counts as part of the given population, then, according to Warren's premiss thus interpreted, he never merits any moral concern. The fact that Warren does say this is evidence that our second interpretation of her premiss is the right one. Now consider the case of someone who decides to bring into existence a person who would no doubt be very happy. By reasoning similar to Warren's, this happy person is henceforth numbered among the given population and thus has interests that ought to be promoted. Hence, there is now a prima facie obligation to bring him into existence. Never mind that the decision was a bit hasty and that now, an hour later, without having done a thing to implement it, the moral agent wishes to change her (his) mind. Because the decision has been made, the happy person's happiness must now be taken into account. What is shaky about this reasoning and hence also about the reasoning which Warren presents in her paper, is the way in which the concept of the given population is used. There is an equivocation. On the one hand, the given population has a fixed size; but on the other hand, it is made to include or not include a hypothetical person, and this at the changing fancy of the moral agent in question. But either the hypothetical person is a member of the given population or he is not. If he is a member of the given population then his existence cannot be put up for reconsideration: it is given. If he is not a member of the given population then, in spite of the fact that the moral agent may bring about his existence, he is still not a member of the given population and thus not an object of moral concern. We can put the same point this way: either one accepts obligations in connection with any possibility of human existence and therefore adopts something like the potentiality principle or else one accepts obligations only in connection with a given population, with a fixed size, and therefore adopts something like the second interpretation of Warren's premiss. If one does the latter then one cannot treat the given population as a flexible conglomeration capable of accommodating any possibility of human existence. If one is not going to accept obligations in connection with all the human lives that might be, then one must be willing to draw a line and say that *these* lives are to count in moral calculations and *those* lives are not. Moreover, even if one of *those* lives is an unhappy one, still it is not to count in moral calculations. Thus it makes no sense to imagine a person starting outside the given population, then entering it, and finally returning whence he came—as if he were a disappointed immigrant! On the contrary. Relative to a given moral agent involved in a given moral deliberation, the given population is, by definition, a class having a fixed number of members.

From what we have said, above, it should be concluded that Warren has not made an adequate reply to the difficulty raised by the symmetry between being obligated to bring happy people into the world and being obligated not to bring unhappy people into the world. The charge still stands against her: 1) that an unhappy person whose existence is a matter of deliberation is not a member of the given population; therefore 2) that he cannot become a member of the given population simply for Warren's convenience; hence 3) that, according to Warren's premiss, there is no obligation not to bring him into existence. But there is an obligation not to bring him into existence. Therefore, Warren's premiss is false.

For the purpose of defending the potentiality principle against Warren's argument, it is actually not necessary to prove that her premiss is false. This is because it begs the question. According to Warren's premiss, morality ought to be a system designed to produce happiness for the sake of a population rather than a system designed to produce a population for the sake of happiness. As Warren puts it, morality "should be concerned with how happy each individual is or will be, not with how many individuals exist and are happy."[5] The proponent of the potentiality principle, however, believes that there is sometimes an obligation to produce people for the sake of happiness. This is a simple corollary if not a mere restatement of his position. Thus, he can hardly be expected to accept Warren's premiss. Warren's argument cannot possibly convince anyone who does not already agree with her.

## *Notes*

1. In this collection.
2. See Jan Narveson's "Moral Problems of Population," *Monist* 57 (1973): 69-78.
3. Jan Narveson, *op. cit.*
4. Timothy L. S. Sprigge, "Professor Narveson's Utilitarianism," *Inquiry* 11 (1968): 337-341.
5. It is this assertion against which I argue in my "Repugnant Conclusion," *Canadian Journal of Philosophy* (appearing in the winter of 1977-78).

# Future People and Us

*JAN NARVESON*

What, if anything, do we owe to future generations? Answers to this question vary widely. Indeed, they range all the way from Nothing to Everything–which would be no cause for alarm, except that both answers, and some in between, have rational support. On behalf of the first option, there is the view that morality is based on a kind of agreement or contract between independent rational agents. Conjoin this with the obvious fact that future people are, just by virtue of being future, not capable of being parties to mutual contracts with us, and we infer that future people are, morally speaking, out of the picture. As the wag says, "Why should I do anything for posterity? What has posterity done for me?" On the other hand, if we take a very different but certainly reputable view of morality, viz., that we ought to maximize human happiness, no matter where or when those humans may be and counting each equally, reflection may drive us toward the opposite answer. For presumably, there is a vast number of generations to come, perhaps an infinite number. Surely, if we make vast sacrifices now, we can leave a heritage which will make a nontrivial positive contribution to the well-being of all future generations; if this is so then, because there are so many, this benefit summed over all generations will outweigh any possible sacrifice. So what we owe the future is Everything.

Though these views are certainly of academic interest, their interest is by no means purely academic. A great many people hold or have held each of them. And beyond doubt, our answer to this general question is of enormous consequence for current practice. We have but to contemplate our light bills to appreciate that. An answer that is reasonably satisfying to our consciences is needed, and the need is of some urgency. Most of us, I suppose, suspect that the correct view lies somewhere between these two extremes. If so, something must be wrong either with the premisses or the reasoning of the two arguments briefly sketched in the foregoing. Of course, the major premise in each represents a very basic and comprehensive outlook on morality. We can hardly hope to adjudicate the conflict between them in a paper of the present scope. It may be of some interest, however, if it can be shown that these very different outlooks do not actually lead to nearly such wide divergence as they at first sight seem to.

Actually, there are three fundamental views of interest to current moral philosophy, or at any rate, to this moral philosopher. The two thus far mentioned are, in effect, Egoism and Utilitarianism. But another, Libertarianism, should also be considered. It holds that we must do nothing which impinges on the moral territory, as it were, of others, though we have no obligation to make improvements on it either. Again, without attempting to argue the relative merits of this as a basic view against the others, I suggest that it does not diverge too widely from the others on the present question. What we will find is that we owe the future something, but not everything, though the amount owed is neither the same for all, nor the same at all times.

What distinguishes the question about future people from the general question of morality, viz., how ought we to deal with our fellow people in general? Future people are, after all, still people; so whatever is true of our dealings with all people *qua* people will be true of our dealings with them. And future people are *real.* They differ from us by virtue of their location in time, just as others do by their location in space. This doesn't make them any more "unreal" than the Chinese, or for that matter, the Pharaohs. But there is a feeling that something about the question of future people makes it very different from the more usual questions of ethics, and the feeling is justified. I find four particularly significant features, as follows:

1. To start, there is the fact mentioned at the outset: our transactions with the future are all one-way. We can leave messages for

them, visit effects on them, but not vice versa. Of course, our thoughts about future people can and do affect us, but that's hardly the same thing as their affecting us.

2. Future generations will–with any luck at all, that is–inherit our stock of *knowledge*, which, apart from food and water, is easily the most important thing we can leave them.

3. The population of all future generations is potentially infinite, and in any case incalculably large. It's potentially infinite because there is no theoretical limit to the duration of things. No doubt the earth will eventually either freeze or burn to cinders, but by then people may have found out how to move on. In any case, what matters is that the size of the population we are dealing with is, in all reasonable expectation, utterly vast and hopelessly indefinite–subject to the qualification implicit in the next point.

4. Finally, and most interesting of all in some ways, there is the fact that the existence of future people is up to us. If the lot of us decide to cease procreating, then there simply won't be any future people–or at any rate, any future people there may be will have come to be as the result of another turn of the evolutionary wheel, and that is beyond our frame of reference. Foreseeably, at any rate, how many people there are in the next generation is due to voluntary activities on the part of people in this one.

Taken together, these features add up to a situation with a rather extraordinary degree of Existential Zap! Not only can we visit enormous good and evil on enormous numbers of people without fear of retaliation or hope of reward, but we even determine the existence of them. Owing to the second feature, however, as well as the third, the situation is significantly indeterminate. Consider the effects of the growth of knowledge over the past half-millenium. Then consider the shape of the curve which would plot that growth. No extrapolation of the exponential function in question can reasonably be made into the remote future; and, of course, what counts is not only the amount of expansion of knowledge but also, and far more crucially, just what sort of things will be found out. Since we cannot in principle know these now–else we would already know what by hypothesis we do not yet know–and since knowledge is known to make huge differences in our lives, it follows that the differences likely to be made by the next couple of hundred years' growth in knowledge are literally unimaginable. Only mystics will engage in futurology over even that time-span, short as it is by historical standards.

Perhaps we can view this latter point as something of a saving grace. Insofar as we are totally in the dark, no rational consideration of a problem is possible, even if the darkness is due to the inconceivability of the amount of light expected! It could reasonably be argued, then, that we should confine our reach to the fairly near future–say, to the next fifty years or so. And, practically speaking, this is wise. Questions about the more distant future may be less pressing; but they are not wholly irrelevant even to the nearer future. We might be able to sort out the issues more clearly by envisaging hypothetical cases more remote from us, and we might find that the results in those cases turn out to apply to nearer ones.

The fourth feature is such as to call for a major division of the issues before us into two: those concerning population size, and those concerning the division of goods and resources between present and future people. The questions are, respectively: How many people should there be? and What if anything must we do for those there will be, however many that is? Obviously these interact. If it doesn't matter how one treats others, then it is hard to see why it would matter how many of them one causes to exist. And if our obligations to whatever people there are are such that they could not be filled if there were more or less than thus many, then surely it would follow that we ought only to produce thus many. But these interactions depend on one's answers to the questions, and they are logically distinct. Moreover, the first seems, somehow, logically prior to the second. If F's are producible by us, the first question would seem to be whether to produce any at all; how to deal with them is a problem which only arises when there are some to deal with. At any rate, we begin with the first.

## *I*

The first question before us, then, is how to decide how many people there ought to be. Let us refer to any reply to this question as a "principle" about the population question; and let us refer to any proposed general answer to the question, how many people there ought to be, as a "policy" about population. Population principles, then, underlie population policies. Policies propose ways of acting by the relevant persons the purpose of which is to affect population size (including as an "effect" that of leaving the population size as it is, and also including the "policy" of having no policy and simply letting people do whatever they please). Principles generalize the reasons for this. Population principles, in turn, may be supported by some still more general principles, the Ultimate Principles of Ethics, for instance. At the most concrete level, of course, will be the particular decisions, made by particular people, to have or not to have children, and the having or refraining from having such children.

It will be assumed here that some possible candidates for Ultimate Principles of Ethics, and/or the population principles which they support, are non-starters. For example, we can imagine some lunatic believing that there are exceedingly hungry human-eating creatures on some other planet, and that the sacred duty of the human race is to multiply to the greatest possible extent in order to provide these creatures with the biggest and best possible diet. More interestingly, let us consider population principles whose basis is simply the desire that the universe be of a certain sort rather than some other sort–say, an "aesthetic" principle. Such grounds for principles amount to sheer preferences, and as such, it will be assumed that they simply do not carry with them the kind of conceptual authority that is required for an acceptable view of morality or of any general moral issue. Were this a textbook on ethics, of course, it would be outrageous simply to "assume" such things; but it is not, and the point, which to be sure is virtually universally agreed upon by philosophers, will not be argued here.

What restriction, then, do we impose in order to confine ourselves to proposals worth taking seriously? The answer, to put it rather vaguely, is that we will only consider principles which are grounded upon the interests of everyone concerned, construing "interests" broadly enough to include the principles of action of those concerned as among the "interests" in question. This leaves, not merely because of its intentional vagueness, a lot of possibilities; but no further refinements will be attempted here, except insofar as the ensuing discussion does so implicitly.

Having laid down this covering restriction, we can now point out that there is a fundamental question facing us, which may be put in the following somewhat paradoxical form: who is "everyone"? But it isn't paradoxical–only baffling! To wit: everyone could be (1) all persons *presently* alive; (2) all persons, including all future persons, or (3) all *possible* persons, including not only all those mentioned in (1) and (2) but also all those who are capable of being born or conceived, whether they actually are or not. The reason for including the third possibility, which may seem a little far out, will shortly be evident, as will the importance of the difference between the first two. To bring out the significance of the differences, let us consider for a moment the idea implicit in such expressions as "our duty to future generations." The idea, namely, is that there are people, in this case future ones, *to whom* we owe something or other. And indeed, it is plausible to generalize this and hold that duties must always be duties *to* someone or other: if no person is affected by an action, then that action (or inaction) cannot be a violation or fulfillment of a duty. This we may call, adopting Derek Parfit's useful terminology, the "person-regarding" view.

The person-regarding view is a natural one to adopt. But it makes for a knotty problem for anyone who wants to hold that we have some such duty as the duty to sustain the human race, or expand it. For *to whom* would we owe such a duty? The obvious suggestion would be that we owe it *to* the "human race," or to all those people out there in the future ahead of us. But this won't do. Given the person-regarding view, we cannot say the former; for the human race is not a person, but rather some such thing as the set of all persons or, worse still, the property of being a person or the idea of humankind. To none of these entities do we owe anything on the person-regarding view, and it is not obvious what could be meant by saying that we "owe" something to any of them in any case. The best we can do is to suggest that we owe the perpetuation of the human race to future persons themselves. But then comes the snag. For if we do not carrry out this "duty," we suddenly find that there is nobody we can claim to have let down, to have defaulted or failed in discharging our duties to them. The existence of the supposed subjects of this obligation is contingent on our fulfilling it. But if there is no subject of obligation, then, given the person-regarding view, there is no obligation. Which means that there can be no such thing as an "obligation to perpetuate the human race," for an obligation that only exists if it is fulfilled, i.e., which logically cannot be violated, is clearly nonsense. One who wanted to maintain such an obligation, then, would have to hold that we owed it to persons other than those who would come into existence as a result of its fulfillment. And that is a perfectly coherent view of the matter; but it does mean that the duty to procreate, if any, is going to be founded on some other duty. For example, it might be that presently existing people will be worse off unless there is a continual supply of new people. Or there might be a need to expand the population in order to make people better off. But then, all this will depend on how things are, and it will also be possible that we need to reduce the population in order to make people better off, or even to keep them from getting worse off. The idea that there is a duty to maintain the human race, as such, will have to be jettisoned.

It will be obvious that on two of the three general accounts of morality with which I am concerned in this paper, this conclusion will stand. If morality is fundamentally a matter of self-interest, modified only by such agreements constraining short-term self-interested activity as may be in the interests of agents to make, then any concern to sustain the race will be purely a personal matter. Most people, no doubt, will be interested in having children, either as a basic, instinctual matter or because they like children, or for any number of other reasons. But nothing which could reasonably be called a duty to procreate will stem from such reasons, except in special cases, as when one person has promised another that he or she will be a co-parent with her or him. And the same, at most, will be true on the Libertarian view. If our basic duty to others is merely to keep off what is theirs except with their consent, then plainly nothing remotely like a duty to procreate will issue directly from the view. For it makes no sense to say that one has done some kind of damage to a possible person by refusing to make that possibility actual. We cannot sensibly say that a possibility is worse off for remaining one than it would be if realized, or that we have violated its right to exist. And, again, anyone who wanted to maintain the very peculiar notion that possibilities have rights, merely as such, would at any rate be departing from our fundamental restriction that when it comes to morality, only persons count. "Possible persons" are not persons: it isn't just that they aren't the usual kind of persons, for neither are they a special kind of persons, as are tall or short ones, male or female ones, and so on.

However, there remains the utilitarian view. Indeed, this may have been the most popular of our three conceptions, for the past century or so, at least in English-speaking countries. Now the utilitarian view, as it turns out, is subject to (at least) two quite strikingly different interpretations in relation to our present subject. (Indeed, it is only on our present subject that there is this kind of difference in interpretation.) These are the interpretations which result from affirming or denying the person-regarding view. Niceties apart, let us say that the utilitarian view is that the right thing for any given agent to do at any given time is whatever will, on the whole, maximize utility for all persons, a given amount of utility counting equally no matter whose it is. Now we get the division of interpretations by asking whether the promotion of utility by producing new people who have pleasant lives is to be entertained on all fours with promoting it by improving the pleasantness of the lives there already are (or would be, in the case of future people, apart from the procreation in question). If we affirm the person-regarding view, then we may well be driven to denying this. For we may reason thus: if we do not produce the new person, then we cannot be said to have done less well by him than the principle asks us to do (viz., as well as possible, subject to the similar treatment of others). For there will then be no "him" to have done well or badly *by*. In order to say that we have the option (let alone the duty) of promoting utility by producing new people who would be happy, it seems that we must deny the person-regarding principle. We must say that the duty to promote happiness is not a duty *to* anyone at all; it is, simply, one's duty. And this seems queer. Duties which are not owed to anybody stick in the conceptual throat.

If the person-regarding view is rejected, of course, then we have the form of utilitarianism which, for instance, Henry Sidgwick explicitly embraced and which Wayne Sumner so lucidly defends elsewhere in this volume. The question before us is what we get if we try accepting this principle. Do we get a coherent sort of utilitarianism at all? More generally, of course, we want to know whether we get a satisfactory population principle. We begin by attacking the former question. In attempting to marshal reasons for preferring it to the Sidgwickian view, we will get into the latter question.

It was once thought that the alternative to the Sidgwickian interpretation is "average" utilitarianism. Given a constant size population, this has the same implications as the "total" view (as Sidgwick's has come to be called): for maximizing the total utility in a given set of people also maximizes the average, by definition. However, their implications diverge when we consider the present question. The "total" view, as its name implies, has it that if a new person's life would have positive marginal utility, then one ought to produce that person, however small that positive quantity was. The average view, however, implies that if a given potential parent's child would be less happy than the average person, then one ought not to have that child. (Less happy among all those currently alive? Or what? This, unfortunately, is a matter which tends not to be raised. But it could plainly make a difference whether the average was, say, that for the entire population throughout time instead of all those currently alive.) As Derek Parfit has pointed out, the conclusion seems quite unintuitive. After all, if the child you would have would be happy, would have a life worth living on balance, why should it make any difference if most others are even happier?

But both the total and the average views imply, apparently, that if the marginal happiness of a child one would have would be great–well above average, say–then it is one's duty to have that child. And *this* seems unintuitive too. It may be said, as Sumner has, that raising a child is a good deal of work, and if one didn't like that work, then the probability of the child's being happy enough to outweigh the disutility involved in raising him is not high. It is not clear to me whether this is true, but let us suppose it is. Still, suppose that one had one's choice of two lives, a childless one and one in which one became a parent; and let us suppose that one would be a quite successful parent and one's child would be very happy indeed. But let us suppose that nevertheless one would enjoy the other life somewhat more. Not a lot more, just *somewhat* more. Well, it still seems to me unintuitive to say that it is then your moral duty to become a parent.

It might also be said that if you could live either of two lives, in one of which you would not benefit others to any appreciable extent but would greatly enjoy the life you did lead, while in the other, you would benefit others substantially, considerably more than enough to outweigh the utility loss to you of living it, but you would have a loss, though not a terribly great one, then it is unintuitive to think it is your duty to live the second life. But I am not clear that this is true. It does seem clear that it is one's duty to benefit others if the benefit is very great and the cost very small; but it does not seem equally clear that one has the duty to have a child if the child would be very happy and the cost to oneself quite small as compared with any other life one could lead instead. If there is indeed this kind of difference, then the non-Sidgwickian view is more plausible. At the intuitive level, it seems to me that there is. But intuitions, it may be agreed, are shifting sands and, at least when not enormously strong, not the sort of stuff to build theories upon. Let us proceed further along the line of theory, then, and see whether something solid emerges.

One shot at formulating the utilitarian principle in person-regarding terms would go somewhat as follows: it is one's duty to perform that action which maximizes the positive difference in utility made in the lives of affected persons. Persons are, so to say, given, and our job is to do the best we can by them. This has the implication (because that's the main point of the formulation!) that the fact that a child we might have would be happy is, *morally* speaking, no reason at all, taken in itself, for having it; since, if we do not have it, it is not the case that the child in question will be worse off, because it won't *be* at all. No comparison, then, between the utility state of the child if we do have it and if we don't have it is possible; one relatum is lacking in the latter case.

But this formulation runs up against a terrible snag, one which has been pressed upon us by Derek Parfit and which I will therefore refer to as Parfit's Problem. His problem gets going when we consider, not happiness-production but misery-minimization. Let us suppose that we are a pair of aspiring parents, and that one of us has a condition such that if we conceive now or in the very near future, the resulting child will be normal, but if we wait for a couple of months, it will suffer from terrible diseases and be deformed for life. It seems obvious to all of us that in this situation, we ought to conceive now or not at all. If we put off having the child in order to have an energetic vacation, and then had the deformed child, surely that would be wrong.

Yet the "comparative" view, as we may call the view formulated in the preceding paragraph, does not imply that it would be wrong. If what matters is how one does by what people there are, then no reason exists to produce people happier to start with, as it were.

The issue here is this. Can we say that the creation of a given life—its conception, say—is the conferring of a benefit on the person who results? Suppose that the resulting person is happy; and suppose too that some of his happiness is due to a fortunate genetic make-up. Since conception is not something which happens to someone who is already around, being instead the creation or production of the person in question, we cannot say that the resulting person is better off than he or she would have been if that event had not taken place. The best one could do is set the utility-state of that possible person at zero if not conceived, and then say that his conception has benefited him to, say, the extent of the contribution to his life-long utility attributable to his genetic make-up as opposed to other contributing factors. But this is to equate the condition of someone who is neither happy nor unhappy with that of one who is dead, and that seems wrong; worse yet, it is to equate it with "one" who was never born in the first place, and thus has no identity at all. And that seems very strange indeed.

The situation here is rather like the one about the treatment of sentences whose referring terms lack reference. Shall we say that "John's children are ill," when John has no children, implicitly asserts that he has some and is thus false? Or shall we say that its having a truth-value at all presupposes that he has children, and hence that it is to be reckoned as lacking truth-value at all? In making utilitarian calculations, do we reckon the utility-level of the unborn at zero, and thus reckon conception or birth as promoting utility on all fours with its promotion in beings who exist independently? Or shall we say that utility presupposes subjects of utility, so that the utility of the unconceived may properly be disregarded? On the one view, we shall say that utilitarianism calls for the maximizing of positive utility in the universe, so to speak, whereas on the other, we will say that it calls for the maximizing of the utility of whatever subjects of utility there are. On the latter view, those who remain childless though they could have been successful parents will not be down-rated for producing less satisfactions all around than they might have; but on the former they will.

Let us see whether the person-regarding view can make any headway against Parfit's problem without also reverting to the impersonal account. On this view, we are not morally obliged to have children just because they would be happy if we did. Are we, then, free to have miserable children when we could have had happy ones instead? Well, if we do that, it is true that we cannot say that we have done the miserable one a disservice, in the sense that *he* would have been happier had we done something else. On the other hand, however, we can say that the person there is if we produce the miserable one is worse off *than the person there would have been had we produced the other one.* And this cannot be said if instead we choose between having a child and not having one.

But what is to be said in that case? It might be argued that, in effect, we always choose between one possible or actual child and another, since we always have the option of, say, adopting instead of conceiving. But this won't really do, for although it is very nearly true, it is not quite true. There could be, and undoubtedly are, occasions when adopting isn't really a feasible option; and of course it is rarely possible to choose between conceiving one sort of offspring and conceiving another sort. Usually the decision is to conceive, and then you find out what you got only after it's too late to consider options. For of course the person-regarding view calls upon us to treat this person, once born, on the same basis of fundamental equality as the impersonal theory. So we must face directly the issue of what to say in the case in which someone's choice is between conceiving and not conceiving. Prima facie, the answer would seem to have to be that on the theory we are considering, this is entirely a matter of free choice on the part of the putative parents, except of course insofar as indirect utilities are concerned, that is, the effects on others of bringing this new child into the world. And this is just the answer we must be able to hedge on, for surely we feel that if one's offspring were to be foreseeably miserable, then one ought not to have it at all.

The question then is: OK, *how* miserable? What controls the standard here? More generally, what enables us to have any standard? One reply to this is that if the child would have been better off dead, then that seems reason not to produce it. Why? Well, because in that event, the case would be one for euthanasia, or at least suicide. And it can hardly be conscionable to bring about the existence of a person whom one knows will then be justified in self-extermination, for this is to ensure that somebody is worse off than he might be, for he would be better off dead!

In saying this, we may seem to risk the following reply. If we can use the notion of being "better off dead," we seem to be attaching a utility-level of zero to death; and that seems to be the high road back to the impersonal view. But I think it is not so. Death is not the same as nonexistence. Death is the terminus of a life, whose subject occupies a region of space-time. There *is someone* to *whom* it happens. Nonexistence, on the other hand, is not a property of individuals. The fifth son of my mother, for instance, does not exist, for she had only four: there is nothing in the universe, viewed temporally as well as spatially, designated by the expression "fifth son of JN's mother." Consequently, there is nobody for whom the question arose whether he would be better off dead *or*, of course, whether he would be better off being born. Questions about the utility of death are therefore meaningful in the person-regarding framework. The person considering whether dying at some particular time would be a good thing for him or not is considering whether his life would be better if it terminated then rather than later. One's death might conceivably maximize his utility. Not so for the case of non-conception. There is nobody who can contemplate the question whether he should or should not be conceived–if he's in a position to contemplate this, then he already has been.

Returning, then, to the question of what standard to use in trying to decide whether some contemplated offspring would enjoy a sufficiently good life to justify us in producing him, it seems to me that adherence to the person-regarding version of utilitarianism requires the following. First, of course, there is what I have previously termed "indirect" utility, that is, the utility of people other than the one there will be if we go ahead. These, in turn, may be importantly divided into two groups: (1) everyone else, present and future, and (2) oneself. Actually, group (1) may further be usefully divided, in nearly every case, into two groups: people one especially cares about, and people one doesn't. The other parent, e.g., obviously has a basic role in this, and in turn there will be various others who will be closely affected, by virtue of emotional ties, proximity, demands on shared resources, and so on. Such considerations can readily influence the decision in either direction. They may benefit from a new addition, or they may be disadvantaged, and these constitute perfectly good reasons to bring to bear on the matter.

But it would be silly to consider only, or even mostly, the utility of others in such a matter, not because they don't count equally but because they aren't as much affected as oneself. Here is where there may be divergence from the impersonal view. For it seems to me that while it may quite possibly be one's duty to avoid having a child on account of the effects on others if one has it, it would only in very extreme circumstances be one's duty to others to *have* offspring. And if, as I have been arguing, the utility of the child, even if it could be expected to be great, constitutes no moral reason in favor of a duty to have the child, then the overwhelmingly decisive factor will be one's own personal values, where the force of the term "personal" is that they are *not* determined by utilitarian considerations.

Since there is a serious risk of being misleading in saying this, let us consider the point at greater length. There is, of course, a reasonable sense of the term in which everything is to be "determined by utilitarian considerations." But this is the sense in which "determined" is a pretty uninterestingly general notion. The question, "will I like the flavor of apples?" is ordinarily not a practical question, but instead a simple question of prediction. Whether to like the flavor of apples isn't ordinarily a question one can sensibly deliberate about. Now, such questions are "determined" by utilitarian considerations only in the residual sense that they are the very stuff of which utilitarian considerations are made. One's likes and dislikes *are* utilities. In deciding whether to buy a dozen apples, on the other hand, we have a practical question which is to be determined by utilitarian considerations in the usual sense of "determined": namely, that one decides by estimating the probable contribution buying or not buying would make to antecedently given utilities. And if there aren't any antecedently given utilities in the case, then that is a case in which it would be proper to say that "no rational decision can be made." It's not a matter of figuring out how best to get what one wants, but rather of formulating or determining what one wants. And it is this sort of thing that I have in mind in suggesting that the decision whether or not to have a child is overwhelmingly, and properly, a matter of personal values. Is the sort of life I will lead if I am a parent the sort of life I really want to lead? Will it be the most satisfying life for me? It is in this connection that considerations of what one's child would probably be like, if one can get them, are relevant. What's relevant isn't just, or perhaps even mainly, his probable utility level. Rather, it's the sort of person he or she would be likely to be. Will the kind of demands he or she will probably make on me be demands which I want to have made on me? That question is just as important as the question whether one would be able to meet them. It is a matter of self-understanding, *not* (mainly) a matter of "calculating" in any very narrow sense.

The implication of the person-regarding view seems to me to be this. Let us suppose that in appraising all these things, but most especially (in any moderately normal case) the latter, we arrive at the conclusion that we would be a bit better off, on the whole, remaining childless (we would lead a slightly more satisfactory life on the whole, than we would even if we had an extraordinarily happy child). Then we should not have the child, on the person-regarding view, whereas on the impersonal view, I take it, we should. That is to say, here is the kind of case where the views really do diverge. And if some think that the implication of the view I am still inclined to press, i.e., the person-regarding one, is heartless or unkind, is it not reasonable to insist on being told to whom we would be being unkind or heartless? Not one's friends, relatives, or fellow-men in general, for we are assuming that their utilities have already been consulted. Surely the objector would have to have in mind the very child one would have. But if one doesn't have it, then there isn't any such child to be heartless *to*!

If, of course, one is inclined to have a child, then it is very much in order to consider whether that child would be happy, for, once born, it is a person to be considered. If there is good reason to think the child would not be happy, then there is moral reason not to have it in the first place. But, unlike either the average theory or the impersonal theory, I don't think that the threshold of unacceptability here can be wholly determined by calculation. Unlike the proponent of the average theory, I don't think that the threshold of unacceptability can be set by considering whether the child in question would be less happy than average. Here, in fact, it would seem that we can agree entirely with the impersonal theorist. His view, I take it, would go like this. Suppose that you could have either child X or child Y, and that X would be happier than Y. And suppose you would rather, so far as your personal utility goes, have Y than X. Then whether you should have X or Y will depend on *how much* you'd rather have Y. If the degree to which your utility is greater if you have Y exceeds the degree to which Y's utility is less than X's would be, then you should have Y. If it is less, then you should have X. This is the view of the matter which would seem to be dictated by the principle that if you are going to produce people, then you should produce the happiest ones consistently with the equal consideration of all others concerned. Where it differs from the impersonal theorist's view is in the "if" clause. The point is that the utility of those to be produced need be consulted only if they actually are produced: the probable happiness of either X or Y does not count in favor of a duty to produce him at all, but only in favor of a duty to prefer one to the other if you decide to produce.

How much difference will this make? Arguably, very little. For the "total" theorist will be able to argue that nearly always, the amount of good which one could do to one's existing fellows (present or future) will be at least as great as the amount one could contribute by adding even quite a happy child to the scene, especially if one is not really inclined toward parenthood by personal inclination. The person-regarding theorist, on the other hand, will point out that nearly always, the production of children is motivated by the inclinations of the prospective parents, rather than by motives of duty. Where the children were not wanted but came about as a result of ignorance about birth-control methods or by accident, both the total theorist and my person-regarding theorist will agree that probably this is not morally desirable anyway. Furthermore, as with all utilitarian theory, it can readily come about on either theory that we have a duty to produce children on grounds of indirect utility, that is, the benefits at stake for our fellows other than the offspring. If the total theorist is correct in his claim about the relative utility of procreation versus alternative activities benefiting others, then the divergence between the two theories will be very slight. There are two questions. First, *is* he right? And second, is that what the duty to procreate should really hang on?

Regarding the first of these two questions, the nub of Professor Sumner's ingenious argument would seem to be the premise that conception, as such, contributes only a small fraction of the utility of the resulting person, most of which is due to ongoing activities of parents, etc., etc. Just how one assesses the size of this fraction is not too easy to say, but it must be admitted that his point is most plausible. Since a person's genetic make-up may be presumed to be a necessary but not sufficient condition for the emergence of many of his salient properties (and within some range, necessary for all of his properties), a marginalist analysis for determination of this fraction seems required. And since his utility, as distinct from his set of desirable qualities, is surely most affected by his environment, especially his human environment, then Sumner's view becomes the more compelling. Nevertheless, it will yield the conclusion that people who could rear many children, each of whom would be more than usually happy, ought to have lots of them as a matter of duty. For once they've had one or two, and provided they can afford to go on, it is very likely that the marginal disutility of each further child for the parents becomes very small, whereas the marginal benefit, given that the child's life-long utility is, even fractionally, at stake, remains virtually constant. Thus if the parents would somewhat prefer to turn to something else, it is hard to believe that considerations of total utility could sanction this unless it were an extraordinarily beneficial activity for mankind. Whereas on the view I have been inclined to accept, it will most likely never become a duty for them to go on to another child. More likely it may be the reverse, for perhaps in biggish families there will be effects of size which work slightly to the disadvantage of the older children, who are increasingly burdened as the family grows larger. But in any case, there will be no a priori ground for a duty to have more. And this, I still think, is intuitively correct.

Intuitions do, however, vary on this matter, as I have said. Some may find it intuitively plausible to hold that people who would make good parents of a large family and can afford to do so also have a duty to produce the said large family. They may find this plausible even if there is no interference, say from religious considerations or other sources of bias on this matter. A strong basis of compelling theory would be preferable in such a situation. One such basis would be provided if the proponent of the view I have been advocating could be shown to be inconsistent. One such charge of inconsistency has been pressed by Sumner, who argues that, contrary to the axiomatic base of utilitarianism, my sort of theorist does not count all equal-sized utilities equally. According to him, my view is biased against certain persons, namely those whom it was in one's power not to bring about. On my theory, he points out, the decision to have a child rests entirely on the utilities of others and not at all on the child's utility, though the reverse is not true—the decision not to have one could well rest in large part on the probable utility of the child if one did have him. But in the case where the decision was positive, it was the case that the child's utility was not counted equally with that of other people.

But *is* this inconsistent? Sumner would agree that the utilities of potential people, as such, are not to be counted. Only actual people matter. And on the present view, if we decide not to have a child, then the utility he would enjoy if we did have him is not utility lost to anyone. Perhaps the following analogy is in order. Suppose that I am a businessman: I imagine an undertaking which would make a sizable profit for my business, but I don't undertake it. Then indeed there is a profit foregone by someone. But suppose I imagine a business which, if established, might make a good deal of money, but the business is never established. Then it is not clear that there is a profit foregone by anyone—certainly not by any business, at any rate. The analogy is, however, admittedly defective at one important point, viz., in my suggestion that other things being equal, one ought to go for the happiest of the possible children one could have, given a choice. In this case, no existing person is worse off than he or she might have been. However, one person is worse off than another would have been if the other option had been taken. And if the option is going to be taken, which is the assumption, then it matters that a better one might have been. It will then be as if a firm was set up in business when another might instead have been set up in a more profitable one. If our concern is that whatever people there are be as happy as possible, we will not be indifferent to this last point. The concern that there be more people, simply in order to maximize instances of happiness in the universe, seems of another order.

The net conclusion remains, therefore, as follows. (1) New additions to population ought not to be made at the expense of those who otherwise exist, even if there would be a net increment in total utility, considered in person-independent terms. But (2) new additions ought to be made if the benefit to all, *excluding* the newcomer, would exceed the cost to all, *including* him or her, as compared with the net benefit of any alternatives which don't add to population. Finally, (3) within those limits, the decision whether to add to population is up to the individuals involved in its production, provided that if they have a choice of which child to produce, they produce the happier one, other things being equal. Though complex in statement, this seems to me a reasonable interpretation of the injunction to go forth and maximize utility for all as applied to the population question. And it seems essentially in accordance with many people's intuitive views on the matter, and probably with most, if they are not adherents of a special religious creed.

It would be rash to imagine that this is the end of the matter. I do have an uncomfortable presentiment that the view presented may have been influenced by an alien conception of what morality is about, viz., the libertarian stance which has it that our duties are fundamentally negative. If at bottom our duty is only not to harm people, rather than to promote utility however and whenever, then it will obviously not be possible to support expansionary population policies as a matter of duty. Whether this conception has had an interference effect on my interpretation of utilitarianism is not easy to say. But I shall have to leave this question to others for the time being.

## *II*

We now turn to the other major department of our general question: what, if anything, can we be said to owe future generations in the way of a heritage from us? What sort of inheritance from us would occasion a justified complaint about us on their part? And what would justify it?

My first task will be to explain why the two extreme answers cited at the beginning of this essay are wrong, even given the moral views from which they may seem to follow. Let us start with the first answer—that we don't owe them anything, because we are not in the kind of communication with them which morality requires, morality being a sort of contract between independent rational agents. The snag in this view is that between us and them is a chain whose links overlap considerably. The next generation comes at a temporal distance of only a third to a half of a typical lifetime. And during the latter years of that lifetime, we are dependent on it, just as it was dependent on us during its earliest years. And of course, that new generation gives rise to another still, with whom its relations will be essentially the same as our relations to it. Its members will not be able to turn to us with a claim for Everything, then turn around and say to the next generation that it owes them Nothing. What it gets from us it will have to get in the light of principles which it must be prepared to apply in similar manner to those who come after. The result of this, I believe, will be that each successive generation can expect a gradual diminution of shares of exhaustible resources. This is because, rightly or wrongly, people in their middle years will expect to require less in their last ones, and hence their legacy to intervening generations will be based on the assumption that a diminished portion for themselves in their declining years will be adequate. Sentiment, of course, may intervene. Most people claim to desire a better lot in life for their offspring than themselves, and for that matter, they can reasonably expect to provide it. But not an increasing share of exhaustible resources: rather, an increasing amount of resources, such as knowledge and skill, which are inexhaustible, plus an improved basic capital in the way of such things as houses or land improvements which last much more than one generation.

Further justifying this basically selfish attitude will be the reasonable insistence that the young, with their lion's share of inheritable knowledge, will find new ways around old problems. Thus, we are told that although nobody at present knows quite how to do it, energy from controlled hydrogen fusion reactions will be on the market in a couple of decades. If this is so, the world's energy problem will be basically solved for the foreseeable future, and our worries about resource exhaustion will be transferred to less immediately essential items.

But let us suppose that resources essential to life are exhaustible. What then? Then surely a given generation would do well to limit severely its production of offspring. For if they are on the brink of starvation, then they surely have reason to make life uncomfortable—or short—for their erring parents. An ounce or two of prevention for this kind of problem is certainly going to be worth the pounds of care which would be required to deal with it later—care, of course, compounded by strife and probably war. Those who think that men are fundamentally justified in doing whatever is in their interest cannot object to harsh treatment by their fellows under such circumstances. It is therefore in their interest to avoid the circumstances and ensure a more equitable distribution of resources between themselves and the immediately succeeding generations. And when the resources are exhaustible and not so very far from exhaustion, the obvious way to do this is to reduce the numbers of those with whom they must be shared. They must strike a balance between those of their interests which favor more offspring and this one.

If we turn to the Libertarian theory, we come up against a fundamental problem. According to it, what we owe our fellow man is merely to keep off his back. Everything is left to the market except respect for the market itself. But what do we say about small children, for instance? Are we to say that a parent has done his duty by his child if he merely leaves the child to its own devices, so long as no actual harm is inflicted on him? What we intuitively think is that to neglect a child is already to harm it, since children are utterly dependent beings. Libertarianism as applied to mature adults has its attractions; but like Mill's Principle of Liberty, it would seem to require qualification in the case of children at least, if not also idiots and "savages." However this problem is to be handled, the theory nevertheless applies in a powerful way to the issue with which we are concerned. For whatever the obligations of parents to their children may be, it is at any rate clear, on this doctrine, that others have no obligations to them. All that a potential parent can expect is to be able to leave to his children whatever he accumulates before they are able to earn their own way. And if among his holdings should be a certain amount of the world's exhaustible resources, then he knows how much of *that* he can expect to leave to them. If he knows that it is not enough to last more than one child its lifetime, he'd better not have more than one if he values his offspring's welfare. Of course, it is unlikely that he will, say, own shares in an oil well. His estimate of his share has to be via his estimate of what he can afford to buy in the way of those resources. But the point remains the same. The premisses are at hand for a purely economic solution to the problem. Among the components of the solution are some which may strike some of us as draconian. For example, suppose that some parent disregards the facts and proceeds to have many children which he then cannot afford to keep up or who cannot, in later life, make enough to keep themselves in the necessities in question, whatever they are. On this theory, the sins of the father will be justly visited upon the children. Society will, in words immortalized on recent bumper-stickers, "let 'em freeze in the dark."

But perhaps it can be argued further that if it is clear that that is what is going to happen, or that the offspring in question are, with good reason, likely to turn to crime in their desperation, others may be justified in such circumstances in *disallowing* the births of excessive numbers of children. This, of course, is just the sort of thing which libertarians want to avoid. But it is not clear that their principles entirely block such an expedient. If so, then the implications of our different moral outlooks are, once again, not very far from one another in practice.

Let us turn to the other possibility mentioned at the outset, viz., that what we owe future generations, on utilitarian grounds, is Everything. Of course, the reasoning in the first part of this paper will, if correct, block this solution in any case. But even if we accept instead the "total" interpretation, the outcome is avoidable. What sets it up, remember, is the assumption that enormously large numbers of people in the future can each be nontrivially benefited by some very large sacrifice made by us now. It will be immediately clear that this outcome cannot be generalized. It cannot be true of *each* generation that if *it* makes the enormous sacrifices, then all future generations are nontrivially benefited, since we should then encounter the "jam tomorrow" paradox: the benefit is always in the future, and each actual generation is miserable. Furthermore, there remains of course the indeterminate but undoubtedly enormous consideration of the advance of knowledge, which may make large sacrifices in the present generation redundant: technological alternatives may well be found which would reduce to trivial proportions the capital requirement for the benefit in question. On top of that, there is the overwhelming plausibility of decreasing marginal utility for these benefits, and increasing marginal disutility for these sacrifices. Large sacrifices, reckoned, say, in material terms, will have a disutility far greater than the ratio of the large material sacrifice to a very small unit of the same sacrificed thing. The disutility of going without food for two weeks, e.g., is much more than fourteen times the disutility of going without it for a day. The sum of these considerations yields the conclusion that self-sacrifice for the sake of distant goods to others is unwise in any considerable dosage.

One might put the conclusion in either of two ways. One might say that the implication is that we ought not to look very far down the road, that a couple of generations or so is all we should worry about. But this is somewhat misleading. Perhaps it is better to say that if we take the longest view possible, as we always ought, what we find is so much obscurity that long-range considerations tell us to confine ourselves to fairly short-range ones.

It will perhaps have been noticed that on none of the theories I have been considering is it held or implied that all persons, throughout time, have, for instance, the right to an equal share of the resources basic to life. Perhaps some will be tempted to entertain some such doctrine. But, I believe, sober reflection shows that no such idea is to be recommended to sane minds. It isn't just that the doctrine, interpreted in such a way that it genuinely extends the alleged right to all future persons, is impossibly abstract or obscure or both. It's also that it fails to take seriously the fundamental point that how many future people there are to be is *up to us*. At the very least, it presupposes that future generations simply fall upon the world from heaven, without the intervention of human forethought. Given that this is not so, the doctrine will become self-extinguishing. Starting with the notion that we all, future and present persons, are entitled to $1/n$th of the exhaustible resources, and assuming (what plainly is false anyway) that we know that there are such things as identifiable finite resources which will always be essential to human life, what happens when in light of this we decide to cut the future generation's size by, say, 1/2? Does this imply that the next generation is entitled to twice as much? Or does it imply that we now can use a larger share than we thought? In any case, where does the notion come from? And what does it even mean? The most plausible answer is that it means that the needs or wants of each person should be counted equally in the determination of who is to have what–but that is the utilitarian view. If any such idea is reasonable, then, utilitarianism is the most likely one, and it has already been considered.

The conclusion, therefore, remains: what we owe to future generations is neither Everything nor Nothing, but merely Something. And the something need not be the same for all, nor can its content be rationally estimated beyond the horizons of technological foreseeability, which are surely very little if any beyond the lifetime of the present youngest generation.

# On Maximizing Happiness

*JONATHAN BENNETT*

1. When it is wrong to bring into existence someone who will be miserable, what makes it wrong is not the threat of misery hanging over the possible person, but rather the fact that if one does it there will be real misery for an actual person. This belongs in the same category as the wrongness of making a happy person miserable, or of failing to make a person less miserable than he is. These are all matters of the (dis)utilities–the ill-fare and welfare–of present and future actual people.

One might even assign (dis)utilities to past people. For instance, one might object morally to using the calculus for military purposes because Leibniz hoped that all his discoveries would contribute to universal peace–'If I use the calculus to help me build a bomb, I am bringing a disutility to Leibniz by bringing it about that he was to that extent a man whose hopes were not going to be realized'. (This would have been acceptable to Aristotle, I understand. He said that someone's *happiness*–according to the standard translation–may be affected by what happens after his death.[1]) I am not endorsing this attitude to past people, but neither shall I quarrel with it here. For my present purposes, I allow it into my scheme because the people in question are at some time actual.

But no sense attaches to '(dis)utility for a person who is at no time actual'. So if a failure to bring someone into existence is ever wrong for utilitarian reasons, these must concern the utilities of people who are at some time actual, not those of the person whose coming-into-existence didn't happen. It might be wrong for me to fail to beget a child because that would deprive my parents of the pleasures of grandparenthood, or because any child of mine would be sure to benefit mankind; in one case my parents are deprived, in the other mankind in general. But it couldn't be wrong because by not bringing the child into existence one deprives *it* of something.

2. 'But it could be wrong because by bringing the child into existence one gives *it* something'.

Well, I submit that in so far as moral questions are to be determined by facts about personal utilities, it should be through the rule:

> The question of whether action A is morally obligatory depends only upon the utilities of people who would exist if A were not performed,[2]

taking this to include people who did or do or will exist whether or not A is performed. Nothing is excluded except the utilities of people who would not exist if A were not performed—those who would exist if and only if A were performed, and also, trivially, those who would not exist whether or not A were performed.

This rule does not express anything that could be called 'negative utilitarianism'.[3] It is not part of any general moral scheme according to which one may be obliged to limit harm but never to bring help, or anything of that kind. Nor does it assume that morality basically tells one what not to do, but doesn't tell one what to do: the difference between 'saying what we should do' and 'saying what we shouldn't do' is just the difference between specific instructions and highly general ones; and nothing like that is involved in the above rule about utilitarian reasons for moral obligations. The rule is 'negative' only in the sense of implying that when I am considering whether I am obliged to do A, the only people whose utilities I need to consider are those who do or would exist if I did *not* do A.

The obvious alternative to my rule is the more generous one which says:

> The question of whether action A is morally obligatory depends upon the utilities of people who would exist if A were not performed, and of people who would exist if A were performed.

Both rules allow that one may be obliged not to bring someone into existence because he is bound to be wretched. What about the obligation to bring someone into existence because he is bound to be happy? The longer rule—the one which makes provision for the larger array of obligations—permits such a reason for such an obligation, whereas my shorter rule forbids it.

Over most of the territory, the two are equivalent. They differ only when there is a question about bringing people into existence: then the short rule confines us to moral injunctions of the form 'Don't do it unless . . .', whereas the long one leaves the door open for further injunctions of the form 'Do it if . . .'. The main reason for preferring the short rule is that it is harmless while the long one opens a Pandora's box of troubles. The long rule doesn't actually force us into trouble: since it merely *permits* us to have a certain sort of moral principle we don't break or flout it if we decline the invitation and keep our morality within the limits laid down by the shorter rule. But attempts have been made to accept the long rule's invitation, i.e., to devise moral principles which are forbidden by the shorter rule—principles which enjoin the creation of happy people, roughly speaking—and so far every one of these attempts has had morally intolerable consequences.

Unless some powerful positive reason can be found for the long rule, therefore, i.e., some reason for wanting a stronger set of principles of obligation than the short rule permits, the case for the short rule will be overwhelming.

3. Some philosophers seem to have thought that they had a case for the long rule, i.e., for the 'Do it if . . .' clause as well as for the 'Don't do it unless . . .' clause. They seem to have relied on the idea that if doing A would bring someone into existence who would then be happy, then not doing A does involve *a loss of utility*— namely the loss of that happiness—even though no actual person is deprived of the utility.

That in its turn appears to depend upon the notion, which I believe to be noxious in utilitarian morality, of *amounts of* . . . The gap can be filled by whatever form of utility you like: I shall say 'amount of happiness', but my concern is with 'amount', not 'happiness'.

Now, it doesn't matter whether it is a total amount, an average amount, or some compromise between these: the mere notion of *amount* lets philosophers introduce a surrogate for the proper notion of utility—it gives them utilities which are not *someone's*, in the form of quanta of happiness which nobody has but which somebody could have. As well as deploring the situation where a person lacks happiness, these philosophers also deplore the situation where some happiness lacks a person; and they speak of the latter situation as being one in which some utility is lost. This, I submit, is a philosophical mistake.

It amounts to the mistake of moving from 'We ought to make people as happy as possible' to the conclusion 'We ought to produce as much happiness as possible'; which doesn't follow.

I don't say that it is a *philosophical* error to hold, as a basic item in one's moral code, that one ought to produce as much happiness as possible. The philosophical mistake is to think that this—or the part of it which doesn't concern actual people—has to do with 'loss of utility' in some reasonable sense of that phrase.

4. With the muddle about 'loss of utility' set aside, perhaps there is some other reason to think that one ought to try to maximize happiness—taking this, loosely, to mean that in some circumstances one would be morally obliged to bring people into existence because they would then be happy. Might one not, for instance, base this on the view that the more happiness there is the better?

Suppose that we have believed that a certain region of the universe is cold and sterile, and then we discover that it is teeming with life and that its sentient inhabitants have very happy lives. Isn't this *good* news?

In my value-system, Yes; but not because I think that the more happiness there is the better. I share Leibniz's liking for rich, organic complexity, and so the discovery that our world has more of it than we had realized would be good news indeed. But amounts of happiness don't come into it. Happiness is relevant only in that the extra organic complexity would not be very welcome if the organisms were desperately miserable. From the fact that I am glad they exist, and wouldn't be glad that they exist if they weren't also happy, it doesn't follow that my gladness stems from a wish for maximal amounts of happiness.

Still, there could be someone whose gladness did have that source—someone who got a lift out of the sheer thought of all that extra happiness. That attitude—which might be expressed as the view that happiness is a good, or that the more happiness there is the better—seems intelligible as a good-hearted response to the thought of happiness in others. But it starts to slip out of my grasp, and to become something which I can only take to be an outcome of philosophical confusion, when it is thought to imply that one is morally obliged to bring people into existence so that they can be happy. I'll return to this point in §9 and §10 below.

5. This issue has a bearing on the question of whether *Homo sapiens* should be allowed to continue. There is obviously a moral case for letting our species die out: that would benefit many other terrestrial species, it would prevent the misery which will be suffered by millions of people if the species does continue, and so on. Against that, there are moral reasons for keeping the species going: reasons stemming from the disutilities to actual people of the phasing out of *Homo sapiens*—the frustration of the hopes of would-be parents, the loneliness of the final few thousand, and so on. From now on, I shall set all of that aside.

If we knew that all of the foregoing reasons pretty much balanced out, so that out of consideration of the (dis)utilities of people who are at some time actual we couldn't make a strong case for or against giving *Homo sapiens* a future, would that be the end of any moral consideration of the question?

Well, I am committed to saying that the question shouldn't be kept alive through any such thought as: We ought to perpetuate our species because if we do larger amounts of happiness will be had than if we don't. But I don't have to say that no other moral considerations could be brought to bear.

For example, someone might accept a principle enjoining the preservation of every species, or every animal species, or every instance of extreme physical complexity, or every form of life which is capable of moral reflection, or. . . . Any one of these could be brought to bear on the 'future for mankind?' question, in addition to all the 'utilitarian' considerations, properly so-called; and clearly none of them enjoins the maximization of happiness or anything like it.

Still, I don't want to make much of that. Although none of those principles is any worse than the principle that we ought to maximize happiness, none of them is much better either: none of them seems to have much to recommend it, considered as an item of basic morality. So I still have not identified any acceptable moral ground for an obligation to perpetuate our species, other than grounds involving the utilities of actual people.

6. When the utilitarian pros and cons are set aside, someone might be simply indifferent about the perpetuation of our species. This attitude, though it is perhaps unusual–even unnatural–should not be found shocking or ugly.

It is not my attitude, however. I am passionately in favour of mankind's having a long future, and not just because of the utilities of creatures who were, are, or will be actual. This is a practical attitude of mine for which I have no basis in general principles. The continuation of *Homo sapiens*–if this can be managed at not too great a cost, especially to members of *Homo sapiens*–is something for which I have a strong, personal, unprincipled preference. I just think it would be a great shame–a pity, *too bad*–if this great biological and spiritual adventure didn't continue: it has a marvellous past, and I hate the thought of its not having an exciting future. This attitude of mine is rather like my attitude to pure mathematics and music and philosophy: even if they didn't have their great utility, I would want them to continue just because they are great long adventures which it would be a shame to have broken off short.

In saying that this is not a principled attitude, I am partly saying that it is not *based on* any principles. If someone doesn't share this attitude of mine, there is little that I can say to him on the topic: I can't reach down for something which produces or confirms these attitudes in me, and appeal to the dissentient at that level.

Some practical attitudes are not based on principles because they *are* principles, i.e., are basic in the person's morality. But my wanting a future for humanity is not like that either. Indeed, it hasn't the right logical shape to constitute a universal principle: it is not a stand in favour of there being animals which answer to this or that general biological or psychological description, but rather a stand in favour of there continuing to be animals descended from members of *my* species, or descended from some of *these* (and here I gesture towards all my human contemporaries). The essential reference to particulars sharply differentiates this from such principled attitudes as my opposition to the causing of unnecessary pain to any creatures which can feel pain.

7. It is because of the unprincipled nature of my pro-humanity stand (as I call it, for short), that I don't regard the stand as part of my morality or, therefore, as a source of moral obligations. Hare's thesis that only universalizable practical attitudes should be accounted moral is true, I believe, and I find it helpful and illuminating. But for present purposes I needn't insist upon it. If you think there can be unprincipled moral stands, then you may count my pro-humanity stand as 'moral' after all; but you won't demand to know what principle(s) it involves, and that is what matters.

It matters because it frees me from the risk of being committed to absurdities. My pro-humanity stance, not resting on any principle, isn't vulnerable to the product of embarrassing counter-examples. You can describe to me a possible world, and ask whether I favour the continuation of *Homo sapiens* in that world (always setting aside the genuinely moral considerations, e.g., utilitarian ones); and I shall answer on the basis of how far it strikes me as a pity, a shame, *too bad*, if the story were to be cut short in that world. There might be patterns and regularities in my answers; you might even come to be able to predict them. But I wouldn't be applying a principle, and so I would never suffer the embarrassment of being committed to saying one thing while wanting to say something different.

Although my pro-humanity stance is not based on a principle, it does have some inner structure and I do have something like reasons for it. My attitude to mankind's future is conditioned by my attitude to its past: my sense that it would be a shame if the story stopped soon is nourished by my sense that it has been an exciting story which involves some long-term endeavours which aren't yet complete. I would probably care less about the 21st century if I didn't love the 17th so much. Thus, if I consider a world where there is no great disutility to actual creatures if *Homo sapiens* dies out, and where the continuity couldn't be more than a purely biological one because all the extrasomatic information and most of the non-genetic information have been irretrievably lost, I have no sense that it would be a great shame if the thread were to be broken then and there, and the species brought to an end.

So if I *had* to find a principle which I could slide in under my pro-humanity stance, it would probably be one about the prima facie obligation to ensure that important business is not left unfinished. Once that principle was clearly formulated, the counter-exemplifying game could begin. But perhaps I could so formulate my principle that no embarrassing counter-examples could be found. Anyway, I would be free from the peculiarly horrid difficulties which beset theories relying on the notion of amounts of possibly unowned happiness.

8. Although I know roughly what principle I would have if I had any, and although I doubt if it would lead me into grave and demonstrable trouble, I don't in fact have a principle. I say this partly because, as I said earlier, my attitude towards *our* great adventure is not an attitude I have towards all great adventures, nor even towards all of some general kind. But as well as that point about the logical structure of my attitude, there is also phenomenological evidence that the attitude is not a principled, moral one. It concerns the way I react to the thought of dissent–including my own possible future dissent–from my present attitude towards the continuation of mankind. I shall explain this.

When we accept something as a matter of moral principle, we engage ourselves to treat it somewhat like a matter of objective fact. I don't think that there are any moral facts, but I still describe moral views as 'correct' or 'incorrect', and I think of moral disagreement as implying that someone is in error. Thus, if I imagine myself coming to relinquish a basic moral view which I now hold, I am imagining a deterioration in my moral sensibility. In contrast, when I imagine myself having a different attitude to mankind's future (still, as always, setting aside the utilities of actual people), I don't see myself as *spoiled* but just as *changed*.

There is an analogous contrast between my attitudes to someone else who disagrees with me on a basic moral matter and to someone who doesn't share my attitude to the future of humanity. With the latter, I might try to bring him around by capturing his imagination with a certain picture of the human adventure; but if I failed, it would not induce the sort of distress which is appropriate when one is faced with fundamental moral disagreement.

If the question of mankind's future became a matter of practical urgency, and the utilities of actual people left the issue evenly balanced (!), then I might have practical reasons for wanting to bring dissentients around to my way of seeing things. That would be a simple matter of wanting them to want what I want, so that they would act to produce what I want: this, I submit, is very different from the sort of pressure towards agreement that obtains in a matter which is clearly classified as moral.

Those remarks imply something which I had better make explicit. Although my pro-humanity stance is not principled, it is thoroughly practical, and it may be at least as strong as some of my principled, moral attitudes. Don't play it down by calling it 'aesthetic' and letting that label suggest that it is merely contemplative. If the occasion arose, I would work for it, and probably even suffer for it.

I would also fight for it. If you try to bring it about that there is no 21st century human species, linked by me (and my contemporaries) to Spinoza and Aristotle, you may not be acting wrongly but I'll fight you all the same.

If my attitude in this matter is just an unprincipled desire, would I be morally in the right if I fought in defence of it, i.e., if I tried to make this desire of mine prevail over the desires of others? I think so. I don't mean that it is morally all right to fight anyone, in any manner, in the furtherance of any desire. But I do hold that each person is morally entitled to give some special weight to his own wants and needs and interests, just *qua* his. Although this 'morality of self-interest', as I call it, seems to be neglected in philosophical writings about morality, it looms very large in almost everybody's moral thinking. I have no hesitation in endorsing it.[4]

9. I suspect that my sort of attitude to the future of mankind is very widespread. It goes naturally with how theists, when not in the toils of the problem of evil, think about God as creator. I'll put this point in a non-theological manner, just for comfort. Suppose that *you* have a chance to bring into existence a race of creatures whose lives will be tremendously worth living. If you take the trouble to create them, they may well bless you for it, praise you, thank you, rejoice in the very thought of you—all the things that go with their

seeing your act as one of supererogation rather than as something you were obliged to do. Why then should you see it any differently?

(I moved from God to you because of general difficulties about moral attitudes towards God–e.g., why lavish praise and gratitude on Him for something which was, for Him, no trouble at all?)

For another slant on the matter, suppose that we came to share this planet with another species who were superior to us in every way except that we still had control (e.g., the Others were vulnerable to radio-waves, and had no comparable means of controlling us). The question might arise as to whether we should hand over dominance to these Others, and, since we could never happily accept a subordinate role, allow *Homo sapiens* to die out. Of course many genuinely moral considerations would come in, especially about the utilities of actual humans and actual Others; but what about the residual question–the question about the sheer idea of humanity's abdicating from its own future?

The example is adapted from Isaac Asimov,[4] whose attitude to the prospect is an enthusiastic *What a way to go!* Many thoughtful people, I believe, would share his feeling that there is something splendid about the idea of a biological species voluntarily ceding its place to another which it judged intellectually and morally superior. And many would feel, instead or as well, that there is something profoundly sad about it. I wonder how many people, if they hadn't been misled by bad philosophy, would want to add to those two civilized responses a moral judgment about an obligation to maximize happiness?

10. By willing the continuation of *Homo sapiens* one is inevitably willing profound misery for many people who would escape it if the species were allowed to die out. It has been pointed out that if that is not to be downright immoral, there must be something one can set against all that misery–something which outweighs it in the moral scales.[5] That is correct, but it falls triply short of re-establishing the amount-of-happiness approach, as I now show.

(a) It is plausible to think that the whole case for the continuation of *Homo sapiens* rests on the utilities of actual people–i.e., ones who were, are or will be actual even if mankind dies out. These utilities are considerable: the phasing out of our species over 150 years, say, would involve ghastly horrors; and the disutilities also include events which, though not intrinsically dreadful, serve to frustrate hopes, abort plans, disappoint expectations, and so on (as when a happy man suffers a disutility by dying quietly in his sleep). Perhaps, if it were not for all that, it *would* be morally inexcusable to sanction the continuation of mankind.

That would probably be the view of anyone who held, as many do, that if we were freely created by a God who knew what was coming, then what He did was inexcusable. Such a view does not commit one to perpetual gloomy discontent: someone who is radiantly satisfied with his own lot might still sincerely judge that the price was, morally speaking, too high. Nor is it implied that one should work for a state of the world in which mankind could be phased out without too much disutility to actual people: improved birth-control techniques, education aimed at discouraging long-term plans and hopes, help for the morale of the gradually shrinking remainder, and so on. Any energies devoted to tackling the problem from that angle could as well be spent on trying to reduce the likelihood that millions will be wretched if *Homo sapiens* does have a long future.

(b) Someone who thinks that there is a moral case for the continuation of mankind, over and above one stemming from the (dis)utilities of actual people, need not immediately fling himself into the arms of a principle enjoining the maximization of happiness. There are other bases he might appeal to, some of them more plausible than any amount-of-happiness principle: e.g., the principle which enjoins the completing of unfinished business, mentioned at the end of §7 above.

(c) Someone who isn't prepared to adopt either of those positions can still escape the conclusion that we are morally obliged to maximize happiness. I shall state this in an abstract form. Suppose someone says something of the form: 'Although if *Homo sapiens* continues many people will be unhappy, this is outweighed–the continuation of the species is made morally permissible–by the fact that if the species is continued then P', where P may be 'many people will enjoy great happiness', or 'certain intellectual and spiritual endeavours will continue', or anything else which doesn't involve the utilities of people who are or will be actual even if mankind does not continue. My point concerns not the identity of P, but rather its formal role in the argument. It is here being adduced as a reason for something's being morally permissible, but does that necessarily imply that it can also help to make something morally obligatory? Unless an affirmative answer to that can be defended, the argument falls at this fence even if it has surmounted the previous two.

The best case I can think of for an affirmative answer goes like this. 'If there is a *prima facie* case against doing A, one is permitted to do it only if it will bring enough compensating good; and if doing A would do a large enough amount of good, as compared with what can be brought about through some (any) alternative to A, then one is downright obliged to do A. Thus, the raw materials for a permission can always be made to serve to generate an obligation'.

Although I cannot disprove that, it is not compellingly self-evident, and I for one don't accept it. In particular, I believe that it fails in cases where the 'goods' in question are personal utilities and the practical issue affects what people will come into existence. I now explain this.

In §2 above I presented and recommended a rule which says that facts about personal utilities are relevant to moral obligations only through arguments of the form: 'It is obligatory to do A because if A is not done then there will be people who . . .'. That lies at the heart of my rejection of the idea that we are obliged to maximize happiness even where this involves creating people to have the happiness.

I stand by that rule because I see no reason not to. So far as the present difficulty is concerned, all I need is to show that the rule allows me to argue: 'The continuation of mankind is morally permissible, despite the predictable misery that will be involved, because of all the happiness that will be involved'. I now show that the rule does indeed present no obstacle to such an argument.

Since we are to relate a rule about obligation to a question about permissibility, the latter should be re-phrased in terms of the former. Our question, then, concerns *the obligatoriness of the NON-continuation of mankind*: the question of whether it is permissible for mankind to be given a future is the question of whether it is obligatory for mankind to be denied a future. For short, let 'A' stand for something like 'bringing it about that mankind has no future'. Then our question is: *Is A morally obligatory?*

Now, my rule in §2 lets us bring to bear upon that question any facts about the utilities of people who would exist *if A were not done*, i.e., if mankind *were* allowed to have a future. As well as making a negative case out of the fact that if A is not done there will be many miserable people, the rule lets us make a positive case out of the fact that if A is not done there will be many happy people. I don't say that it *is* all right thus to balance the bliss of some against the misery of others; but if it isn't, *cadit quaestio*. What I am saying is that my rule gives me access, in considering the obligatoriness of the non-continuance of mankind, to all the facts about all the people who will exist if mankind's non-continuance does not happen, i.e., who will exist if mankind continues. And so I have a clear, coherent basis upon which to maintain that the proposition *If mankind has a future then there will be many happy people* has some tendency to make it morally permissible to give or allow mankind a future, while having no tendency whatsoever to make it morally obligatory to give or allow mankind a future.

## *Notes*

1. Aristotle, *The Nichomachean Ethics*, Bk. I, ch. 10.
2. In this, as indeed throughout this paper, I follow the excellent lead of Jan Narveson, 'Utilitarianism and New Generations', *Mind* vol. 76 (1967), pp. 62-72.
3. As is suggested, against Narveson, by Jonathan Glover, *Causing Death and Saving Lives* (Penguin Books, 1977), p. 67.
4. I discuss it at more length in a book, tentatively entitled *Consequences*, which should be published in 1979.
5. R. I. Sikora, 'Utilitarianism: The Classical Principle and the Average Principle', *Canadian Journal of Philosophy* vol. 5 (1975), pp. 409-419, at pp. 414-415.

# Environmental Ethics and Obligations to Future Generations

*ROBERT SCOTT, JR.*

Almost every policy advocated by participants in the environmental crisis debate would if adopted have significant and widespread effects on the people of both present and future generations, and this gives rise to a difficult aggregation problem. The problem is how to weigh the effects on future people against the effects on present people.[1] Since almost every environmental policy affects both present and future people, no argument for the view that a given policy ought to be adopted will be sound unless its normative premise correctly "solves" this aggregation problem.

Consider the problem of non-renewable resources. According to some analysts (Cloud; Lovering; Meadows, *et al.*), if present rates of consumption continue, there are only enough of certain important minerals to last another 100 years. If, however, such rates were halved by adopting contractionist population policies, reduced per capita consumption, and/or recycling, known reserves would last for 200 years. Adopting any of these three policies would at least inconvenience, and probably cause a great deal of unhappiness to, present people. On the other hand, future people would be benefited. What ought to be done?

---

*Work on this paper was supported by NSF Grant OSS76-16382 (Dr. Mary B. Williams, Principle Investigator) from the Ethics and Values in Science and Technology Program. I would like to thank the editors of this issue of *Philosophical Monographs*, especially Dick Sikora, for helpful comments and criticisms.

The aggregation problem for effects on present and future people is at least as difficult as the (still unresolved) aggregation problem for effects on contemporaneous people—how much unhappiness may justifiably be caused to some present people for the benefit of other present people? Of course almost every utilitarian principle offers *a* solution to both the present-present and present-future aggregation problems. Most philosophers would, I expect, want to say that these utilitarian solutions are unacceptable for one reason or another.

There are, however, many different "dimensions," to use a term of David Lyons', along which utilitarian principles can differ. And as might well be expected, different forms of utilitarianism solve the aggregation problems in different ways. That is to say, there are situations where both present and future effects are involved where one form of utilitarianism prescribes one action and another form prescribes a different action.[2]

In this paper I will restrict attention to two such dimensions—those which give rise to total versus average utility principles and those which give rise to principles which do versus principles which do not "discount," or weigh less heavily in the utilitarian calculus, future effects of present actions. With some important qualifications to be set forth below, I will argue that one good solution to the present-future aggregation problem is provided by a classical or total utility principle which discounts effects on future people.

## *I*

That there is a difference between total and average utility was, as far as I can tell, first explicitly noted by Sidgwick (pp. 414-415).[3] For present purposes we can restrict attention to varieties of act utilitarianism having the following form: "A person ought to do an action at a time if the utility of that action is greater than the utility of any alternative action he could do at that time."[4] The difference between the total and average utility versions of this form of act utilitarianism is just a difference about how the utility of a person's doing an action at a time is defined. According to the total utility version, the utility of an action is the sum of the utilities for everyone affected by the action; whereas, according to the average utility version, the utility of an action is the sum of the utilities for everyone affected divided by the number of people affected. For the purposes of this paper we will assume that the utility for some individual person of someone's doing an action is just the net amount of happiness over unhappiness or pain which he experiences as a consequence of that action.

As noted by most people who have written on the differences and relative merits of total versus average happiness versions of act utilitarianism, each version has precisely the same implications for what ought to be done whenever none of an individual's alternative actions will affect population size. In all such cases, the action which produces the highest total utility must also produce the highest average utility, and conversely. However, in almost every situation involving a decision on environmental policy, there will be some alternative course of action which will make some difference for population size. Issues of population policy are the most obvious cases, but decisions involving the use of either renewable or non-renewable resources can also affect population size. Moreover, an alternative which is almost always available to every moral agent is to kill someone. Hence, there will almost always be at least the possibility of conflict between the total and average happiness principles.

Now if the total and average happiness versions of utilitarianism even occasionally conflict, then anyone who admits the moral importance of utilitarian considerations is faced with a problem. He must either reject one of the two versions or treat each as having some weight and try to find some method of weighing them against one another or attempt to formulate and justify a different sort of utilitarian principle. How might a decision on this matter be justified? Well, as a start we can consider objections to the various possible utilitarian principles in hopes of finding one principle which fares best.

There are of course several problems which afflict the total and average happiness principles equally. I have in mind cases where enslaving a minority, breaking a desert island promise, or torturing innocent people is happiness maximizing in both the total and average senses. According to one canonical diagnosis of these difficulties, utilitarian principles are important but they must be supplemented with principles of justice (Frankena, pp. 43-52; Brock, pp. 261-269; Rescher, pp. 40-41, 47-48; Cornman, pp. 504-508). If we grant, as seems reasonable, that all purely utilitarian principles are subject to justice-counterexamples,[5] then we should be suspicious of any reason for preferring the total over the average happiness principle, or vice versa, which is based on an injustice. If we allow, again as seems reasonable, that any correct moral code will contain both a utilitarian and a justice principle (and perhaps some other principles as well), then whichever of the versions of utilitarian principle we pick, the justice principle will presumably save it from the justice-counterexamples.

## *II*

As it turns out, there are a number of objections not based on injustices which seem to affect only one or the other of total or average happiness utilitarianism. Consider, for example, a case widely held to favor average over total happiness utilitarianism:

> If [total happiness] Utilitarianism should be true it would be one's duty to try to increase the numbers of a community, even though one reduced the average happiness of the members, so long as the total happiness in the community would be in the least increased. It seems perfectly plain to me that this kind of action, so far from being a duty, would quite certainly be wrong [Broad, p. 250. Cf. Rawls, pp. 162-163; Vetter, pp. 445-446; Rescher, pp. 27-28; Narveson, p. 80; Singer, p. 83; Green, p. 4; Brandt, p. 53; Henson, p. 324; Sartorius, p. 22].

A very simple situation of this sort is represented by the diagram below:

| Case #1 | | I | II |
|---|---|---|---|
| | *A* | 10 | 9 |
| | *B* | 10 | 9 |
| | *C* | | 3 |
| | TOT | 20 | 21 |
| | AVE | 10 | 7 |

*A*, *B*, and *C* are people, and I and II are outcomes, showing respectively the utility which accrues to the people as the result of not expanding or expanding the population under the conditions described above. The absence of a utility number for person *C* in outcome I indicates that *C* does not exist in I, and the fact that outcome I is circled indicates that it is supposed to be intuitively preferable given the facts about the case. According to the total happiness principle, II is preferable, yet surely, all other things being equal, I is better than II. Thus, the intuitively correct result would be dictated by the average happiness principle.

The average happiness principle, however, would prohibit people from having any children who were only just a bit below the average in happiness level (Henson, p. 325; Singer, p. 84; Narveson, pp. 80-81). Such a situation may be represented as follows:

| Case #2 | I | II |
|---|---|---|
| *A* | 10 | 10 |
| *B* | 10 | 10 |
| *C* | | 9 |
| TOT | 20 | 29 |
| AVE | 10 | 9 2/3 |

This diagram could also represent a situation where the average happiness could be increased only by killing off people whose happiness level was below the average.[6] Clearly, all other things being equal, such a course of action would be wrong, and the total happiness principle would dictate that the relatively unhappy people not be killed. Both the total and the average happiness principles, however, could dictate killing off "absolutely" unhappy people (Henson, p. 327), as is evident from Case #3:

| Case #3 | I | II |
|---|---|---|
| *A* | 10 | 10 |
| *B* | 10 | 10 |
| *C* | −10 | |
| TOT | 10 | 20 |
| AVE | 3 1/3 | 10 |

Another objection to the average happiness principle is that it could prescribe the extinction of the human race for trivial present gains (Williams, pp. 10-11; Sikora, pp. 410-411). Williams formulates the objection as follows:

> Consider a social system which maximizes the happiness of every person who is born, but does so by using up resources in such a way that the number of births permitted must be decreased every year.

> Suppose that this continues, without any decrease in the average happiness, until no further births can be permitted. . . . When the people alive at that point die, the species becomes extinct. . . . Note that the extinction could have been avoided, with very little sacrifice in average happiness, by restricting the number of births to the number which could be sustained indefinitely at that happiness level.

Case #4 represents an extremely simplified version of this situation:[7]

| Case #4 | | I | II |
|---|---|---|---|
| | *A* | 51 | 50 |
| | *B* | 51 | 50 |
| | *C* | | 50 |
| | TOT | 102 | 150 |
| | AVE | 51 | 50 |

Here again, the total happiness principle yields the intuitively correct result.

The only other objection I am aware of which works against exactly one of the two versions of utilitarianism is the following:

> The average happiness postulate will not do . . . if we have to decide whether new people should be brought into existence. Let there exist a few men on earth, all in extreme misery. Another man could be brought into existence who would be a little less miserable, so that the new average happiness would be a little higher. The average happiness postulate would demand that the man's existence should be started–an unacceptable consequence [Vetter, p. 446].

This sort of situation seems to be captured by the diagram below:

| Case #5 | | I | II |
|---|---|---|---|
| | *A* | −10 | −10 |
| | *B* | −10 | −10 |
| | *C* | | −7 |
| | TOT | −20 | −27 |
| | AVE | −10 | −9 |

Case #5 clearly favors the total over the average happiness principle.

## *III*

Thus far, we have found (i) some cases which seem to favor the average over the total happiness principle; (ii) some cases which seem to favor the total over the average happiness principle; and (iii) some cases which seem to count against both principles (the justice problems). Should we then conclude with Sikora (pp. 411-412) that when the average and the total happiness principles conflict, "we should sometimes do the thing that will bring about the highest average level of happiness; sometimes the thing that will bring about the greatest excess of happiness; and sometimes accept a trade-off between the two"? Such a conclusion would, I think, be premature.

First of all, someone might try to show that despite Case #1, the total happiness principle ought to be preferred over the average happiness principle. It might be urged that Case #1 is highly unlikely; and if a principle has counterintuitive implications only in highly unlikely situations, and if all of its competitors have such implications in situations which are not highly unlikely, then all other things being equal that principle should be preferred over its competitors.

I think that it is reasonable to hold that apart from their different counterintuitive implications, all other things *are* equal between the total and average happiness principles. Moreover, Williams has argued that a case somewhat similar to Case #1 is highly unlikely (pp. 15-16). Unfortunately, Case #1 seems to be enough different from Williams' case to make it very difficult to see whether her argument for unlikelihood could be made to carry over.[8] Still, since Case #1 is the only sort of case which seems to favor the average over the total happiness principle, the project of trying to show Case #1 to be highly unlikely deserves more attention.

If no argument could be made for the view that cases of #1's sort are highly unlikely, would we then be justified in accepting a trade-off position? No, for there has recently appeared a new competitor–a utilitarian principle formulated by Singer which is alleged to contain the strengths of both the total and average happiness principles, but the weaknesses of neither. According to Singer, the following principle fits this bill:

> If a possible future state of affairs is a world of P people at an average level of happiness A, it is wrong to bring into existence any greater number of people, P + N, such that no sub-group of P + N

> contains P people at an average level of happiness equal to or higher than A [Singer, p. 89].

As Sikora has pointed out (p. 417), this is not exactly the principle Singer wants, for in discussing some applications of his utilitarian principle, Singer argues as though he also holds the view that:

> If a possible future state of affairs is a world of P people at an average level of happiness A, it is wrong not to bring into existence a greater number of people, P + N, if some sub-group of P + N contains P people at an average level of happiness higher than A.

From here on, when I speak of Singer's principle I will mean the conjunction of the two principles just quoted.

As Singer correctly notes (pp. 89-90), his principle yields intuitively correct verdicts in some of the cases which are problems for the total and average happiness principles. Thus, Singer's principle would favor outcome I in Case #1, since no group of two people in outcome II has an average happiness level greater than or equal to 10. Moreover, like the total happiness principle, Singer's principle does not entail that outcome I is obligatory in Case #2. Hence, there is some reason to prefer Singer's principle to both the total and average happiness principles. There are, however, problems facing Singer's principle.

Sikora has argued that Singer's principle entails that "it would be wrong to prevent the existence of anyone whose existence would increase–no matter how little–the average happiness of the crucial sub-group, even if the person in question would be so wretched that he would wish that he had never been born" (Sikora, p. 418). A very simple version of the sort of case Sikora seems to have in mind would be the following:

| Case #6 | | I | II |
|---|---|---|---|
| | *A* | 20 | 21 |
| | *B* | 20 | 21 |
| | *C* | | –9 |
| | TOT | 40 | 33 |
| | AVE | 20 | 11 |

This seems to be a case which favors both the average and total happiness principles over Singer's principle, since clearly, Singer's principle entails that it would be wrong to bring about outcome I, whereas both the average and total happiness principles entail that I is obligatory. However, by slightly modifying Sikora's example, it is possible to construct a case which is a problem for all three principles. All we need do is suppose that *A* and *B* get even more benefit out of *C*'s misery:

| Case #7 | I | II |
|---|---|---|
| *A* | 20 | 36 |
| *B* | 20 | 36 |
| *C* | | –9 |
| TOT | 40 | 63 |
| AVE | 20 | 21 |

Fortunately for Singer, both Sikora's objection and my modification of it are based on an intuitively impermissible injustice. Cases #6 and #7 are exactly like the problems mentioned earlier of the innocent man, enslaving a minority, etc. But surely, if we allow that any acceptable moral code must contain both a utilitarian and a justice principle, we must allow that Sikora's objection would be blocked. Thus, although it would appear that Singer thinks that his principle *alone* "can serve as a basis for choosing a population policy" (Singer, p. 81), we should not allow Sikora's objection to refute Singer's principle. So far, then, we have found no tenable objection to Singer's utilitarian principle.

Ironically, Singer himself provides what seems to lead to a fatal counter-example to his principle. According to Singer, his principle entails that "under certain conditions (for instance, a world in which resources were so limited that we would have to sacrifice our own standards for the sake of future generations) it would be wrong, other things equal, to continue the human race" (Singer, p. 97). If we imagine that the sacrifices which would have to be made by the present generation are sufficiently small, then Singer's case becomes equivalent to Case #4, where the human race is made extinct for the sake of trivial present gains. Surely no principle with such an implication is acceptable.

Singer would probably reply to this objection as he does to his own weaker objection:

> The result does go against some of our most cherished convictions

> about the duty of preserving our race, and so on. I do not think we should be too dismayed by this. Our convictions have been formed in circumstances in which the prevailing conditions were almost the exact opposite of the imaginary conditions we are now considering. . . . Intuitions which have their origin in this kind of background should not be relied upon when we are faced with situations, real or hypothetical, in which the background is radically different [Singer, p. 98].

I think that we can agree with Singer that appeal to counterintuitive implications should not be the only criterion by which moral principles are evaluated. However, having counterintuitive implications does seem to be a bad-making characteristic of moral principles, just as having implications which run counter to observation is a bad-making characteristic of scientific theories. Moreover, Singer himself appeals to counterintuitive implications of total and average happiness principles, as well as to the intuitively correct implications of his own principle, in arguing for his own utilitarian principle. If intuitions do not count either for or against a moral principle, then we needn't give up both total and average happiness principles in the first place.[9] Moreover, surely the circumstances envisaged in Case #4 are no more bizarre or unusual than the circumstances Singer (among others) envisages in Cases #1 and #2.

## *IV*

So far we have examined three utilitarian principles, each having strengths and weaknesses, none entirely satisfactory. And since we have restricted attention to weaknesses which do not involve injustices, it seems unlikely that a moral code which contained only one of the utilitarian principles plus some justice principle would avoid all objections. Why, then, does Sikora say only that we should admit the relevance of two utilitarian principles—the total and the average happiness principles? Why aren't we stuck instead with three principles to balance against one another?

Although he does not discuss this possibility, Sikora could argue that there are no cases where of all three principles *only* Singer's principle yields the intuitively acceptable verdict. There are such cases for both the total and average happiness principles, however;

and so if we are not to multiply principles beyond necessity, we are justified in throwing out the Singer principle. Hence, Sikora might argue, as far as utilitarian considerations go, we need only admit the relevance of the total and average happiness principles; and where they conflict, attempt to weigh them against each other.

If we grant with Sikora, however, that both the total and the average happiness principles ought to be given some weight, it would be hard to argue that we have found a plausible solution to the aggregation problem concerning effects on present and future people. These two utilitarian principles amount to different aggregation procedures, but if Sikora's view is correct we must now aggregate the two principles themselves.

Fortunately, we needn't worry about this latter aggregation problem, for there is a form of total happiness utilitarianism which can avoid all of the non-justice problems discussed in this paper.

## V

Rawls suggests that total happiness utilitarians might want to discount effects on future people in order to avoid what Rawls takes to be a counterintuitive consequence of total happiness utilitarianism. According to Rawls, because there could be so many people in future generations and so many future generations, situations might arise where utilitarian principles would dictate imposing extreme sacrifices on the people of the present generation so as to slightly increase the total happiness of future generations. However, if the happiness of future people were discounted, this result could be avoided. Hence, says Rawls, a total happiness utilitarian could improve his theory by incorporating discounting (Rawls, pp. 297-298).[10]

The sort of situation Rawls is discussing as a problem for the total happiness principle *sans* discounting is somewhat similar to Case #1 above. Rawls's case, however, seems to involve an injustice–the present generation bears an unfair burden–whereas Case #1, it is possible to imagine, involves no injustice. Nevertheless, by following Rawls's suggestion and adopting some form of the doctrine that the happiness of future people should be weighted less heavily than the happiness of present people,[11] it would appear that a proponent of the total happiness principle could avoid all problems of Case #1's sort.

Moreover, all of the cases which favor the total happiness principle without discounting over the average happiness principle without discounting, favor the total happiness principle with discounting over the average happiness principle with or without discounting. In Cases #2, #4, and #5, the total happiness principle with discounting would yield the correct result so long as in each case *C*'s happiness was not totally discounted–i.e., disregarded–and the total happiness principle with discounting could easily be formulated so as never totally to disregard any future effect. On the other hand, the objections to the average happiness principle based on Cases #2, #4, and #5 would be even stronger against a form of average happiness utilitarianism which incorporated discounting. Cases #3, #6, and #7 involve injustices and, hence, for reasons by now familiar, need not be discussed here.

It might be objected that a total happiness principle which incorporated future-discounting would be open to a new objection–namely, that in discounting future effects, it becomes more likely that there will be situations where present people can justify on utilitarian grounds living it up at the expense of future people. Two replies might be made to this objection.

First of all, the situation described above clearly involves an injustice. It would be unfair for the present generation say, wantonly to use the earth's finite supply of fossil fuels so that the people living two or three generations in the future have to suffer a lower standard of living. Yet, as I have said several times before, we are working under the assumption that a satisfactory normative ethical theory will contain both a utilitarian and a justice principle; and it is likely that the justice principle would prohibit any such gross present prodigality.

The second reply which might be made to the objection above is that until we know exactly what the discount factor is, it is very difficult to know whether the total happiness principle which incorporated that factor would countenance any morally unjustified present prodigality. It should be obvious that there are infinitely many different possible discount factors,[12] and to justify selecting one from among them would require a close examination of many more particular cases than space allows here. On the other hand, I do not think that it is necessary to have some precise discount formula at hand in order to evaluate either my case for the total happiness principle with discounting or the present objection against it. Even a cursory examination of the cases discussed in the body of this paper should suffice to convince anyone that there is *some* discount factor which allows the total happiness principle to avoid the objection in Case #1 while still yielding intuitively correct results in Cases #2, #4, and #5. By the same token, it seems at least possible that incorporating this factor into the total happiness principle would block the objection now under consideration.

## *VI*

To sum up, I have argued that the classical utilitarian principle with future discounting when it is part of a moral code which includes some plausible principle of justice provides a satisfactory solution to the present-future aggregation problem. I do not believe that any utilitarian principle by itself would constitute an acceptable moral code.

One problem for my solution is the problem facing any code which admits the moral relevance of more than one consideration, viz., the problem of weighing those considerations when they conflict. In this case, the problem is how to balance justice against total utility. Surely, however, this problem is less difficult than weighing justice and total and average utility.

Finally, I should reiterate that my solution is proffered only as *a* good solution to the present-future aggregation problem. In order to justify my solution as the best solution, I would need to examine some of its competitors–e.g., Sartorius' purely utilitarian solution (Sartorius, pp. 21-24) and the various solutions via principles of justice (v. Rawls, pp. 284-297; Cf. Hubin, Delattre, Kavka, Green, Mueller, and Dyck). But this is a topic for another paper.

## *References*

Bentham, Jeremy. *The Principles of Morals and Legislation*. New York: Hafner, 1970.

Bergstrom, Lars. "On the Formulation and Application of Utilitarianism." *Nous*, 10 (May 1976): 121-144.

Brandt, R. B. "Some Merits of One Form of Rule Utilitarianism." *University of Colorado Studies in Philosophy*, 3 (January 1967): 39-65.

Broad, C. D. *Five Types of Ethical Theory*. London: Routledge and Kegan Paul, 1930.

Brock, Dan W. "Recent Work in Utilitarianism." *American Philosophical Quarterly*, 10 (October 1973): 241-276.

Cloud, Preston. "Mineral Resources in Fact and Fancy." *Environment: Resources, Pollution, and Society*. Edited by William W. Murdoch. Stamford, Connecticut: Sinlauer Associates, 1971.

Cornman, James W. "The Problem of Justifying an Ethical Standard." *Philosophical Problems and Arguments*. James W. Cornman and Keith Lehrer. New York: Macmillan, 1974.

Delattre, Edwin. "Rights, Responsibilities, and Future Persons." *Ethics*, 82 (April 1972): 254-258.

Dyck, Arthur. "An Ethical Analysis of Population Policy Alternatives." *Monist*, 60 (1975): 29-46.

Frankena, William K. *Ethics*. Englewood Cliffs, New Jersey: Prentice Hall, 1973.

Golding, Martin. "Obligations to Future Generations." *Monist*, 56 (January 1972): 85-89.

Green, Ronald M. "Intergenerational Distributive Justice and Environmental Responsibility." *Bioscience*, 27 (April 1977): 260-265.

Henson, Richard. "Utilitarianism and the Wrongness of Killing." *Philosophical Review*, 80 (1971): 320-337.

Hubin, D. Clayton. "Justice and Future Generations." *Philosophy and Public Affairs*, 6 (Fall 1976): 70-83.

Kavka, Gregory S. "Rawls on Average and Total Utility." *Philosophical Studies*, 27 (1975): 237-253.

Lovering, T. S. "Mineral Resources from the Land." *Resources and Man*. Edited by the Committee on Resources and Man of the National Academy of Sciences. San Francisco: W. H. Freeman, 1969.

Meadows, Donella H. et al. *The Limits to Growth*. New York: Signet/The New American Library, 1972.

Mueller, Dennis C. "Intergenerational Justice and the Social Discount Rate." *Theory and Decision*, 5 (1974): 263-273.

Myrdal, Gunnar. *The Political Element in the Development of Economic Theory*. New York: Simon and Schuster, 1969.

Narveson, Jan. "Moral Problems of Population." *Monist*, 57 (1973): 62-86.

Paley, William. *The Principles of Moral and Political Philosophy*. London: R. Faulder, 1790.

Parfit, Derek. "On Doing the Best for Our Children." *Ethics and Population*. Edited by Michael D. Bayles. Cambridge, Massachusetts: Schenkman, 1976.

Rawls, John. *A Theory of Justice*. Cambridge, Massachusetts: The Belknap Press of Harvard University Press, 1971.

Rescher, Nicholas. *Distributive Justice*. New York: Bobbs-Merrill, 1966.

Sartorius, Rolf E. *Individual Conduct and Social Norms*. Belmont, California: Dickenson, 1975.

Segerberg, Krister. "A Neglected Family of Aggregation Problems in Ethics." *Nous*, 10 (May 1976): 221-244.

Sidgwick, Henry. *The Methods of Ethics*. New York: Dover, 1907.

Sikora, R. I. "Utilitarianism: Classical and Average." *Canadian Journal of Philosophy*, 5 (November 1975): 409-419.

Singer, Peter. "A Utilitarian Population Principle." *Ethics and Population*. Edited by Michael D. Bayles. Cambridge, Massachusetts: Schenkman, 1976.

Smart, J. J. C., and Williams, Bernard. *Utilitarianism: For and Against*. Cambridge University Press, 1973.

Vetter, Hermann. "The Production of Children as a Problem of Utilitarian Ethics." *Inquiry*, 12 (Winter 1969): 445-447.

Williams, Mary B. "New Foundations for Environmental Law?" Mimeograph, 1976.

## *Notes*

1. I assume in this paper that effects of present actions on future people ought to be given *some* weight. Such a view seems to follow from another view which I find quite reasonable–namely the view that each person has a prima facie duty of beneficence and a prima facie duty of non-maleficence. I have attempted a fuller articulation and defense of this in my paper "Environmental Ethics and Obligations to Future Generations," read at the conference *Obligations to Future Generations*, University of Delaware, December 1977.

2. Not all differences in utilitarian principles are relevant to the present-future aggregation problem. For example, "Right" versus "Ought" forms of act utilitarianism do not diverge in any interesting way in such cases.

3. Myrdal, however, maintains that Mill held an average happiness principle to be best regarding population policy (Myrdal, p. 38). Paley, who was an unambiguous exponent of the total happiness principle (Paley, pp. 345-347), seems to have appreciated the difference between average and total happiness principles, but he is not very clear on this point.

4. Utilitarianisms can differ with respect to how the notion of an alternative action is unpacked. There is a large literature on this subject. For recent discussions, see Brock (pp. 249-250) and Bergstrom. In this paper, I will understand "$x$ is an alternative to $y$ for $s$ at $t$" as "$s$ is able to do $x$ at $t$, $s$ is able to do $y$ at $t$, and $s$ is not able to do both $x$ and $y$ at $t$." It should also be noted here that I have formulated act utilitarianism as providing only a sufficient condition for the obligatoriness of an action.

5. I exclude "ideal" utilitarianism–i.e., forms of utilitarianism which define utility in terms of intrinsic goods, where one intrinsic good is a just distribution of other goods–from the class of purely utilitarian principles.

6. Case #2 is also a problem for Rescher's Effective-Average principle (Rescher, pp. 35-38). According to Rescher's principle, the best outcome is the outcome with the greatest effective average, where the effective average for an outcome is just the average for that outcome minus one half the standard deviation for that outcome. In Case #2, the standard deviation for outcome I is 0; hence, the effective average for outcome I is 10, the same as the average. For outcome II, on the other hand, the standard deviation is $\sqrt{2}/3$, or approximately 0.47. Hence, the effective average for outcome II is approximately 9.43. So Rescher's Effective-Average principle, like the average happiness principle, favors outcome I.

7. This objection to the average happiness principle is similar to a much weaker objection propounded by Smart. Smart argues in effect that intuitively, $N$ people at an average happiness level $A$ is not as good as $N + M$ people at an average happiness level $A$, where $N$, $M$, and $A$ are positive numbers (Smart, p. 28). Obviously, however, the average happiness principle would entail that these possibilities are equally good; whereas the total happiness principle would favor the larger population. The main difference between Smart's case and Case #4 is that Smart's case is concerned only with different possible present populations. Smart rightly does not place much weight on his case, nor does anyone else I know of.

8. Williams' case is exactly like Case #1 except that in outcome II, $A$ and $B$ have 10 instead of 9 units of happiness. Williams argues that her case is highly unlikely in part on the grounds that such a case assumes that adding additional minimally happy people would *not* decrease the happiness of already existing people. However, Case #1 makes just the opposite assumption, since $A$ and $B$ *are* made worse off by the addition of $C$.

9. Another objection to Singer's principle is allegedly that it leads to intransitive preferences–i.e., there are supposed to be possible circumstances where according to Singer's principle an outcome I is better than an outcome II, and outcome II is better than outcome III, but outcome I is not better than outcome III (Parfit, pp. 104-108; cf. Singer, pp. 94-96).

10. Rawls, however, ultimately denies the utilitarians this expedient on the grounds that it is *ad hoc* (Rawls, p. 298). Yet surely even if amending a principle is motivated by a desire to avoid some objection, if the principle with the amendment is more plausible, then the amendment is justified. Moreover, there are other arguments for discounting (e.g., Golding, pp. 92-98; Passmore, pp. 90-92). I discuss some of the main arguments for discounting in my paper "Environmental Ethics and Obligations to Future Generations."

11. A more precise formulation of this doctrine would be a recipe for calculating the utility of an action as follows: first determine the amount of happiness which the action would produce for each individual affected, then multiply that happiness number by some factor, $n$, such that $0 < n \leqslant 1$ (cf. Bentham, Ch. IV). Segerberg (p. 225) suggests that the form of the factor might be something like the economist's discount factor $(1 + r)^{-t}$, where $0 < r \leqslant 1$ and $t$ is the temporal distance from the action to the effect in question.

12. Consider, for example, that there are uncountably many substitutions in instances of the Segerberg formula if $r$ is a real number.

# Classical Utilitarianism and the Population Optimum

*L. W. SUMNER*

The current human population of this planet is approximately 4 billion persons. It increases at an annual rate of 1.9%. If this growth rate continues global population will double in 37 years. The population of India is just over 600 million. Its annual growth rate is 2.1%. At that rate the population of India will double in 33 years. The population of Canada is presently about 23 million. Its annual growth rate is 1.3%, and its doubling time is 54 years.

Reflection on facts like these, and on estimates of the planet's stock of resources, have led many to conclude either that the world is already overpopulated or that it soon will be if its current growth rate is sustained. Most would agree that a country like India *is* already overpopulated. Conversely, some might feel that a country like Canada, with a relatively small population and a low growth rate, is underpopulated.

Conclusions like these suggest that a given population can exceed or fall short of some ideal level and/or growth rate. If a country can be over- or underpopulated then presumably it can also be well-populated, and perhaps some countries are well-populated in this sense. Those who take this suggestion seriously employ the notion of a *population optimum*, the idea being that it ought in principle to be possible to

*Earlier versions of this paper were read at the University of Calgary and at the Annual Congress of the Canadian Philosophical Association. I am grateful to my commentators and audiences on those occasions for their many acute and constructive challenges to the paper's conclusions.

define a best-of-all-possible-population-levels for a given unit (a city, or a nation, or the world) for some given period of time, and that this optimal level might then be an appropriate goal for public policy. My concern here will be with the method to be used in defining such an optimum.

In order to make my way through some very complex matters, I shall first record a number of working assumptions about the problem:

1. *It is possible to distinguish among ends, means, and procedures.* A population optimum is an end. It is tempting to think of the optimum as a fixed level of population to be aimed at and then maintained once it is achieved, but this is too simple for at least two reasons. First, it is too static in not allowing that different population sizes might be appropriate for the same society at different times. There is no reason to limit optima to steady states; an ideal profile for a society over a given time period might allow for limited increase, or decrease, or some combination of both. An optimum is better construed as a *pattern* defined by specified population levels for selected points in time. It may also be defined by the *status quo* population and then some sequence of rates of increase and/or decrease.

The resulting notion is still too simple because merely aggregative. It may be just as important to aim at some desirable *composition* (a profile of the aggregate by age, say, or sex) and geographic *distribution* for an optimal population level. This additional complication will be ignored in the discussion to follow.

As means we may think of the various policies which might be implemented in order to achieve a particular optimum. Some (not all) of these are appropriately called *population policies*. Leaving migration aside, the direction and rate of change in a population size are fully determined by the relation between its birth rate and its death rate. Both of these factors, at least within certain limits, are responsive to selective social control. Thus the birth rate may be raised or lowered by limiting or increasing access to such family planning methods as contraception, sterilization, and abortion, or by changing standards of perinatal care. Economic incentives may be offered for bearing, or for forbearing to bear, children. Controls may be legislated on family size by establishing either a minimum or a maximum; birth control methods, or pregnancy itself, may become compulsory. Likewise, the death rate is responsive to standards of hygiene and nutrition, the control of infectious diseases, provisions for the care of the aged, the vigour with which new medical technologies are developed, and so on. In so far as effects upon the population level are the principal aim or outcome of a policy, then we may treat it as a population policy.

It is easy to assume that population policies are the only, or the most effective, ways to control population. But it is quite clear that population levels and rates of change respond to a wide variety of general social and economic conditions: the kinds of opportunities available to women and their tendency to enter the labour market, the level and distribution of education, patterns of religious affiliation, the extent of economic development and urbanization, the distribution of wealth and the availability of a secure social minimum, the nature and extent of warfare, etc. While all of these factors affect population, each has a much wider sphere of operation and none would be pursued simply for its population effects. Most studies give us reason for thinking that the more dramatic changes achievable in, say, the birth rate are by-products of policies which are not in themselves population policies.[1] In any case it is obvious that the regulation of population is not an isolated social activity: population policies all have non-population effects and most broader social policies have population effects.[2]

Since I shall have little to say in the sequel concerning the means of achieving and maintaining a population optimum, I will register one fairly obvious observation here. Even if we were all to agree on the optimum to be aimed at none of us would be indifferent concerning the means to be used. Assuming that we would want to order available policies in terms of their acceptability, it is not difficult to imagine some of the criteria which we would be likely to employ: efficiency, economic cost, direct personal cost (raising the death rate is less desirable than lowering the birth rate), respect for individual freedom (voluntary programmes are preferable to compulsory ones and, perhaps, positive incentives are preferable to negative ones), side effects, and so on. Any ordering of available means will of course be controversial, but for our purposes it is enough to have the rough sense that, at least in the circumstances we usually contemplate, permitting the distribution of contraceptive devices is a more acceptable method of controlling population growth than shooting every tenth member of the populace. I shall be claiming later that one form of utilitarianism threatens to violate even these very weak sensibilities.

By procedures I mean the decision mechanisms which are necessary if those means which we deem ideal for our chosen ends are to be selected and implemented. Were we to pursue this issue we might want to ask whether democratic governments are capable of selecting the best means, whether there is any proper role here for government at all, whether global population control can be achieved without the sacrifice of national sovereignty, and other such political questions. However, we shall not be pursuing this issue.

2. *The concept of a population optimum is a meaningful one.* Since a society's population level is not utterly beyond its control, I shall assume that any given society (by which I mean any unit which has a population) possesses a number of possible patterns which it can pursue. These patterns comprise its *feasible set* of population objectives. The optimum is the pattern which is judged by some specified criteria as that which it would be best to achieve. Of course there need be no unique optimum in that sense: the criteria may pick out a number of feasible patterns as equal best, in which case all of them will count as optima. But there must be some standard or set of standards which can be used to order the members of the feasible set in terms of their desirability. If a single standard is used then the options are compared in terms of the extent to which they satisfy it; if a set of independent standards is used then there must be some means (a system of weights perhaps) for ranking patterns which satisfy different standards to different extents. This is to require that population patterns be commensurable.

3. *The problem of defining a population optimum has a maximizing solution.* Given the foregoing constraints on the problem, there is a weak sense in which any solution must be a maximizing solution: the optimum must maximally satisfy whatever standards are employed.[3] So far we have placed no limits on the standards to be employed; thus we could select a given pattern because it best achieves God's plan for the world or promotes the manifest destiny of our favoured race, or whatever. Some standards, but not all, compare alternatives according to the extent to which they increase some selected quantity. The optimum is then that pattern which maximizes that quantity—produces at least as much of it as any other alternative. The simplest such rule would be "Maximize the number of persons," which provides an easy, though not especially plausible, solution to the problem of locating the optimum. Other rules will treat the number of persons as a de-

pendent variable, the optimal number being that, whatever it is, which maximizes some other commodity. I shall be assuming only that a maximizing solution is a possible one, not that it is the best. The latter claim will, I hope, receive some support in the argument to follow.

4. *The problem of defining a population optimum is a moral problem.* That the problem is a normative one is obvious enough, since it concerns what we should aim for or what it would be best to aim for as a population level. Thus economists have considered this question as one aspect of welfare (i.e., normative) economics. That it is a moral problem may sound a bit stranger to ears accustomed to identifying morality roughly with sex. In the more philosophical sense of the term, the purpose of a morality is to establish norms which are to regulate (perhaps among other things) the relations of persons to one another. Thus morality includes (and perhaps is coextensive with) the realm of the interpersonal. Prominent among our modes of relating to one another is our capacity for affecting one another's interest or welfare. Thus morality includes norms regulating the ways in which we can harm or benefit each other. Those ways are limitless, but in a crowded world they include both creating new lives and terminating extant ones. Thus the vital activities (in the literal sense) are interpersonal ones in that they affect the welfare of others. (Note that we need not here raise the touchy issue of whether creating a person can be a benefit or harm to that person; it is enough that it can be a benefit or harm to the rest of us.)[4] Indeed it is difficult to think of a matter which affects the future welfare of our species (and of all other species, for that matter) more profoundly than the growth of our population.

When the issue is seen in this light then saying that it is a moral issue may appear to be merely insisting on the obvious. (I hope so, because it *is* obvious.) But it has one implication worth dwelling on for a moment. If this is a moral issue, and if the point of a moral theory is to provide us with guidance on moral issues, then we may legitimately expect of a moral theory that it provide some solution to the problem of a population optimum. If any theory is incapable of doing so then it is *ipso facto* incomplete. Now most of the traditional moral theories that we learn, or teach, in the classroom were devised in and for a world in which population was not a pressing problem. They therefore focus on the sort of person we should be or how we should treat others—issues which take the existence of individuals as a stable boundary condition. Let us call those moral issues which take for granted some particular number of persons *fixed pool* problems. Then the classical theories have been developed for and largely concern themselves with fixed pool problems. But some moral issues are *variable pool* problems: they consider the number of persons itself as on the agenda. There is no guarantee that a theory which works very nicely for fixed pool problems will have anything at all to say about variable pool problems. If not, then the theory is incomplete (this incompleteness may, of course, be symptomatic of some deeper defects in the theory). Though I cannot argue the point here, it seems to me that many classical theories are incomplete in just this sense: they imply little or nothing for population problems.[5] Utilitarianism is an exception to this rule: it may generate what one regards as the wrong solution, but at least it generates a solution. Already it has a leg up on many of its traditional rivals.

The remainder of this discussion will be devoted to exploring, and defending, a utilitarian solution to the problem of defining an optimum population. It seems to be widely believed that the theory handles this problem in a particularly disastrous manner. Thus Robert Nozick, for instance, has claimed (with, as usual, little supporting argument) that "utilitarianism is notoriously inept with decisions where the *number* of persons is at issue"–though he did have the grace to concede that in this area "eptness is hard to come by."[6] I interpret this to mean that while utilitarianism is not silent on population questions, its answers to them are obviously, even laughably, deficient.

The other problem impeding discussion is that the theory is now marketed in a number of distinct models. What I shall call the classical theory was first assembled in modern form by Bentham and given further refinement by J. S. Mill and by Sidgwick.[7] It had enough initial plausibility as a moral (and political) theory to elicit three sorts of reaction. The true believers embraced it in its pure form as a general procedure for moral decision-making. The theory's opponents, who have always constituted a majority, at least among philosophers, found it godless and pernicious, a solvent of such central values as the dignity of persons, individual rights, and social justice. The middle ground has belonged to the revisionists. They will neither accept nor reject the theory as it stands–they are potential customers but only if a few alterations can be made. Revisions are the food additives of theory construction. In the case of utilitarian revisionism the junk theories which have flooded the market have been particularly indigestible.

Luckily most of them—ideal utilitarianism and rule utilitarianism, for example—have by now sunk into a well-deserved obscurity, and it will not be necessary here to disturb their slumber.

Recently, however, a version of the theory called average utilitarianism has been riding a modest wave of popularity. Though some have (incorrectly) attributed it to Mill, it seems to have originated early in this century among welfare economists.[8] When J. C. Harsanyi, in some well-known papers published in the 1950's, sought to derive utilitarian principles from a contract base, it was the average theory which he chose to defend.[9] Following this lead, John Rawls in *A Theory of Justice* settled on the average theory as the main rival to his own principles of justice; ironically, the theory's current popularity is probably in large measure due to Rawls' hostile treatment of it. In any case, both utilitarians and their critics seem to be drifting toward average utilitarianism as a plausible alternative to the classical theory.

This trend is of interest to us since the average theory was devised precisely because it was thought to fare better than the classical theory with problems of population (indeed, as we shall see, they diverge only for such problems). It will therefore be convenient to conduct our investigation as a comparison between the two theories. I might as well confess openly at the outset that on the issue of utilitarian revisionism I am of a decidedly old-fashioned turn of mind. Having once settled into a moral theory I am loath to abandon it for some newfangled invention unless given good reason to do so. In this case, therefore, I need to be shown both that the classical theory performs badly on population questions and that the average theory does considerably better. Luckily for my innate stubbornness, exactly the opposite is true.

Both theories are best defined as possible specifications of a more primitive theory which I shall call proto-utilitarianism. The proto-utilitarian accepts the following theses:

1. A moral theory is a decision-procedure for moral problems which
   (a) identifies the alternative actions available to the agent (the feasible set),
   (b) ranks these alternatives in terms of some dimension(s) which the theory deems morally significant, and
   (c) requires selection of the top-ranking alternative (if there is a unique best) or any one of the top-ranking alternatives (if there are a number of equal best).

2. The only morally significant dimension of actions is their utility.
3. Utility is the satisfaction of wants or preferences.
4. The utility of an action is some function defined over the utilities of the various individuals whose welfare is affected by the action, equal utility of different individuals counting equally; actions are ranked in order of their tendency to increase this function.

The proto-theory, so defined, is fully comparative (it selects what ought to be done by comparing the utilities of all available alternatives) and maximizing (it requires maximizing some function defined over individual utilities). However, it does not specify what that function is.

The classical theory requires maximization of the net *sum* (total) of individual utilities while the average theory requires maximization of the *average* (mean). It is obvious that these alternatives by no means exhaust the possibilities. Thus one could easily imagine maximizing the median, the mode, or the standard deviation divided by the square root of your telephone number for that matter. Some of these outcomes I should be reluctant (for reasons I will not present here) to call utilitarian, which suggests that not all theories descended from proto-utilitarianism are themselves utilitarian. And anyway, most are just crazy. I shall stick to the selected pair.

A moment's reflection will show that in most decision situations the classical and average theories will yield identical results. Consider a given population $p$. For simplicity I shall ignore the influence of migration, so that $p$ fluctuates only with the number of births and deaths that occur within the pool. Let us say that a particular action or policy has *population effects* just in case it affects (or would affect if carried out) the size of $p$. (Effects, of course, need not be changes.) Now suppose that some agent is deciding between two actions which would produce different utility sums but neither of which would have population effects. The pool of persons among whom these alternatives distribute their utility is constant—namely $p$. Then maximizing the sum of utility must produce the same choice as maximizing the average, since the averages for the alternatives are obtained simply by dividing their sums by a constant. Thus it is only in a decision situation in which different alternatives would produce different population levels that the two theories can diverge. Suppose that the question is whether to add an additional person to the existing population. Imagine that the utility of 'doing nothing' (the status quo) is $u$; its average is therefore $u/p$. Imagine further that the utility added by the additional person would be positive but less than the status quo average. Then expanding the population by this one person will produce a greater sum but a lesser average than the status quo. It will therefore be preferred by the classical theory, but not by the average theory. It is no accident that the average theory was devised strictly to handle questions of population.

The two theories obviously have a good deal in common. They both propose maximizing solutions to the problem of defining an optimal population. Neither requires maximizing (or indeed any other operation upon) the number of persons itself; in both theories the optimal population level is whatever will maximize some other commodity (the optimum is a dependent variable). Both would require utilitarian calculations of a rather mindbending complexity–one must be able to compute the sums of utility "contained in" a number of alternative futures, each flowing from a different population policy and each involving (perhaps) millions or billions of persons. (Indeed, I would want to make the operation even more complicated by requiring some consideration of the effects upon other animal species of the level of our own population.) Since this computational burden is equally shared by the two theories, and is therefore not an issue between them, I shall assume that the usual shortcuts are available in actually making the theories work.

So we have come at last to the main question–given that you wish to purchase a utilitarian solution to the problem of a population optimum, should you opt for the classical or the average product? My tactic will be to subvert the average theory by stages, first by removing one of its principal supports, next by showing that it violates one of the basic values of any utilitarian theory, and finally by outlining its singularly implausible implications.

Historically, utilitarianism and theories of a social contract have been rivals, especially in the realm of politics. Rawls' efforts to revive the contract theory have superseded this incompatibility by employing a hypothetical contract (or rather a hypothetical individual choice under uncertainty) as a device for justifying a moral and/or political theory. Although Rawls tries valiantly to show that from an appropriately defined original position his own (non-utilitarian) principles of justice can be derived, some commentators have concluded that his real achievement has been to construct a contractarian justification of utilitarianism itself–an expanded and more thorough version of the argument of Harsanyi. We need not decide whether this is so. (I am very much inclined to the view that a contractarian derivation of utilitarian, or any other, moral principles is an activity possessing at best heuristic value.) What is significant for our enterprise is Rawls' claim that the only version of utilitarianism obtainable by this contract method is the average theory; indeed in his view the contract method reveals that a "different complex of ideas" underlies the two theories despite their surface similarities.[10] Be this latter point as it may, the fact remains that *if* one is tempted by hypothetical contract arguments and *if* Rawls is right then one cannot be led to the classical theory. Thus the average theory would possess one possible means of support denied to its rival.

As long as we define the contract situation as Rawls does then he *is* right. Imagine being asked to choose between joining two societies, S1 and S2, while being denied all information concerning who you will be in either society. On the assumption that your aim is to maximize your own utility, then you might reason as follows. Since you know nothing about who you will be assume that you have an equal chance of being anyone in both S1 and S2. If their populations are $p1$ and $p2$ respectively then the probabilities of your being any particular person are $1/p1$ and $1/p2$ respectively. If the total utilities of the two societies are $u1$ and $u2$ then you maximize your expected utility by choosing the larger of $(u1 \times 1/p1)$ and $(u2 \times 1/p2)$. But that is the same as choosing the greater of $u1/p1$ and $u2/p2$–i.e., maximizing average utility. Of course if the populations of the two societies are the same then your choice will also maximize total utility. But if they are not then you will always opt for the higher average; the prospect of larger numbers living at a lower average will hold no attraction for you.

Implicit in the contract situation as just described is the provision that you have an assured place in both S1 and S2, however their populations may differ. You have a confirmed reservation and, unlike hotels and airlines, these societies do not overbook. It is only when this provision holds that you may safely disregard numbers and concentrate on average utility. Let us now suppose that the provision does not hold. (The decision situation is admittedly a little bizarre, but then it is pretty bizarre already and anyway in contract arguments we are free to design any situation we like. So why not this one?)[11] Imagine that the number of hypothetical contractors is known to you and that it is equal to the population of S1. By choosing S1 each member of this pool of $p1$ possible persons is assured that he/she will be an actual person–though still with no idea of *which* actual person. You are now offered the alternative of S2, whose population you know to be less than that of S1 but whose average utility is greater. Since there are $p1$ possible persons competing for $p2$ places (and $p1 > p2$) you will have to participate in a lottery to determine whether you will have any place at all. Assuming that everyone has an equal chance of winning this lottery then you are confronted with the following alternatives: the expected utility of S1 is, as before, $u1/p1$; the expected utility of S2 is $u2/p2$ discounted by the probability of winning the lottery, namely $p2/p1$. But then the expected utility of S2 becomes $u2/p1$; eliminating the constant divisor, you maximize utility by choosing the larger of $u1$ and $u2$, i.e., by maximizing total utility.

More exotic variants of this game can be played, and it is by no means certain that the classical theory will always result. But it *is* clear that the average theory will *not* always result, and that alone is sufficient to defuse the contract argument to the average theory. To carry the issue further one would need to show that one conception of the original position, and of rationality in such a position, is (non-questionbeggingly) superior to another–and that is no easy matter. Until a clear resolution of this problem appears, the less that utilitarians have to do with contract arguments the better both for them and for the cause of moral argument.

We turn now to a consideration which ought to be much closer to a utilitarian's heart. One feature of the proto-theory outlined earlier was what I will call *utilitarian impartiality*: in calculating the utility of an action each individual's utility is included and the equal utility of different individuals will count equally. Historically, this provision is captured in the dictum which Mill (inaccurately, as far as I can see) attributed to Bentham: "each to count for one, no one to count for more than one." This is of course the only sort of impartiality or equality which the theory guarantees, since (notoriously) as an aggregative theory it is capable of justifying unequal treatment of persons. Equal consideration at the input stage yes, equal treatment at the output stage not necessarily.

Utilitarian impartiality is an absolutely essential element of utilitarian morality. It ensures that utilities are not weighted or otherwise manipulated so as to favour individuals distinguished only by what (for the theory) are in themselves morally irrelevant characteristics: sex, race, nationality, species, etc. Equal consideration is extended to all sentient creatures; this is, surely, one of the grander ideals inherent in any utilitarian ethic. Among the characteristics of individuals which are morally irrelevant must be included spatial and temporal location. If a person is (or will be) affected for better or worse by an action then that effect must be reckoned in whether it is proximate or remote over space and/or time. It is, after all, equally *real* regardless of where and when it occurs. This is the reason for the theory's insistence that the consequences for future (as yet nonexistent) generations must be taken into account in deciding on a population or resource policy.

Jan Narveson has defended a version of the theory which openly violates this impartiality requirement by counting for nothing certain utilities of persons who would be added to a population if the decision were made to expand.[12] The classical theory would count these additional utilities fully in favour of an expansionist policy. It does not exclude or in any way discount them on the ground that the very (future) existence of these persons is dependent on the policy which we (now) select.[13] (And anyway it should be kept in mind that in a world in which total depopulation is a member of our feasible set, *everyone's* future existence is dependent on the population policy which we now select.)

The kind of consideration which the average theory accords to future (and contingent) persons is more ambiguous. In a sense it is faithful to utilitarian impartiality since it always includes everyone's utility in computing the sums from which it then derives its averages. But let us look more closely. It will help if we expand slightly the situation sketched earlier to illustrate the divergence between the classical and average theories. Imagine that the status quo population is $p$ and that the question is whether to expand by precisely one person. We have a choice among one policy with population effects (one-person expansion) and a variety of policies each of which will have no population effects and will distribute a different utility sum through this pool of $p$ individuals. The best of these latter alternatives will produce a total utility of $u$ and so will one-person expansion. To sharpen the issues even more we may imagine that under the status quo alternative all the utility gain accrues to one person, Smith, while everyone else is left exactly as before; while under the expansionist alternative all of the resulting utility gain accrues to Jones, the new person to be added. Since they produce the same totals, the classical theory will be indifferent between these policies; benefitting some existing person and creating some new person are simply different ways of increasing the overall sum of utility. On the other hand, because the expansionist policy distributes its utility over a pool of $p + 1$ persons, its average utility will be lower. The average theory will therefore dictate steady state.

But on what grounds? We are invited to choose between equal gains by Smith and Jones (though they are not of course both gains in the same sense).[14] In favouring steady state over expansion it is difficult to avoid the conclusion that the average theory favours Smith over Jones *simply because he already exists.*[15] But that is to favour a person simply on the ground of his temporal location and that contradicts utilitarian impartiality. The average theory (in effect) discounts utilities which belong to future and contingent persons. The theory will not be indifferent between the alternatives in this case until Jones' added utility is greater than Smith's–indeed until it is equal to the sum of Smith's gain *plus* the average under the best non-expansionist alternative. Note that, *ex hypothesi*, no one is affected by the choice except Smith and Jones. The preference which the average theory exhibits is a pure (and arbitrary) preference for the living over the as yet unborn.

The first line of attack on the average theory was intended to appeal to contractarians and the second to utilitarians. We still lack, and need, a straightforward comparison of the implications of the two theories for questions of population. The classical theory bids us consider population expansion as one possible method of maximizing the welfare of a given society. Changes in the population level are so closely interlocked with other social changes that no expansionist policy will be just a population policy; it will also contain provisions affecting the well-being of already existing individuals. Similarly, non-expansionist alternatives will not aim solely at the purely negative goal of no increase but will also feature programmes designed to raise the overall level of social utility (redistribution of resources, economic development, or whatever). The point is that any government possesses an array of means for advancing the collective interest of its present and future populace; all that the classical theory stipulates is that the dividends returned by population expansion, including the utilities of the additional persons who would not have existed save for such expansion, be counted in on the same footing as any other dividends. It must of course be remembered that the classical theory is fully comparative: it requires choice of that policy in the feasible set which will produce a maximum of utility. It therefore ensures that population expansion will be dictated only when it promises a *greater* overall return than *any* non-expansionist policy. More precisely, it will dictate expansion to the point at which further expansion will return no more overall utility than some (any) non-expansionist alternative.

It is generally considered to be a weakness of the classical theory that it tends to be expansionist on population questions. The average theory was invented precisely to avoid this tendency while retaining some of the other features of utilitarianism. (And it does avoid this tendency, with a vengeance, as we shall soon see.) But what criticism can be offered of a theory which counsels expansion when and only when that alternative outranks *all* non-expansionist policies in terms of total utility? What criticism, I ask, except one based on a pure preference for present over future persons, or for smaller numbers for their own sake? And how could any such preference be defended? (For those who fear that the classical theory would require further growth in an already overpopulated world some reassurance should be offered. Though it is difficult to be certain, it seems overwhelmingly likely that the planet as a whole has already passed the point at which further growth is the *best* means of promoting human welfare. If so, then perhaps we should begin aiming at overall zero growth for the system (which might still require growth for some societies) and concentrate our energies and resources on providing a better standard of living for those numbers already among us. But this is to say that the classical theory could be used to support the intuitions about over- and underpopulation with which I began. It is therefore unlikely to generate consequences which are absurd or even seriously counterintuitive.)

The average theory is certainly more conservative about population increase—any growth must contribute *more* additional utility than the *best* non-expansionist alternative. When this condition is not met increase will be ruled out. But our population options are not restricted to increase and steady state. When we consider the possibility of contraction then the theories reverse roles. The classical theory becomes conservative, since any contraction (whether through lowering the birth rate or raising the death rate) is so much utility lost. It therefore demands some counterbalancing gains. But the average theory calculates its average over that pool of persons who will actually exist as a result of adopting a particular policy (that is why it is conservative about population increase). Thus if we choose to contract to a smaller pool, the average is calculated only over the members of that pool; the utility losses involved in eliminating existing persons or not producing new ones do not in themselves figure in the theory's calculations at all. Furthermore, contraction is dictated as long as it is the most efficient means of raising the average. That it will be *an* efficient means seems assured, since the average will rise every time we decline to add to the pool some persons whose utility contribution would be below the existing average. Thus at least a rapid decline in the birth rate would seem to be in order. But there is no reason for the theory to stop here. Lowering the birth rate while holding the death rate constant produces a gap of several decades before population growth stabilizes, let alone begin to decline. A much surer means is to raise the death rate, by eliminating members of the current population pool. After all, every time we get rid of someone whose utility contribution is below average the average instantly rises (which means that still more persons are below it, whose elimination will raise it again, and so on . . . . ).[16] Earlier I suggested a very weak ordering of means of controlling population in which killing off those already among us ranked rather low. There is the distinct danger, because the victims' utility losses would in themselves count for nothing and because getting rid of them could quickly raise the average, that the average theory would reverse these priorities. But that result *is* counterintuitive and absurd.

On the classical theory, it is likely that a global population optimum is no greater, and perhaps somewhat smaller, than the numbers which we currently possess. What kind of optimum would the average theory dictate? What is that number of us such that their average welfare is as high as it can be? Presumably there is some critical minimum such that further decline would lower the average. But what will this minimum be and how far would we go before we reached it? While it is again impossible to be certain, it seems likely that the optimum population defined by the average theory would be very small indeed, as compared with our current level, and that the theory would not be squeamish about the means to be used in achieving that optimum. (As a comparable micro-situation, imagine that you are among the passengers in an over-crowded lifeboat and you discover that the sole aim of the officer in charge is to ensure the survival of that pool of persons whose average welfare would be highest. How small would that number be?)

I am here assuming that we would be disposed to reject any theory which could require us to reduce our present population level to, say, the million (or thousand or hundred) best-off persons and to use genocidal tactics in doing so. But then, until some way of avoiding these implications is available, I am much inclined to think that the classical theory offers us a safer bet as a solution to the problem of defining a population optimum. If so, we have a somewhat surprising result: far from posing a particularly nasty threat to the classical theory, population questions turn out to highlight its virtues. Nozick notwithstanding, where the number of persons is at issue some versions of utilitarianism are considerably more ept than others.

## *Notes*

1. For one sociologist's defense of this view see Goldscheider (1971), especially ch. 6.

2. The only adequate model for understanding population fluctuations is an extremely complex feedback mechanism which captures the interactions among narrow or focussed factors (those with specifically vital effects) and wider social factors. Within any such model the distinction between ends and means becomes artificial, though not too artificial for the purpose of the present discussion.

3. It is in this weak sense, for instance, that Rawls' principles of justice are maximizing principles. See Rawls (1971), p. 211.

4. The issue of whether one can benefit a person by bringing him/her into existence will not be raised in this paper, since it is not itself pertinent to a utilitarian treatment of population. It is enough that producing new persons can create utility gains, whether or not they are, strictly speaking, gains *to those persons*. For a discussion of these issues whose main lines I endorse see Parfit (1976).

5. One example: the Kantian imperative that persons not be treated merely as means receives in liberal social theory the interpretation that individuals have the right to be free and that any use of coercion which violates that right is illegitimate. Question: can merely

creating a person be a use of that person as a means or a violation of his/her rights?

6. Nozick (1974), p. 41.

7. I ignore here the mistaken claims of those who hold that, in important respects, Mill was himself a revisionist.

8. For an early, and explicit, formulation of the classical position on population expansion see Paley (1814), Book VI, Ch. 11. I know of no evidence that Bentham ever entertained the average alternative. He explicitly regarded population increase as *one* possible means of maximizing the aggregate of happiness (Stark [1952], Vol. III, pp. 307-312, 261-363), though an unreliable one. He was also aware that population growth might result in an increase in total, but a decrease in average, wealth (*ibid.*, Vol I, pp. 360-361). However, in the one place where he considers the alternatives of a larger population at a lower living standard, *v.* a smaller population at a higher standard, he prefers the latter because of its greater likelihood of maximizing long-range *total* utility (see *ibid.*, Vol. I, pp. 111-112). Sidgwick seems to have been the first to formulate, and reject, the average theory (see Sidgwick [1907], pp. 415-416) and he was followed on this issue (as on most) by Edgeworth (1881). However, for a discussion rather friendlier to the average theory see Sidgwick (1919), pp. 317-318. As for Mill, it is difficult to understand why he has been located in the average camp in such discussions as Rawls (1971), p. 162 and Sikora (1975), p. 409. Their acknowledged source is Myrdal (1953) who, however, limits himself to the following statement without documentation: "Although it is nowhere very clearly stated, it can be shown that his ideal is a population in which average happiness per head is maximized" (p. 39). Admittedly, Mill's formulations of his own moral principles are rather loose but, in the absence of any explicit treatment by him of the point at issue, it is left quite unclear *how* this can be shown. Narveson (1967) seems to be unique in thinking that both Bentham and Mill were average utilitarians (see p. 62), but again so supporting evidence is offered. The more sober view is that in its modern form the average theory was the creation of Edwin Cannan and Knut Wicksell: see the discussions in Dalton (1928) and Gottlieb (1945). It should be noted that in the Cannan-Wicksell formulation the optimal population is that which maximizes average *product* (or average product per man-hour), not utility. I have benefitted much from the treatment of these question in "The Ethical Foundations of Population Policies," an unpublished 1974 paper by Simon Blackburn and Partha Dasgupta.

9. See Harsanyi (1953) and (1955). Harsanyi did not, however, deal

with situations in which the average and classical theories diverge and it is not clear that he was addressing himself to this issue. See Harsanyi (1955), p. 316n.

10. Rawls (1971), p. 189. The argument from the original position to the average theory (which Rawls rejects) is given in pp. 161-166.

11. Although this point is somewhat overstated, the fact remains that, as in any deductive arguments for normative conclusions, there *must* be a high degree of circularity in hypothetical contract arguments. Since the product of any such argument is controversial it cannot be obtained from a set of merely innocuous premises. Rawls himself admits (p. 141) that *in part* his original position is designed so as to yield his favoured outcome. The alteration of this position suggested in the text could (like Rawls' construction) be given an independent justification but I confess openly that its main virtue is that it yields *my* favoured outcome. Since writing this paper I have encountered an argument similar to my own in Kavka (1975). As I do, Kavka suggests that "it might be illuminating to extend the veil of ignorance to shroud the question of existence and to think of the parties in the original position as rational and self-interested *possible* persons choosing principles for governing the fundamental institutions of the society whose population policies will affect whether or not they will exist and in which they will live *if* they come into existence." Kavka's conclusion is the same as mine: "if we make certain assumptions which seem reasonable for representing the conditions of choice for possible persons in the original position, we can easily show that rational self-interested possible persons in the original position would choose those principles expected to lead to the highest total utility for the society in question in preference to principles expected to lead to a higher average but lower total utility" (pp. 240-241). The argument is rather more fully worked out than mine but we agree in most essential respects. Kavka works with the special case of an equal distribution of utility but also observes, correctly, that the distributive pattern is irrelevant to an argument to either variant of utilitarianism. He also assumes that utility scales will contain both positive and negative regions whose crossover point (zero) is assigned to nonexistence. While this construction *may* be innocuous enough, it can also lead to embarrassing problems for utilitarians. See Henson (1971) and Sumner (1976). In any case the assumption is unnecessary for the argument. I am grateful to Brian Barry for bringing Kavka's article to my attention.

12. See Narveson (1967) and (1973). Narveson's (complex) position is that the fact that an additional person would be happy does not

count at all in favour of producing that person, but the fact that he would be unhappy does count against producing him.

13. Some have found strange or objectionable this requirement of impartiality between present (actual) persons and future (possible) ones and (more generally) the counting of the utilities of merely possible persons. However, the sense in which the theory demands consideration of possible persons appears to be quite innocuous. Any comparative utilitarian theory must calculate the utility of each alternative in the feasible set in order to select the preferred choice. If these alternatives are (as they ought to be) mutually exclusive then *ex hypothesi* at most one of them will ever actually be done. Therefore at most one set of possible consequences will be actual ones. In coming to a decision it is still necessary to compare these (as it turns out) actual utilities with all of the other (as it turns out) merely possible ones. The projection of alternative possible futures, and alternative possible quanta of utility, is unavoidable. Population questions merely add one new dimension to this projection, since now some of the *merely* possible (never realized) futures contain persons who never actually exist at all. If it is impossible even to identify these unlucky individuals (except, of course, as those who would have existed had we chosen to . . . ) that is a matter of indifference to a utilitarian who considers persons just as so many utility locations anyway. What remains crucial for the utilitarian is that he count equally *all* the utilities which *would be* generated by *all* the available alternatives, regardless of *whose* utilities these are. The utilities of possible persons are just so many possible utilities.

14. See note 4, above.

15. That this conclusion is somewhat too simple may be seen by considering the following case. Suppose that we are to choose between the status quo policy and *substituting* one new person for one old, the total utilities being equal. Now both the classical and average theories will be indifferent, which shows that the average theory does not necessarily favour present persons over future ones. (I owe this point to Alister MacLeod.) Perhaps the average utilitarian discriminates more selectively against *additional* persons; in any case it remains true that he violates utilitarian impartiality by giving unequal consideration to equal utility gains.

16. This implication of the average theory was first pointed out by Henson (1971). Earlier in the argument it was shown how an *additional* person must on the average theory pay a utility premuim in order to *come to exist*. Though he does not put it in this form, Henson's argument demonstrates that, in addition, *extant* persons must pay a utility

premium in order to *continue to exist*. The premium in both cases is the same: the person's utility contribution must be at least as great as the average would be if he/she did not begin/ceased to exist. Of course eliminating below-average individuals would result in some circumstantial disutilities for those survivors who cared about the departed. The problem is that on the average (but not the classical) theory these disutilities *to others* are the *only* ones which attend killing: the victim's losses do not count for anything at all if his/her death raises the average. I have argued in Sumner (1976) that any acceptable utilitarian treatment of killing must locate its wrongness primarily in the harm it does to the victim. I have also shown there how the classical theory can satisfy this demand. The average theory cannot. It might be thought, however, that the classical theory is susceptible to a weakened version of the objection Henson makes to the average theory. Suppose, as seems plausible, that death is not the worst possible fate: some continuations-of-life would be worse than no-longer-existing. In that case there might indeed be a utility gain in killing such people. I can certainly imagine cases in which a person would (literally) be better off dead, but I do not think that many such cases exist (see again, Sumner, 1976). Where they do, they are precisely the sort of case in which many morally serious people (utilitarian or not) regard euthanasia as a viable option. This is not the place to investigate the morality of euthanasia, although I am quite willing to defend a utilitarian treatment of it. The fact remains that the average theory threatens to justify killing large numbers of persons who, while below average utility, are decidedly not better off dead.

## References


Dalton, H. "The Theory of Population," *Economics*, March, 1928.

Edgeworth, F. Y. *Mathematical Psychics*. London: C. Kegan Paul & Co., 1881.

Goldscheider, Calvin. *Population, Modernization and Social Structure*. Boston: Little, Brown and Company, 1971.

Gottlieb, M. "The Theory of Optimum Population for a Closed Economy," *Journal of Political Economy*, December, 1945.

Harsanyi, J. C. "Cardinal Utility in Welfare Economics and in the Theory of Risk Taking," *Journal of Political Economy*, October, 1953.

——— "Cardinal Welfare, Individualistic Ethics, and Interpersonal Comparisons of Utility," *Journal of Political Economy*, August, 1955.

Henson, Richard G. "Utilitarianism and the Wrongness of Killing," *Philosophical Review*, July, 1971.

Kavka, Gregory S. "Rawls on Average and Total Utility," *Philosophical Studies*, 1975.

Myrdal, Gunnar. *The Political Element in the Development of Economic Theory* (translated by Paul Streeten). London: Routledge & Kegan Paul, 1953.

Narveson, Jan. "Utilitarianism and New Generations," *Mind*, January, 1967.

———. "Moral Problems of Population," *The Monist*, January, 1973.

Nozick, Robert. *Anarchy, State, and Utopia*. New York: Basic Books, 1974.

Paley, William. *The Principles of Moral and Political Philosophy*. Twentieth Edition. London: J. Faulder, 1814.

Parfit, Derek. "Rights, Interests and Possible People," partially printed in Samuel Gorovitz *et al.*, eds., *Moral Problems in Medicine* (Englewood Cliffs: Prentice-Hall, 1976).

Rawls, John. *A Theory of Justice*. Cambridge: Harvard University Press, 1971.

Sidgwick, Henry. *The Methods of Ethics*. Seventh Edition. London: Macmillan and Company, 1907.

———. *The Elements of Politics*. Fourth Edition. London: Macmillan and Company, 1919.

Sikora, R. I. "Utilitarianism: The Classical Principle and the Average Principle," *Canadian Journal of Philosophy*, November, 1975.

Stark, W., ed. *Jeremy Bentham's Economic Writings*. London: George Allen & Unwin Ltd., 1952.

Sumner, L. W. "A Matter of Life and Death," *Nous*, May, 1976.

# Is It Wrong to Prevent the Existence of Future Generations?

*R. I. SIKORA*

Most people would probably agree that anyone deciding whether or not to do something that could conceivably lead to the destruction of mankind–for example, whether or not to start a revolution that might escalate into a nuclear war–should concern himself not only with the possible consequences of his action on those currently alive but should also consider the fact that his action might prevent the existence of future generations. It might seem that for practical purposes it doesn't matter whether or not it is wrong to prevent the existence of future generations because in order to prevent their existence you would have to do something drastic to everyone alive such as making them all sterile or destroying them all, and *that* in itself, aside from any other consequences, would certainly be wrong. But there could be a good reason for doing something that involved a *slight* risk of causing something terrible (such as, for example, the death of everyone alive); and a level of risk that would be tolerable if that was *all* that one should worry about might *not* be tolerable if the possible prevention of future generations had to be taken into consideration as well.

Though it seems eminently reasonable to hold that we have an obligation to refrain from preventing the existence of future generations (provided they have good prospects for happiness), it is a claim that some able philosophers reject. The obligation not to prevent the existence of future generations is supported by what is perhaps a more fundamental obligation–*that it is prima facie wrong to prevent the existence of anyone with reasonable prospects for happiness*. I am not claiming that this obligation is always overriding: it is in fact commonly overridden by other obligations. But that we have such a *prima facie* obligation relating to possible future persons is the basic thesis I want to establish in this paper. I will call my theory (or any theory that holds that it is *prima facie* wrong to prevent the existence of a person with reasonable prospects for happiness) an "obligation theory," and any theory which denies this, an "anti-obligation theory."

Moral systems have commonly considered only our obligations to those who are currently existing. Once future generations are taken into consideration, new moral issues arise which are not just a problem for utilitarians (though they have generally been brought up in the context of some sort of utilitarian system); they are problems for any ethical system which purports to be complete. Because I am a kind of utilitarian I consider the issues within a utilitarian framework, but analogues to the kinds of utilitarianism I discuss could be given for other moral systems. For instance, there could be semi-consequentialist analogues in the style of W. D. Ross or Aristotelian analogues where the questions would be, not what it is right or wrong to do, but what it would be virtuous or vicious to do.

What I take to be the two main objections to saying that we have an obligation not to prevent the existence of future persons is that this obligation relates to someone whose existence is not actual but only *possible* and who may in fact never exist; and that it commits us to what Derek Parfit calls the repugnant conclusion: that if an extremely populous world with a happiness-average barely over neutrality would have a greater happiness-total than a much less populous world with a far higher happiness-average, we would be forced to choose the first. In its more plausible form, the obligation theory cannot escape Parfit's objection; but I will attempt to blunt it by arguing: (a) that the most plausible anti-obligation theories face the same problem; (b) that the possible-persons objection is incompatible with Parfit's objection because any theory that implies that we never have an obligation to create happy people even at the cost of some sacrifice to those alive—because their existence in only possible—could conceivably be confronted with a situation in which the low-average alternative world in the repugnant conclusion could only be avoided by the creation of those happy people; (c) that this more populous world with a low happiness level might in fact be quite similar to the actual world we live in; and (d) that no currently defended version of an obligation theory would require us in actual practice to make the repugnant choice. I spend what may seem a disproportionate amount of space on the repugnant conclusion because it strikes some people, including, e.g., Peter Singer, as the most formidable objection to an obligation theory.[1]

The main body of my paper is not about the repugnant conclusion, however, but attempts to make the following points:

(1) that timeless utilitarianism (the view that the utilitarian principle applies to everyone who exists in the timeless sense) is incomplete on the question of our obligations to future generations because it is compatible with both obligation theories and anti-obligation theories;

(2) that the common view that it is at least permissible, taken in itself, to bring into existence a large group of people almost all of whom would be happy even if one of them would be utterly wretched can be justified only if it is admitted that it is a good thing to bring about or not to prevent the existence of happy people;

(3) that classical utilitarianism can be defended by a new argument which again relies on the intuition that we can only justify allowing groups of people some of whom will be wretched being brought into the world if it is admitted that it is a good thing to bring happy people into the world;

(4) that those who take the view that the preservation of mankind is not a moral but an aesthetic matter–that it would be a shame not to have people in the future mainly for the sort of reason that it would be a shame not to have elephants, giraffes, and other interesting and complicated forms of life, or for some other non-moral reason–are mistaken. It *is*, I argue, fundamentally a moral matter; though if one accepts my *meta*-meta-ethical theory, it doesn't really matter whether it is a moral question or not as long as the reasons that can be given for the preservation of mankind can prove persuasive to an epistemically rational person.

## 1. *Anti-obligation Theories & the Repugnant Conclusion*

It has commonly been thought that average utilitarianism can avoid both the possible-persons objection and the repugnant conclusion objection. Average utilitarianism, which seeks to maximize the happiness average rather than the happiness total, differs from classical utilitarianism only on matters affecting population size: it would direct us, for example, to aim at a smaller population with a lower happiness total if this would result in a higher happiness average. Average utilitarianism avoids the repugnant conclusion because it allows the average to be raised by adding people whose existence at the time the decision is made is merely possible which, of course, makes it vulnerable to the possible-persons objection (though in actual fact this isn't a real problem).

Taking the problem of the repugnant conclusion first, consider the following case. There has been a nuclear war. Only a million people are left in the world all of whom, because of radiation, are sterile. Once they die, unless something extraordinary occurs, no one will exist. Because of the effect of radiation on their health, the death of most of their families and friends, and the tremendous destruction in the physical world, their prospects for happiness are very low. However, if they want to they can repopulate the world with test-tube babies whom previous experimentation has shown will have a high level of happiness. Producing and rearing these children will unavoidably require a good deal of time and effort from them which will lower their own level of happiness still further. There are then two possible worlds: one in which the average happiness level would be very low and the other, the world of the test-tube babies which their sacrifice could bring about, in which the happiness level would be very high.

*Any theory that takes it to be wrong to require those alive to make sacrifices to bring about the existence of possible persons must choose the first of these alternatives, the world with a very low happiness level: that is, it must embrace the repugnant conclusion.* Average utilitarianism, however, can choose the second alternative, the happier world: since its sole objective is to maximize the happiness average, it will tell us to choose the happier world even if it requires a sacrifice from actual persons for possible persons.[2] Average utilitarianism only avoids the repugnant conclusion because it allows that there can be obligations concerning possible persons. *Any theory which denies that there can be an obligation to add possible people is open to the repugnant conclusion objection so that in fact no theory can avoid both the repugnant conclusion and the possible persons objection.*

As I see it, the main problem for average utilitarianism is this. Suppose you could cause someone to exist (that is, you could "add" an "extra person") whose net effect on others would not be harmful and who would enjoy a happy life though his happiness would be below the average. An average utilitarian has to assert not merely that we have no obligation to add this extra person but that it would be *wrong* to add him, and that it would be wrong no matter how happy he would be so long as he would not be as happy as an average person in that world. And it would be wrong to add him even if, besides being happy himself, he would have a beneficial net effect on others so long as that effect was not as great as the difference between his own happiness level and that of other people because if it were not, he would bring down the average. This can go further: it would be wrong to add him even if adding him satisfied the conditions of Pareto optimality, that is, even if each of the other people whose condition he affected was the better for it. In fact, it could even be wrong to add a happy person or group of persons who would satisfy what might be called the "Pareto-plus optimality requirement" by having a beneficial effect on *everyone* already there so long as doing so would lower the overall average. To take a simple case, suppose you have a world with a population of two people each with a happiness level of ten, and that you add another person with a happiness level of five who through his actions would make each of the others happier so that each of their happiness levels would go up to eleven. The Pareto-plus optimality principle would tell you to add him, but an average utilitarian would have to say that it would be wrong to add him: you would be reducing the average from ten to nine (i.e., 27/3). Sometimes showing that an ethical view has counter-intuitive consequences is not totally decisive because our initial intuitions may prove to have been mistaken, but this is surely not the case with the Pareto-plus optimality objection. It is enough by itself to demolish average utilitarianism.

### 2. *Is the Repugnant Conclusion Really Intolerable?*

Since any theory which denies that we can have an obligation to future generations (as well as the most plausible theories which do not deny this) entails the repugnant conclusion, it behooves me to see whether it is not something we can live with after all. It strikes me that the world we actually live in may be no better than the low-average alternative in the repugnant conclusion. All that would have to obtain for this to be the case is that the average person in the world should not have *significantly* more happiness than unhappiness, and it is certainly arguable that this is so. Furthermore, although one tends to think of the low-average alternative world as one in which everyone's happiness level is always just barely over neutrality, it doesn't *have* to be like that to get the required average; and even if it were, it wouldn't be as bad as it seems for if no one experienced more than mild pleasure, there wouldn't be much room for pain either; otherwise, the average wouldn't be above neutrality.[3] And many people would, I think, take a life in which there wasn't much pleasure but in which there wasn't much pain either to be an acceptable sort of existence. In actual practice, one wouldn't expect a world in which the average person's pleasure barely exceeded his pain to be either a world of continuous mild pleasure, or a world of hedonically neutral experiences with just enough mild pleasure to yield a positive net balance. One would expect instead a world rather like ours in which there was, among other things, a lot of intense suffering and even more moderate suffering and unpleasantness; and in order to balance this painful experience and come out with a slightly positive hedonic balance there would have to be some intensely pleasant experiences–joyful, even ecstatic experiences–or, lacking that, a great many moderately pleasant experiences.

If hedonistic utilitarianism is true, then in order for the low-utility-average alternative of the repugnant conclusion to contain more utility than disutility, that world must contain at least somewhat more pleasure than pain. Such a world may be no worse off hedonically than the world we actually live in. But if ideal utilitarianism or an interest theory is true, a world with considerably more pain than pleasure could still contain more utility than disutility because intrinsic value and disvalue in those systems is not solely a matter of pleasure and pain. Consequently, an ideal utilitarian or a philosopher who holds an interest theory could assert that the highly-populated low-utility-average alternative world of the repugnant conclusion although it contains more utility than disutility might nevertheless contain considerably more pain than pleasure, and considerably more pain than pleasure than is the case in the actual world. Though I would like to claim that the low-average alternative of the repugnant conclusion would not be worse than the actual world, showing that this is so is not essential to my case.

### 3. The Repugnant Choice in the Actual World

While both obligation and anti-obligation theories are open to the repugnant conclusion in theory, it might be claimed that while this is only a logical possibility for an anti-obligation view, there is a real chance that any obligation theory will be forced to it. In order to consider the merits of this contention, I need to look at some particular obligation theories. Classical utilitarianism requires actual people to make sacrifices to add extra people whenever doing so will maximize happiness (or whatever is taken to be the basically valuable thing). If one didn't want to go this far—and this is, I think, the commonsensical stance—one might take the position that while the happiness of extra people should be given *some* weight, it should not be given equal weight with the happiness of actual people. This is what I will label compromise principle 1, since another way of looking at it is as a compromise between a theory attributing no value to adding happy people and classical utilitarianism. The question is, given the world we live in, is it likely that either theory would force us to add great numbers of people till we have a large drab world instead of a much smaller, much happier world? Consider the sorts of effect that adding population could have on the average and the total happiness in the world: it could (1) increase the total without lowering the average; (2) increase the total but lower the average; or (3) decrease both the total and the average. It is only in the second case that there is any danger of the repugnant conclusion, but the world as a whole is now obviously so crowded that adding extra people is likely to lower both the total and the average happiness.[4]

If it is indeed unreasonable to think that the world's happiness will be increased by adding extra people, it is unlikely that the moral beliefs of a classical utilitarian or someone holding compromise principle 1 will force either of them to make the repugnant choice. Actually, there is a reason why it is even more unlikely. To be forced to the repugnant conclusion, you must not merely advocate a policy that will decrease the average in order to increase the total but *the decrease must be from a high average to an average barely above neutrality*. If there is to be such a decrease, the original average would have to be many times as great as the new average for, to be high, the average must surely be many times as great as an average that is barely above neutrality. Thus the new population would have to be many times as large as the old one. Consequently, in order for you to be confronted with the repugnant choice it must not only be possible for you to raise the total by increasing the population: *you must be able to raise the total by increasing the population to many times its current size.* But that is clearly out of the question for the world as a whole and if it is attempted in some part of the world with a relatively small population such as Canada, there is the further fact that both space and natural resources desperately needed elsewhere would be used up, not to speak of the enormous increase there would be in world pollution problems.

Jonathan Bennett has suggested that since Parfit's objection runs into these difficulties, we should look for some other form of the objection which does not. It might be urged that it would not only be repugnant to choose a world with an average barely above neutrality over a world with a high average, but it would also be repugnant (though perhaps less so) to choose a world with a lower happiness average than some other possible world even if the disparity isn't as great as that in Parfit's example. But this is average utilitarianism again—which is, of course, open to the Pareto-plus optimality objection. In order to avoid it, the principle could be modified to: it is always wrong to increase the total by lowering the average except when doing so would not be detrimental to the interests of some privileged group (such as those currently alive). The repugnance would then consist not in choosing a world with a lower happiness average than some other possible world, but in lowering the average in order to increase the total happiness by adding extra people at the expense (however little that might be) of those in that privileged group. A crucial assumption underlying this seems to be that there is no, or only marginal, moral worth in adding happy people to the world. But that is just what the objection seeks to establish so it suffers from circularity. Still this doesn't show that the intuition is mistaken. I will try to show that in §§ 8, 9, & 10.

### *4. No Plausible Ontological Preference Theory Can Avoid the Repugnant Conclusion*

I have argued that a strict anti-obligation principle is no better off with respect to the repugnant conclusion than the most plausible obligation theories: they are all open to it in theory but not in practice.

At this point I ask whether it is possible to find a plausible moral theory for my opponents which is in the main against adding extra people if this would require any sort of sacrifice from what might be called the ontologically privileged, but which nonetheless avoids the repugnant conclusion even in theory. A reader who is satisfied that there is no such theory can skip this section. In order to cover the most promising alternatives, I mean to examine systematically the main theories based on different answers to the question, "How much weight ought to be given to the interest of the ontologically privileged, and how much to the interest of those who are not members of that group?" (By the ontologically privileged, I mean that class of people whose ontological status is thought to make the promotion of their happiness of greater moral importance than that of "extra people," i.e., those not included in that group. The ontologically privileged might, for example, be thought of as the class of all actual persons.

1. *It is always obligatory to add happy extra people when the ratio of happiness gained through adding them compared to the happiness loss of the ontologically privileged is satisfactory.* Obviously, a ratio of less than 1/1 is unsatisfactory: no one supposes that the happiness of extra people should count more than that of the ontologically privileged.
   1.1. *Any ratio higher than 1/1 is satisfactory.* (the position taken by classical utilitarianism)
   1.2. *Only some ratios over 1/1 are satisfactory.* (compromise position 1)
2. *There is no ratio of gained happiness for added people versus loss to the ontologically privileged such that whenever that ratio is attainable it is obligatory to add happy extra persons.*
   2.1. *It is never obligatory to add happy extra people but it is not wrong to add them unless their addition would be detrimental to the interests of the ontologically privileged.* (That it is not wrong to add happy extra people whose addition will not be detrimental to the interest of the ontologically privileged is to be taken as included in all of the following views.) This avoids the main objection to average utilitarianism: it permits us to add extra people who will be happy if adding them is not detrimental to the interests of the privileged group. However, it entails

the repugnant conclusion because it prohibits raising the overall average at the expense of the ontologically privileged.

2.2. *It is sometimes obligatory to add happy extra people but only when it is compatible with the maximization of happiness for the ontologically privileged.* This clearly entails the repugnant conclusion. In addition, it is what Rawls calls a lexicographic principle (or, for short, a lexical principle), i.e., a principle which treats two distinct sorts of consideration as morally significant but gives one strict precedence over the other. When two sorts of consideration rather than just one appear to be morally relevant, lexical principles embodying the two considerations seem to have a decided advantage over principles which allow room for only one of them; but the problem is that if two distinct things are really morally significant, it seems unlikely that one of them should always take complete precedence over the other. For example, it would seem that if we have any obligation at all to add happy people, the obligation, say, to visit your elderly ailing aunt should not take precedence over your obligation to add a very large group of very happy people. A second problem is that in actual practice the second-rank obligation is usually given no real role. In the present case, for example, the obligation to add happy extra people is only meant to be a tie-breaker when two alternate policies would work out equally well for the ontologically privileged. It seems unlikely that there would ever be any such ties to break.

2.3. *It is sometimes obligatory to add happy extra people but only when doing so involves no net loss to the ontologically privileged* **or is needed to avoid the repugnant conclusion.** This is 2.2. modified by the addition of the boldface clause. It is an ad hoc modification of a strict ontological preference theory, hence, the "ad hoc theory." Since it avoids the repugnant conclusion without involving the consequences of an average theory, it is worth serious attention. Unfortunately, it is open to stiff objections:

(a) In a world with a high happiness average there would be no obligation to add extra people no matter how happy they would be and no matter how small a sacrifice would be needed to add them. On the other hand, in the sort of world with an average barely over zero envisaged by the repugnant conclusion, major sacrifices could be required, and these extra people for whose existence major sacrifices could be required might be far less happy than extra people for whose existence members of a happier state would be required to make no sacrifices whatever. But: (i) This runs counter to our ordinary tendency to think that it is more appropriate to ask for sacrifices from those who are well-off than from those who are badly off; and (ii) if we are required to make sacrifices to bring about the existence of happy extra people, it would seem that the happier those extra people would be, the greater the obligation would be: instead, the ad hoc theory calls for a sacrifice to bring about the existence of extra people with even a modest degree of happiness if they are needed to avoid the repugnant conclusion, and there is no obligation whatever to bring about the existence of even extravagantly happy extra people if they are not needed to avoid the repugnant conclusion.

(b) It is not just that people in an unhappy world would have a greater obligation to make sacrifices to add happy people than those in a happy world; the obligation would be infinitely greater because those in a happy world have no obligation to make any such sacrifice at all. It is simply something they should do if no sacrifice is required.

(c) According to the ad hoc principle, there is no obligation to make sacrifices for slightly less improvement than just enough to avoid the repugnant conclusion, and no obligation to bring about more improvement than is necessary to avoid it (even if such improvements could be achieved at the cost of proportionally far less sacrifice than those that the principle would require.)

(d) The ad hoc principle is, like the last, a lexical principle.

(e) The ad hoc view is an ontological preference theory (a theory that favors the ontologically privileged); but in abandoning the claim that we are *never* obligated to make sacrifices to bring about the existence of happy extra people, it gives up the main attraction of ontological preference theories.

2.4. *It is obligatory to add extra people whenever the ratio of gained happiness for those extra people versus the loss to the ontologically privileged exceeds some specified ratio higher than 1/1, except when doing so will lead to the repugnant conclusion.* Although this is a lexical principle in that avoidance of the repugnant conclusion is given strict priority over compromise principle 1, it is atypical in that it allows ample room for the application of the second-ranking consideration. In fact, if I am right, a situation will never arise in which the top-ranking consideration comes into play because compromise principle 1 will never in fact require us to make the repugnant choice. If so, this principle is extensionally equivalent to compromise principle 1.

Thus if anyone objects that compromise principle 1 leads to the repugnant conclusion in theory, this principle is an alternative that avoids the objection but is still for all practical purposes equivalent to compromise principle 1. However, I cannot accept it myself. I cannot because, if one is a utilitarian and if one admits (as the principle does) that there is some finite good in adding an extra person with even a slightly positive happiness balance, one will have to hold that it is infinitely *bad* to shift to the "repugnant" average, in order to justify the claim that it would be better to avoid the repugnant conclusion than to add even an infinite number of extra persons at a low but still positive happiness average. In fact, since the principle would allow one to accept a decrease in the overall average for a suitable increase in the total (so long as the average did not decline all the way to a "repugnant" average), infinite importance would have to be attached to the last bit of the decline, and that I can't accept.

2.5. *One should follow the classical principle except when it would lead to the repugnant conclusion.* Here again the original principle and its lexical counterpart designed to avoid the repugnant conclusion are extensionally equivalent. Again, I am bothered by its being a lexical principle although I am happy with it for all practical purposes.

I realize that I've given these seven possible theories in perhaps tiresomely complicated detail. Let me characterize them once more in a briefer way, which will, I think, show more clearly the relationship they have to each other:

1. The classical principle;
2. Compromise principle 1;
3. It is not wrong to add happy extra people when it is not detrimental to the interests of the ontologically privileged;
4. It is obligatory to add happy extra people unless it is detrimental to the interests of the ontological elite;
5. Principle 4. modified to avoid the repugnant conclusion;
6. Compromise principle 1 modified to avoid the repugnant conclusion;
7. Classical utilitarianism modified to avoid the repugnant conclusion.

### 5. *All Ontological Preference Theories Are False*

One of the first objections to any theory that holds that it may be obligatory in some cases for us to make a sacrifice for future generations is, put first in its crudest form, that it is never justifiable to require a sacrifice from an existing person for someone who does not exist. People who are currently existing constitute a kind of ontological elite whose interests are to take strict precedence over the interests of everyone else. The commonsensical root of this lies, perhaps, in something like this: suppose you are thinking of having another child. In weighing the pros and cons, you consider the interests of people who are currently living, the sacrifice that would be required, for instance, from yourself and from the other members of your family. You do not consider the interests of the unborn child one way or the other. Why should you? He or she is just a possibility.[5] But the case is not as simple as that, it turns out. As soon as much thought is given to the matter, it is clear that the ontologically privileged class must be extended to include not only existing but inevitable people, though just what it is to be an inevitable person is not immediately clear. Some writers seem to think that the class of inevitable persons is the class of all those who exist in the timeless sense except for those who have existed in the past and those who exist now. But this won't do because it is also supposed that you may in fact bring about the existence of a person (thereby making him exist in the timeless sense) who does not belong to the class of inevitable persons because you could have refrained from bringing about his existence. Furthermore, an inevitable person is not one who will exist no matter what *anyone* does: that would result in there being virtually no inevitable people. An inevitable person must instead be someone who will exist regardless of what a particular agent or group of agents (smaller than all mankind) does. Thus the notion of an inevitable person is always relative to some agent or agents. For example, a person whose existence is inevitable from my point of view may not be inevitable from his prospective parents' point of view: they could, for example, use a birth-control device or copulate at a different time. This means that there is no single class of inevitable persons. Therefore, if in framing our population policies the interests of inevitable people are to be set above the interests of merely possible people, different individuals should favor different population policies.

Peter Singer (following Derek Parfit) has quite a different objection to having the privileged class contain only actual and inevitable people. From the point of view of a population planner, it is inevitable that there be some minimum world population at a given time in the future—say, 1985—regardless of which of the policies open to him is put into effect.[6] On the other hand, the number of *particular* individuals whose existence is inevitable from his point of view is much smaller than the minimum world population because his policy will affect the lives of most of the world's population either directly or indirectly, and even a minute effect on the time of impregnation will result in a different individual being born. Suppose that from his point of view, the smallest possible population for 2025 is five billion, but that only three billion of them will be inevitable from his point of view. Clearly, it would be wrong for him in framing population policy to be concerned only, or even primarily, with those three billion so that the class of the ontologically privileged must clearly include not only actual and inevitable persons. It needs to be supplemented at the very least by the class of those filling what I will call "inevitable slots." Consider the following case. I know a couple who plan to have a child. I can alter their lives slightly so as to change the time of conception, thereby causing a different child to be born. Accordingly, any particular child they have will not be an inevitable person from my point of view. Still, because there is no morally acceptable way in which I can completely prevent them from having *some* child, there can be said to be a slot that will inevitably be filled though the particular child who fills it will not be an inevitable person. He or she will be the occupant of an inevitable slot. Will it do then to say that the top priority in population policy should be the welfare of actual and inevitable persons and the occupants of inevitable slots, and that the interest of others should count only as tie-breakers? Is this at last the combination of classes of persons whose interests can justifiably be placed above those of extra persons? No. The reason is again that the minimum possible population size for some given time in the future would exceed the number of people who would fall in the favored group of ontological categories for the population planner. In this case, the time in question would be somewhat farther into the future because we now have the occupants of inevitable slots as well as actual and inevitable persons. It still doesn't have to be so very *far* into the future, however, because there would soon come a time when a comparatively small part of the population was made up of the descendants of those alive at the time of the population planners' decision, and only those people could qualify as the occupants of inevitable slots.

The notion of an inevitable slot can be expanded in two ways. First, the class of occupants of inevitable slots could be expanded by allowing inevitable as well as actual persons to count as prospective parents of the occupants of slots; and secondly, the requirement for a child to be an occupant of an inevitable slot could be lowered so that it is only necessary that one rather than both of his parents is bound to have a child. But these changes wouldn't really make a significant difference; they would simply move the time at which the ontologically preferred persons would fall short of the minimum possible population somewhat farther into the future.[7]

It should be clear by now that any ontological preference theory will have consequences that none of us would for a moment be willing to accept. This applies not merely to relatively restricted ontological preference theories which restrict the ontologically privileged to actual and inevitable persons but to the various extensions of such theories with their increasingly far-fetched ontological categories. One consequence of this is that any theory that claims that there can be no obligations concerning possible persons, happy as well as unhappy ones, can be dismissed out of hand.

## 6. *Peter Singer's Minimum Number Theory*

At least some anti-obligation theories avoid the repugnant conclusion; namely, average theories and what I have called the ad hoc theory; but average theories are decisively refuted by the Pareto-plus objection, and the ad hoc theory is excluded for other reasons—among them, the fact that it is an ontological preference theory. Peter Singer's anti-obligation position while neither an ontological preference nor an average theory, still seems to avoid the repugnant conclusion. Following Parfit, Singer sees that it will not do to be concerned only with actual and inevitable persons:

> If a possible future state of affairs is a world of $P$ people at an average level of happiness $A$, it is wrong to bring into existence any greater number of people, $P + N$, such that no sub-group of $P + N$ contains $P$ people at an average level of happiness equal to or higher than $A$.[8]

This is not in any way an ontological preference theory. It doesn't matter to Singer whether or not the persons whose average is to count in deciding on an ideal population size are actual or inevitable, and although he doesn't use the notion of occupants of inevitable slots in any of the ways I've discussed, it is clear that someone would not be entitled to special consideration on his theory simply because he occupied one of my slots. It might be argued that Singer's concern with the minimum number enables him to use "occupant of an inevitable slot" in a way I haven't considered: aren't all the people in whose happiness he is interested (except insofar as they are tie-breakers) occupants of the minimum number of slots? Perhaps so, but a more appropriate term would be "*degree of happiness* slots" because, for Singer, it is the degree of happiness rather than ontological status that gives someone priority in a population planner's consideration. By rejecting ontological preference theories, Singer avoids the troubles they entail; but he also gives up their supposed advantage—denying that there can be obligations concerning persons who are neither actual nor in some sense inevitable.

What Singer wants (as he makes clear earlier and as is only reasonable) is a principle that will ensure the highest possible happiness average for the group of *P* persons; but his formula does not meet this requirement because it would allow population planners to limit the population to *P* persons even if adding additional people would make it possible to have a sub-group of *P* persons whose happiness level was higher than the happiness level of *P* persons would be if there were only *P* persons. To avoid this, his principle should be modified to:

> If a possible future state of affairs is a world of *P* people at an average level of happiness *A*, it is wrong to bring into existence any greater number of people, *P* + *N*, such that no sub-group of *P* + *N* contains *P* people at an average level of happiness equal to or higher than *A*, *and it is wrong to fail to bring into existence additional people if they would increase the happiness of a sub-group of* P *people*. (My change in his principle is in italics.)[9]

This is equivalent to:

> If the smallest possible population at some time in the future is *P*, we should aim at a population size such that the happiness level of a group of *P* members of it will be as high as possible.

I have objected[10] that, as it stands, this principle tells you to add an extra person even if he would be extremely wretched as long as his addition will increase, no matter how little, the average for the privileged group. Singer could of course add a suitable proviso to avoid this, though this would, I think, run counter to the spirit of his work. In the event of a tie where two alternate population plans would result in the same average happiness level for the privileged group, Singer thinks that the welfare of those not in this group should be weighed simply as a tie-breaker. In other words, he is using a lexical principle where the welfare of extra people is the second-ranking consideration.

Though I have a high regard for Singer's theory, which is the logical next step after an ontological preference theory, it is ultimately untenable for the following reasons:

*Objection 1.* Suppose that you could have either (i) a relatively small population with a high happiness average (its size will provide the minimum number); (ii) a population twice as large with half of them, the minimum number people, at a slightly higher average than in alternative (i) but with the other half at a happiness level only slightly over neutrality; or (iii) a population three times as large with a third of them (the minimum number people) with a higher happiness average than in alternative (i) though a bit lower than they would be on alternative (ii), and the remaining two-thirds only slightly less happy than the minimum number people. On Singer's view, we must choose (and this, I think, is counter-intuitive) the *second* rather than the third alternative. He is forced to this because, in the second alternative, the minimum number people would have a slightly higher average than in either of the others. This is hard to swallow but there is worse to come.

*Objection 2.* Suppose that the minimum possible population for a given time in the future is one, and that you will get the happiest subgroup of one in a fairly large world, World *A*, in which the average for the rest will be barely above neutrality; but that in a slightly smaller world, World *B*, everyone would be just a bit less happy than the minimum number person in World *A*. Singer would obviously be forced to choose World *A*. In choosing it, he would not only be opting for a world with both a lower happiness average *and* a lower happiness total (and one in which these characteristics could not be excused by considerations of ontological preference); he would have fallen into the repugnant conclusion: he would be choosing a world with a happiness average only slightly above neutrality (for the single happy person of course wouldn't significantly increase the average in his world) rather than a world with a high happiness average. And if it is argued that he would never be confronted in practice with a situation that would require him to make this objectionable choice, the same holds for the classical and the compromise principles. The minimum number theory lacks the very feature which had seemed one of its prime recommendations.

*Objection 3* (the *ABC* objection). If an ethical system tells you to bring about state of affairs *A* in preference to state of affairs *B*, and then tells you that once you have *A* you should abandon it for *B*, the system is in trouble. If over and above this, circumstances could arise in which once *A* was brought about, *B* would no longer be possible but the system went on to tell you to bring about state of affairs *C*, which is in fact inferior to *B*, the system is in even worse trouble. Singer's minimum number principle combined with his traditional utilitarianism for actual persons is open to this objection—for short, the *ABC* objection. Singer's principle (as I have amended it) is that if the smallest possible population size for a given time is *P* (the minimum number), you should have just that size population that will give you the happiest possible sub-group of *P* persons. Thus, if the alternatives for some given time in the future are: *state of affairs AA*: 10 billion people with a happiness average of 9; *state of affairs A*: 20 billion people with the top ten billion at a happiness level of 12 and the other 10 billion with a happiness average of 1; and *state of affairs B*: 21 billion people with 10 billion at a happiness level of 11 and the other 11 billion at a happiness level of 10; it is clear that Singer must pick *A*. Suppose now that when *A* has been brought about, *B* is no longer a possible alternative but that one could instead (say, by drastically redistributing the wealth of the country) have *state of affairs C* with 20 billion people, 10 billion of them with a happiness level of 7 and the other 10 billion with a happiness level of 6. Singer's traditional utilitarianism for actual people would force him to choose *C*, despite the fact that he would initially have regarded *C* as the *worst* of the four alternatives. Thus, the *ABC* objection.

It might be argued that if you know that your moral convictions will force you to change from *A* to *C* later, you should not have chosen *A* originally. To take care of this, a proviso could be added such as: in determining what population size will result in the happiest minimum number, take into account any redistribution of means of happiness that utilitarianism for actual people will eventually require. Reasonable as this sounds, it leads to paradoxical consequences:

(a) The augmented rule would still tell you to bring about *A* rather than *B* or *C*, provided that you couldn't later reduce the happiness of the minimum number people by changing to *B* or *C*. But it would surely be odd for a rule to tell you to bring about *A* rather than *B* or *C*, despite the fact that it would also tell you that once you had brought about *A* (if only you could) you should abandon it for *B*, or, barring that, for *C*.

(b) In cases where you would choose *A* only if you knew that state of affairs *B* or *C* would *never* be future alternatives which your principle would force you to choose, you might sometimes be able in some way to tie your own hands–say, to pass a law so that once you had brought about *A*, alternatives *B* and *C* were no longer open to you. But it is surely peculiar to say that you should tie your own hands so that in the future you won't be able to do what you ought to do if only you could.

*Objection 4.* Derek Parfit provides the principle which is the basis for this objection.[11] He says that if a woman means to have a baby in any event but if a baby conceived at time *t* would be happier than one conceived at time $t^1$, then she should conceive the baby at time *t*. The interesting thing about this is that instead of the usual situation where the choices are between two alternatives in one of which a person would be happier than he would be in the other, the choices in this case are between two entirely different people, the reason being that if conception occurs at a different time, a different individual results.

The underlying assumption here seems to be that if you are going to create one of two possible people, you should create the happier one. If there is no conflict of interest this seems intuitive enough, but in a case where having the happier child would cause a loss to an actual person, it is not clear how much weight should be given to the interest of the actual person as opposed to the difference between the interests of the possible persons. I can formulate three possible versions of this principle, each giving progressively less weight to the interest of the actual person. First, the mother could have an obligation to conceive a baby at one time rather than the other only if it would involve no loss to herself. But this is too weak for Parfit's purposes. Consider next a case where the mother must make some sacrifice to conceive the baby at time *t* rather than at time $t^1$. Let us say that her loss would be 10. This must be weighed against the difference in happiness between the two possible babies (let's say that this difference is 11). The moderate version of the principle would say that the difference between the babies' welfare should count *somewhat* less than her own welfare but not infinitely less. The strong version would say that the mother should count her own welfare as on a par with the difference between the respective welfare of the possible babies and that since this difference is 11 which is greater than her own loss, she should conceive the baby at time *t*.

The last two alternatives are both incompatible with the minimum number theory. Suppose that the minimum number is two and that the two persons are prospective parents who will benefit slightly more from having a child at time $t^1$ than from having a child at time *t* but that the child conceived at *t* would be a good deal happier than the one conceived at $t^1$. Both versions, strong enough to be plausible, would tell them to have the child at time $t$ but (provided that neither of the possible children would be happier than their parents) the minimum number theory would tell them to have a child at time $t^1$. (Parfit holds the strongest version of the theory. I agree with him, but I consider the other two because, when added disjunctively to the strong version, they are much harder to deny but still strong enough to be useful in attacking a number of important positions.)

*Objection 5* (the timeless persons impartiality principle). Suppose that we know that roughly 10% of the population in the future will be born with some sort of congenital disease which will make them relatively unhappy and that we plan to make the population larger than it needs to be so that these people will not fall in the minimum number category. In terms of Singer's principle, this means that the interests of living persons are to take strict precedence over those of persons born in the future with the congenital disease. Suppose further that there is a scarce natural resource which, if it is not consumed by those now alive, could be used to relieve the distress of those future people with the congenital disease; and that, though those now alive would get some pleasure from the resource, it would do them far less good than it would do the diseased people. According to the Singer theory, it is perfectly justifiable for those alive to use up the resource. This violates what I will call the timeless impartiality principle, that we should be impartial in weighing the respective interests of everyone who exists in a timeless sense.

Or imagine another case: where the more those now alive suffering from this congenital disease use the natural resource, the better for them; but where at some point the law of diminishing returns sets in dramatically, so that they derive progressively less and less benefit from larger doses. Since they fall into Singer's privileged category, his theory directs us to use up the resources on them; whereas the timeless principle would tell us to save some for more efficient use on future persons with the same disease.[12]

## 7. *Timeless Utilitarianism Is Incomplete*

The timeless impartiality principle coupled with the core of utilitarianism (that the utilitarian principle applies at least to everyone currently alive) yields timeless utilitarianism (that the utilitarian principle extends to everyone existing in the timeless sense). Because most utilitarians are likely to find timeless utilitarianism hard to reject, any version of utilitarianism which can be derived from it will be equally hard to reject. I believe that Narveson, Sumner and Warren think that their particular kinds of utilitarianism can be derived from timeless utilitarianism, despite the fact that Sumner takes a pro-sacrifice, and Narveson and Warren, anti-sacrifice positions. I mean to show that these derivations are not possible because timeless utilitarianism does not give an answer one way or the other to the question of whether there is intrinsic worth in adding happy people.

First off, for an action to be obligatory, it is necessary not only that it not be wrong itself but that no alternative action be permissible. Given this, it can be shown that it is neither obligatory to add happy people in order to increase the total happiness at the cost of a sacrifice from those currently alive nor obligatory *not* to add them. If you add them, they will always have existed in the timeless sense so that it will not have been wrong by adding them, to have treated their happiness on a par with the happiness of currently existing persons. If you don't add them, they will not have existed in the timeless sense so it will not have been wrong, by adding them, not to have treated their happiness on a par with the happiness of those alive. But if both adding them and not adding them are permissible, neither is obligatory. Consequently timeless utilitarianism is incomplete: it doesn't help us to decide whether or not there is intrinsic worth in adding happy people to the world.

Timeless utilitarianism is, for a similar reason, incomplete in Parfit's baby case. If the happier baby is conceived at a time which involves some inconvenience to his parents, it will not have been wrong, provided the loss is not too great, because the happier baby will have existed in the timeless sense so that it will not have been wrong to have given his happiness full weight. If on the other hand, the less happy baby is conceived at the more convenient time, this will not have been wrong either because the happier baby will not have existed in the timeless sense so that his happiness did not have to be counted.

## *8. The Eclectic Position and the Transitivity Argument*

At this point, I am tempted to make a final try to take the bits and pieces that are left and to construct a plausible position for those who hold that there is no intrinsic value in the preservation of mankind. The theory I have come up with is a minimum number theory, and it seems to me that it should have the following characteristics, for reasons I'll make clear as I go along:

(i) Because timeless utilitarianism seems right to utilitarians as far as it goes (even though it is incomplete), it should contain the principle of timeless utilitarianism.

(ii) It needs to be supplemented by either a moderate or a strong version of Parfit's principle.

(iii) To avoid the objections to ontological preference theories that led Singer to reject them, it must require us to take the welfare of at least the minimum number of persons into consideration even though many of them will not belong to an ontological elite.

(iv) As a minimum number theory, it must require us to be concerned with the future welfare of many prospective persons who don't belong to any ontological elite. Otherwise it would be vulnerable to the manifold objections to ontological elitism.

(v) To avoid conflict with timeless utilitarianism, it must require that if we add people in order to benefit the minimum number, the happiness of all the added people must be counted on a par with that of actual persons.

(vi) In order to be an anti-sacrifice view, it must hold, of course, that there is no intrinsic value in adding happy persons (unless they will be happy enough to be included in the minimum number group).

The resulting eclectic position can't be supported by arguments based on either the repugnant conclusion objection or the possible persons objection. I suspect that whatever attraction the eclectic position may have derives from the fact that it is a philosophical descendant of theories which were supported by arguments on which it can't itself rely. Mongrel as this conglomerate of principles may be, it deserves attention since it seems to be the best that can be done for those who don't want to hold that there is intrinsic value in the preservation of mankind.

Both (ii) and (v) can require us (though in different ways) to make sacrifices when we add people in order to get the particular people who will be happiest.[13] Since there might be other ways in which we could be called upon to make sacrifices for the same sort of objective which the eclectic position doesn't say anything about, it is not yet complete. For a philosopher with the consequentialist orientation of a utilitarian, the next move would be to make some general rule of which (ii) and (v) would be corollaries. But in order to do this one must first choose between the two versions of Parfit's principle. In fact, one must choose the stronger of the two to get a principle that will match (v) in its indifference regarding whether the total happiness should be raised by increasing the happiness of those alive or by arranging that the happiest possible people should be born. Still, whatever version of Parfit's principle you choose, you will be led inevitably to a pro-obligation theory. If you select the moderate version, it will be a compromise principle; if you accept the strong version, it will be the classical principle. I mean to show this first with the moderate version because I suspect it is the one that most people would find hardest to reject.

I am not claiming that either version of Parfit's principle implies a pro-obligation view. It is rather that there is no satisfactory utilitarian rationale for accepting either version unless you hold that there is intrinsic value in adding happy extra people. Narveson accepts Parfit's principle as part of an overall principle that is like the eclectic position I've just constructed except that it lacks (iv) and (v) (those pertaining to Singer's minimum number theory) and includes the weak rather than the moderate version of Parfit's principle. Narveson takes his overall principle (including the part from Parfit) to be implicit in timeless utilitarianism, which he regards as providing a utilitarian rational both for an anti-sacrifice view and for Parfit's principle. But timeless utilitarianism is incomplete with regard to both.

I can think of only two ways in which a utilitarian could justify Parfit's principle (or rather, its moderate version). The most obvious and, I think, the correct way is to claim that a prospective mother should make a small sacrifice to get a considerably happier child because: (1) other things being equal, a world that contains a happier person will be better than a world that contains a less happy person in his place; (2) happiness added to the world through adding the happier rather than the less happy person should be discounted in relation to the effect it will have on the happiness level of those currently alive; and (3) one should always do the thing that will result in the best of the possible worlds one's action might lead to. If one can improve the world by adding a happy rather than a "neutral" person (i.e., a person, so to speak, with equal amounts of utility and disutility) and if (as a utilitarian must hold) adding a neutral person does not make the world better or worse than adding no person at all, then (given the normal transitivity relation) one can improve the world by adding a happy person. How much the world is improved by adding someone with a given happiness level is a function of the discount rate chosen in step 2. A similar line of reasoning starting from the strong version of Parfit's principle would lead directly to classical utilitarianism because with the strong version, no discounting is required.

A second rationale could conceivably be given for accepting Parfit's principle: (1) given that the world is to contain a certain number of people, following Parfit's principle will indeed make the world better but (2) one can't make the world better by adding extra people no matter now happy they will be unless they will have a beneficial net effect on the people already there.

The transitivity argument would seem to show that given (1), it is implausible to hold (2). It could conceivably be claimed that transitivity doesn't hold in this case, but how could such a move be justified? It won't do to object that it may be obligatory to add extra people on the grounds that there can be no obligations concerning possible people, because the denial that there are such obligations leads to totally unacceptable conclusions. Nor will it do to say that there can be no obligation relating to what Mary Warren calls "merely possible persons," where a "merely possible person" is a possible person who will never exist; it won't do because there *can* be an obligation relating to a merely possible person who would be wretched if he existed–namely, the obligation not to add him. Nor will it do to say that a world can't be made better or worse by the addition of someone who would have no net effect on those existing. Clearly, the world *would* be worse if the person added was unhappy. Instead the claim will have to be that there is an asymmetry here: that although the world can be made worse by adding unhappy people, it cannot be made better by adding happy ones. This claim is the subject of § 9.

## *9. An Argument for the Obligation Theory*

In actual practice, it would never be justifiable *per se* to add any large group of people to the world unless there is at least some intrinsic moral worth in adding happy people to the world. The reason for this is that one can be virtually certain that at least *some* members of any large group that might be added to the world will, for one reason or another, have wretched lives, which of course counts negatively; so, unless adding happy people is to count *positively*, no matter by how much the happy outnumber the wretched and no matter how happy they are, it would be as wrong to add the whole group, happy members included, as it would be if it contained only its most wretched members.[14]

An alternative form of this argument: it would always be wrong, taken in itself, not to prevent the existence of any large group of people unless it is *prima facie* wrong to prevent the existence of happy people; otherwise, there would be nothing to offset the *prima facie* wrongness of failing to prevent the existence of the wretched people who would inevitably be members of any large group.[15]

William Anglin objects[16] that the most I have proved is that it is a supererogatory good deed to bring into existence (or not to prevent the existence of) happy people. My response[17] is that a utilitarian cannot admit that bringing about a given outcome is a supererogatory good deed unless we have at least a *prima facie* obligation to bring about that sort of outcome.

Bennett makes three objections to my argument,[18] the second of which is by far the most interesting:

> Someone who thinks that there is a moral case for the continuation of mankind, over and above one stemming from the (dis)utilities of actual people, need not immediately fling himself into the arms of a principle enjoining the maximization of happiness. There are other bases he might appeal to, some of them more plausible than any amount-of-happiness principle; e.g. the principle which enjoins the completing of unfinished business. . . .[19]

(Although the core of Bennett's objection is contained in this passage, I will draw on the rest of his paper as well to make his case as strong as possible.) He thinks that we can get something adequate to offset the wrongness of bringing the wretched people into existence without holding that it would be *prima facie* wrong to prevent the existence of the happy members of the prospective group. He is right in holding, in effect, that an action that is *prima facie* wrong may sometimes be permissible even if it would not be *prima facie* wrong *not* to do it. For example, suppose that I have a life preserver which someone else needs but which I also need. It is *prima facie* wrong for me to keep it because he needs it. It would *not*, however, be *prima facie* wrong for me not to keep it but to give it to him. Even so, it is *permissible* for me to keep it because of my own need. My own need makes it *prima facie* permissible (and indeed permissible *tout court*) to keep it without making it in any way wrong for me not to keep it. My need is a factor in the situation which tends to make keeping the life preserver permissible without making not keeping it in any way wrong.

Typically, such characteristics of actions are egoistic. Is there a characteristic of actions, some sort of balancing factor, which is egoistic, which tends to make the act morally permissible, and which would allow the bringing about of the existence of a large group of people despite the fact that some of that group will lead miserable lives? It is conceivable (though unlikely) that such a characteristic can be found if the number of miserable people the act would cause to exist is very small. Bennett thinks, however, that there is a balancing factor strong enough to offset even the bringing-into-existence of a great *many* miserable human beings—as would be the case, for instance, if the future of humanity were involved. Let me construct a case with an incredibly large number of possible people. Jones is the sole survivor of a nuclear war. People who are now dead and toward whom Jones has no obligation have started a batch of test-tube babies. Because they will be extremely small even when they are full-grown, the earth will be able to support a truly *enormous* number of them, in fact, $1{,}000{,}000^2$, all of whom but a very unhappy million will have rich and happy lives. If Jones chooses, he can totally prevent their existence, and the prospect of the very unhappy million little people makes it *prima facie* wrong for him not to prevent the existence of the whole lot. Suppose that Jones has some sort of interest in these possible people, an interest which has nothing to do with the well-being of the enormous number of happy ones—perhaps an aesthetic interest in having mankind continue. Surely it is obvious that if there is only Jones's own aesthetic interest to counterbalance the great moral weight of the *prima facie* wrongness of not stopping the birth of a million wretched people, that interest wouldn't even *begin* to be weighty enough.

However, Bennett makes it clear that his own "pro-humanity stance" is not aesthetic but "intensely practical." Furthermore, his central stance is that it is not a matter of principle: he wishes to avoid principles because they may commit him to unacceptable consequences. He offers as his reason for being prepared to make sacrifices and even to fight for the preservation of mankind, not the principle that one should not prevent the completion of unfinished business (or even business of some particular kind) but his interest in the particular unfinished business of the human race, an essential factor being the fact that *he* is a member of that race.[20] He urges that "each person is morally entitled to give some special weight to his own wants and needs and interests, just *qua* his." Suppose then that my man Jones, like Bennett, has an intense interest in seeing certain human projects completed and that he has reason to suppose that if the existence of the test-tube babies is not prevented they will complete those projects. Would this interest, even granting Bennett's point that special weight should be given to the fact that it is *his* interest, be of sufficient weight to offset the evil of causing a million wretched lives? Obviously not.

Alternatively, Bennett can take the line that he *is* appealing to a principle to get his counterweight, a "principle that enjoins the completing of unfinished business." Previously, his proposed counterweight was egoistic. This time, it is non-egoistic, which makes it more promising. However, it still won't do. Let's change the previous case slightly and have the test-tube babies initiate a new set of projects of their own rather than choosing to complete mankind's unfinished business. Despite the fact that there is now no unfinished business in this situation which could serve as a balancing factor, it still would be morally permissible not to prevent their existence even though there would still be a million wretched lives.

But perhaps some other non-egoistic reason can be found to outweigh the moral reason for preventing the existence of these future generations. It cannot be a consideration having to do with the pleasure, wellbeing, or fulfillment of interest of the almost $1{,}000{,}000^2$ happy people because that would be a moral consideration and of no use to Bennett. But if the balancing factor is meant to be some value in the completion of the various projects that is *independent of* the contribution to the interest-fulfillment,[21] pleasure, or wellbeing of the $1{,}000{,}000^2$ people those projects may make, I am at a loss to see how this could counterbalance the weight of the million miserable lives. I would be equally at sea if the counterweight were supposed to consist in something like the value sometimes attributed to preserving particular species—apart from the wellbeing of their members, apart from their ecological role, and even apart from the aesthetic pleasure that some people might take in looking at them or knowing that they were there. Here again, I can't for the life of me see how it could be enough to make it morally acceptable to let a million wretched people be born.

## *10. A New Defense for Classical Utilitarianism*

In §9, my argument was for the obligation view in general; here I will give a new argument for classical utilitarianism, based on the same underlying intuition.

(1) To prevent the existence of a person who would have, by a given amount, more unhappiness than happiness in his life is as important morally as it is to prevent an equal amount of unhappiness for a person who is alive.

(2) Other things being equal, if it is expected that the total happiness and unhappiness of a given group of people will be equal, it is not wrong to add them.

(3) But (2) would not hold unless there is at least as much positive value in increasing the happiness total of mankind by adding happy people as there is negative value in adding unhappy ones.

(4) Given (1) and (3) plus timeless utilitarianism, we can infer that classical utilitarianism is correct.

Some of those who disagree with me on whether or not it can sometimes be obligatory to make sacrifices for future generations may attack premises (1) and/or (2) under the mistaken impression that if those premises are weakened, the argument will result in some sort of anti-obligation theory. But the only sort of conclusion to which plausible forms of (1) and (2) can lead is still an obligation theory.

Perhaps the most fragile of these steps is (2). Though I think that (2) is in fact correct, one could assert instead that a group of people ought not to be added unless their total happiness will considerably exceed their unhappiness. (2) could be modified to avoid this objection but that would weaken the argument's conclusion. The argument would then be:

(1) To prevent the existence of a person who will have, by a given amount, more unhappiness than happiness is as important morally as to prevent an equal amount of unhappiness in a person who is alive.

(2a) Other things being equal, it is wrong to add a group of people unless one expects the happiness of the group to exceed its unhappiness by a ratio of $x$ to 1.

(3a) But (2a) would not hold unless there is at least $1/x$ times as much positive value in increasing the happiness total of mankind by adding happy people as there is negative value in adding unhappy ones.

Given (1) and (3a) plus timeless utilitarianism, we can infer (4a): there is at least $1/x$ times as much positive value in increasing the happiness total of the world by adding happy people as there is in preventing an equal amount of suffering (or adding an equal amount of happiness) for those alive (compromise principle 2).

Though he is bound to regret losing the simplicity of the classical principle, a utilitarian might tolerate (4a) provided the ratio isn't *too* far from the one-to-one ratio of classical utilitarianism. But might we be forced to accept such a high happiness-excess ratio in (2a), say, 10 to 1, that it would result in a conclusion really quite far removed from classical utilitarianism? I think not, because such a ratio would lead to counter-intuitive results. If it were taken to be wrong, other things being equal, to add a group of people unless it is probable that their happiness total will be at least three times (let alone ten times) their unhappiness total, one would be forced to regard it as wrong *per se* to add *any* future generations unless one were extremely optimistic, because it is highly unlikely that they would on the average have three times as much happiness as unhappiness.

Alternatively, the first premise might strike some people as mistaken on the grounds that it is not, in fact, always wrong to add a person whose unhappiness would exceed his happiness–it is only wrong when the ratio would be fairly high–let's call this level Φ. If one wishes to go along with this, my original premise could be replaced by another according to which it is *prima facie* wrong to add a person only if his ratio of unhappiness to happiness exceeds level Φ. If, say, one held that there was negative value in adding a person only insofar as he would have more than five times more unhappiness than happiness and a given person would be likely to have six times more unhappiness than happiness, 5/6 of his unhappiness could be disregarded in deciding whether it would be wrong to add him. This would provide a basis for another attempt to reconcile our normal intuitions about which groups of prospective people it would not be wrong to add with a high happiness-excess demand in the (2a) ratio: we would have such a little excess of unhappiness to count negatively that a high ratio of good to bad could be required in (2a) without violating our intuitions as to which groups it would not be wrong to add. With these revisions the argument would lead to compromise principle 2.

It is doubtful that utilitarians will embrace the resulting argument, however, because not only is compromise principle 2 unwieldy when compared to the elegance of classical utilitarianism, the choice of a particular ratio for (2a) will inevitably be somewhat arbitrary as well—which will be reflected in the conclusion. Besides, taking account only of a fraction of the unhappiness excess of a terribly unhappy person, in deciding how much negative value there would be in adding him, is inconsistent with a hedonistic version of timeless utilitarianism.

It has been claimed that hedonistic utilitarianism is implausible because it would result in the outrageous requirement that people who have more unhappiness than happiness should be killed. Surely this is not the case because, among other things, any such policy would not only evoke violent and widespread revolution but would cause such enormous dread and misery that it could not be defended on hedonic grounds. Even so, there is no question that a hedonistic utilitarian must hold something that many people could not countenance: that is that it is irrational to regard one's life as having intrinsic worth if it contains more unhappiness than happiness. I am willing to go along with this myself in that I think that although we shouldn't go around killing unhappy people, we also shouldn't knowingly bring them into the world.

The problem for a hedonistic utilitarian is that his system forces him to hold that a life with more pain than pleasure, even a little bit more, is not worth living and is not worth bringing into existence. A non-utilitarian can avoid the problem by holding that a life with more dis-utility than utility can be worth living and can be worth bringing into existence, but a utilitarian can't. If a philosopher cannot swallow this stiff consequence of hedonism but wants to remain a utilitarian, there are two things he can do—be an ideal utilitarian or hold an interest theory. If he does the first, he can hold that unpleasant as well as pleasant experiences have intrinsic value, and that the intrinsic value of a pleasant experience is not solely a function of how good it feels but can far exceed the value of the pleasure alone. Could an ideal utilitarian then argue that, with these new sources of intrinsic value, there would be so much excess intrinsic value (even in the case of groups of people whose addition was taken to be only marginally permissible) that we could justify the decision to add them even if the happiness-excess ratio in (2a) was so high that it would lead the argument far from classical utilitarianism? In order to do so, some method of measuring intrinsic value must be found, a notorious headache for ideal utilitarians. If one gives up the whole job of measurement as hopeless, one will not be in a position to decide between (2) and (2a). Nevertheless, if my argument for classical utilitarianism is sound in other respects, one will still be forced to accept some form of obligation theory. The particular form will depend on whether one accepts (2) or (2a): if (2), classical utilitarianism follows; if (2a), some other pro-obligation view. But without a way of measuring intrinsic value, there is no reasonable way of choosing between (2) and (2a). If on the other hand, one tries to come up with a workable method of measurement, the best I can think of is something like asking people at the end of each day whether that day has been worth living; or, putting this in more technical terms, whether they felt that their experiences contained more that was intrinsically good or more that was intrinsically bad. I suspect that those who want a high ratio for (2a) so that they can hold the compromise position instead of classical utilitarianism, won't find much support in the answers they get. Nor do I think it will do them much good to claim that the goodness of the good days exceeds the badness of the bad days sufficiently to get the kind of overall excess of intrinsic value that their strategy requires.

The other possibility is an interest theory. Sumner argues that, on an interest as opposed to a hedonistic version of utilitarianism, one would very rarely find a life in which there was an excess of negative over positive value. If one holds such an interest theory and one also holds (as Sumner would) that most lives have far more positive value than negative value, one can again adopt a very high ratio in (2a), so that although one's conclusion will attribute some value to adding happy people, it will be relatively little. Sumner's claim is that most lives have more positive than negative value; but for a large number of people, life is more a matter of the non-fulfillment of negative interests than the fulfillment of positive ones. That is, their life is more a matter of occurrences that they would like to avoid but can't than of occurrences which they positively desire. Work occupies a large part of most people's lives and many people, perhaps most, seem unfortunately to find their work something that they hope at best to get through with relatively little pain rather than as a source of positive fulfillment.[22] Think how many people would rather sleep than work, not to speak of all the physical and mental illness in the world, the misery, injustice and loneliness, a list as grim as it is long. One might argue that even people whose lives are more a matter of having their negative interests frustrated than of having their positive interests fulfilled usually have an extremely intense though irrational interest in avoiding death as such, i.e., an interest over and above their desire to avoid it because it will prevent them from fulfilling any more of their positive interests. Given this, it can be urged that even though living involves a great deal of frustration of their negative interests, dying would involve even *more* because of the sheer intensity of the desire not to die and that therefore we should try to keep even such unhappy people alive. Except for extreme cases, this conclusion may well be true; but though it provides a reason for preserving the life of a person in this unhappy position, it does not provide a reason for denying that, taken in itself, it is a bad thing to add him to the world.[23]

When I look back at the intricate series of arguments and counter-arguments in this section, I am consoled to note that at the very least they show that some sort of theory which allows for the value of adding happy people must be correct. However, this was already quite clear. As for the case I've tried to make for classical utilitarianism, I think if one begins with a favorable attitude toward hedonistic utilitarianism, the argument is hard to resist. But for those who hold an interest theory or ideal utilitarianism, the case for classical utilitarianism doesn't look quite so strong. A revision of (2) that would allow them to reject it in favour of a compromise principle quite close to it is somewhat plausible, and a revision that would allow them to have a compromise principle quite far removed from it would not be *totally* implausible. But who wants a compromise principle anyway? Furthermore, a form of the argument which is neutral as to what is intrinsically valuable can be given:

(1) To prevent the existence of a person who would have, by a given amount, more of what is intrinsically bad in his life than whatever is intrinsically good is as important morally as it is to prevent an equal amount of what is intrinsically bad for a person who is alive.

(2) Other things being equal, if one expects the total amount of

whatever is intrinsically good to equal the total amount of whatever is intrinsically bad for a given group of people whom one could add, it is not wrong to add them.

(3) But (2) would not hold unless there is at least as much positive value in increasing the total of whatever is intrinsically good for mankind by adding people with an excess of whatever is good as there is negative value in adding people with an excess of whatever is bad.

(4) Given (1) and (3) plus timeless utilitarianism, we can infer that classical utilitarianism is correct.

The new version of the argument should seem much more compelling that the old one for a non-hedonistic utilitarian. The second premise is still the crucial one. Isn't it in the last analysis implausible to deny it now that it is neutral as to what is intrinsically valuable? If one expects equal amounts of positive and negative value (whatever one takes them to be) for a group of possible people, isn't it hard, other things being equal, to deny that it is not wrong to create them? And why resist this highly plausible premise when one's only reward is a compromise principle one would rather do without? Given a choice between the classical principle coupled with premise (2) and the unwieldy compromise pro-sacrifice principle coupled with premise (2a), surely not many philosophers would choose the latter. If what one really wants is neither of them but a theory that assigns no worth whatever to adding happy people to the world, the price is preposterously high—it is to wreak havoc with our other intuitions.

## *11. Meta-ethics, Meta-meta-ethics and the Obligation Principle*

Up to now my strategy has been to bury anti-sacrifice views under a heap of moral intuitions that go against them, and my discussion has remained strictly within the bounds of normative ethics. Now I turn to meta-ethics to consider various analyses of the concept of obligation; also, to what might properly be called *meta*-meta-ethics, to ask how much, if anything, in practical deliberation about future generations hinges on which meta-ethical theory turns out to be correct.[24]

*Brave New World.* Smythers and Green are two of the few sterile survivors of a nuclear war. Smythers is a musician with a bad heart. He would like nothing better than to spend the rest of his life with his

Steinway, just where he is, working on the late piano works of Beethoven. Green is a scientist who has a formula for making test-tube babies to repopulate the world, babies who will have excellent prospects for happiness and achievement. They will, among other things, be able to take full advantage of the cultural resources left behind by past generations. Because Smythers has enormous respect for Green, he will do whatever Green tells him. If they didn't have the babies to take care of, they could have lives of ease and pleasure with the other survivors whereas they know that taking care of the children will require major sacrifices from both of them. Smythers in particular realizes that the effort will shorten his life. Despite this, Green decides to make the babies and Smythers accepts his decision. The babies grow into a god-like race of intelligent, strong, happy and loving people who not only fully appreciate the works of the great composers, writers and artists of the past but who create even greater works themselves. Although Smythers enjoys seeing the results of his sacrifice, the enjoyment he derives does not equal the sacrifice he made. Still, in retrospect, he is glad that Green persuaded him to make the decision he did and he would be ready to make the same decision again. (It seems to me, incidentally, that Smythers could well have been glad to have made the sacrifices he did for the new race, even if they ignore the unfinished projects of mankind and start their own instead.)

There is, I believe, a broad sense of "obligation" such that, given Smythers' attitude, a strong case[25] can be made that he had not just an aesthetic or other non-moral preference for the preservation of mankind but a moral *obligation* to make the sacrifices he did to repopulate the world. There is perhaps a narrower sense of the word as well in which he did not; but I will argue that even if there is, the broader sort of obligation takes precedence. I hope that most of my readers will find my account of Smythers' response plausible, and that they would go so far as to say that, in the same situation, they would be glad if they had done the same thing he did. Even so, I am sure that some people will think that I am wrong, that there is no sense of "obligation" such that Smythers had an obligation to make the sacrifices he did; or that even if there is such a sense, it lacks the precedence I claim for it. In order to meet this objection—which I regard as formidable—I need to make a considerable detour into meta-ethics. Thirty years ago, philosophers paid too much attention to meta-ethics rather than normative ethics, but we are now doing the opposite. With the exception of Hare, none of the main writers on obligations relating to possible persons deals with the meta-ethical aspects of the problem. This is, I think, a mistake.

To begin. Non-naturalism, the theory that ethical judgments cannot be translated into non-ethical terms and that ethical terms therefore refer to distinctively ethical qualities, has been shown to be unsatisfactory because there are no distinctively ethical qualities. Ethical naturalism can be divided into two kinds, "subjective naturalism" and "objective naturalism." Subjective naturalism is the theory that ethical judgments can be translated into non-ethical terms and that the rightness of an action is a function of some actual or ideal person's attitude towards it, while objective naturalism takes the rightness of an action to be independent of any such relation. Moore's open-question argument is not enough to show that all forms of ethical naturalism are false: it only shows that ethical terms are not overtly synonymous (i.e., obviously synonymous) with non-ethical terms, not that they are not covertly synonymous with them (i.e., synonymous but not obviously so).[26] The same would hold for tests in which we try to show that a given non-ethical term is *not* synonymous with an ethical term on the grounds that it does not strike most normal users of the language as contradictory to say that one of the terms applies to an action but not the other. For example, you can't show that "right" is not covertly synonymous with "conducive to the maximization of happiness" by noting that most people don't regard it as contradictory to say than an action is right but that it will not maximize happiness. However, you can show that "right" is not even covertly synonymous with "conducive to the maximization of happiness" by showing that many normal users of the language do not even take the two terms to be entirely or even approximately coextensive. You may use two terms as synonyms without realizing that you are doing so and therefore fail to pass the open-question test, but you can hardly use two terms as synonyms and yet firmly and repeatedly contend that one of the terms applies to a given action and the other not. The same attack may be repeated against any of the other objectivist candidates for synonymity with ethical terms. More important in meta-meta-ethics: even if some objectivist term did turn out to be synonymous with an ethical term, it wouldn't make any practical difference.[27] Though I am very sympathetic to hedonistic utilitarianism, I wouldn't feel I had done much for it if I managed somehow to show that "right" really is synonymous with "conducive to the maximization of pleasure." The fact that the word "right" happened to have that meaning might be interesting but it wouldn't give me another reason to decide to maximize pleasure. Imagine two worlds, in one of which the word "right" is not used at all but only the expression "conducive to the maximization of pleasure," while in the other the two expressions are used as synonyms. A person in the second world would have no more reason to maximize pleasure than someone in the first.

The simplest form of subjective naturalism is the view that what it means to say that an action is right is that the speaker favours it. This view is clearly wrong because it doesn't allow for the possibility of mistaken ethical judgments (except in those cases where the speaker doesn't know what he favours). Simple emotivism, the view that to say that an attitude is right is not to make a statement about one's attitude but simply to express it, is open to the same objection. C. L. Stevenson's attempt to save emotivism from this objection by saying that ethical judgments have descriptive meaning which varies from one group to another as well as emotive meaning is unsuccessful. It enables us to account for some but not all of the ways in which ethical judgments can be mistaken.

*Ideal observer theories.* In an ideal observer theory, an action is taken to be right if it is the action that an ideal observer would choose to have performed. Very generally, the ideal observer is said to be benevolent and calm and it is stipulated that his choices are not to reflect cognitive defects. More precisely, it is stipulated that his choices will not be affected by logical errors or by failure to make the logical inferences relevant to (i.e., capable of influencing) them; he will have all the conceptual apparatus relevant to those choices; and he will have the relevant factual information as well as a vivid idea of the relevant consequences of his choice.

Such a person is said to be epistemically rational, calm and benevolent. (The qualification "epistemically" is necessary because without it, "rational" might be taken to imply something over and above epistemic characteristics.) Having a vivid idea of the consequences of an action is part of epistemic rationality, because one would like the observer to have knowledge by both acquaintance and description of the consequences of an action; and a vivid idea of the consequences is what thoroughgoing knowledge by acquaintance would give him. An advantage of acting in the way you would if you had knowledge by acquaintance of the results of your action is that it would keep you from being sorry for what you had done when you saw what it led to. Smythers acquired knowledge by acquaintance of a good part of the results of his action and the fact that this led him to be pleased with what he had done would provide an advocate of the ideal observer theory with the beginnings of a case that he had made a good decision.

I am happy with the requirement that the ideal observer be calm and epistemically rational, but serious problems arise from the stipulation that he be fully benevolent. First, it means that we would sometimes be required to perform actions that are beyond the call of duty: it would require us to categorize behaviour that we usually regard as supererogatory, such as that of Albert Schweitzer, as obligatory. Secondly, it is, I think, desirable that ethical terms be defined in such a way that most people would have strong motivating reasons for being moral. Suppose that in order to persuade someone to make a genuine sacrifice for someone else (who will gain more than the agent will lose) I tell him that he ought to do it. On the ideal observer theory, this is the same as saying that an ideal observer would choose to have him do it. Because the ideal observer is by definition benevolent, it follows analytically that he will make the benevolent choice; but the person I am trying to persuade could well reply that what a benevolent person would choose is of no significance to *him* because he is not benevolent himself.

Another problem. It is by no means clear that we have been told enough about the ideal observer to be able to decide what he would say about such questions as whether it would be wrong to prevent the existence of future generations. If additional characteristics were ascribed to him, there would be a risk of circularity as well as a repetition of the problem I just found in attributing benevolence to him. Suppose that the ideal observer is defined as a person who, among other things, cares as much about adding happy people as about the happiness of already existing people. If I try to persuade someone to make a sacrifice to create a happy person on the grounds that that it what an ideal observer would want, he can say, "But I'm not like your ideal observer. I'm just not the kind of person who cares about adding happy people." This problem cannot be avoided by stipulating that the ideal observer, besides being epistemically ideal and benevolent, be normal in other respects, because one would then have to decide what the normal person's attitude towards happy extra persons would be; and even if a normal person would have the attitude you wanted, someone could say, "Well, yes, the ideal observer may have the attitude of a normal person but I don't, and I don't care if I am not normal. And to this there is no answer.

My theory avoids this impasse by dropping the stipulation of benevolence, and by substituting the agent himself in an epistemically rational state for the ideal observer. To say that I ought to do a given thing is to say that I would choose to do it if I were calm and epistemically rational.[28] Now there is a good answer to the question, "Why should I be moral?" or "Why should I do the moral thing?" "Because it's the thing I would do if I were epistemically rational." Most people would regard this as a strong reason for doing it. Sometimes, of course, this won't persuade us to do what we ought to do but this enables the theory to account for *acrasia*: the theory would make the conviction that one ought to do a given thing about as persuasive in getting one to do it as such convictions usually are. Some readers may worry that, with the stipulation of benevolence removed, the theory won't require fully benevolent behavior from any typical human being because typical human beings, even if they were epistemically rational, would probably not choose to be fully benevolent. This is true, and consequently my meta-ethical theory cannot support straight utilitarianism.

Actually, I take this to be an advantage, because traditional utilitarianism with its insistence on complete benevolence is forced to construe supererogatory behavior as obligatory. My meta-ethical theory would serve as a basis for a kind of utilitarianism without supererogation where, while it is never wrong to do the optimific thing, one is not *obligated* to do it when doing so requires a personal sacrifice, unless other people would gain proportionally more than the agent would lose: the ratio of the gain to others versus the loss to oneself is the one an individual would choose if he were epistemically rational.[29] I believe that most of us, if we were epistemically rational, would be willing to make sacrifices for others. I am relying heavily here on the fact that although epistemic rationality does not logically require that we be sympathetic towards others, the requirement that we be vividly aware of others' experiences would, when combined with the other aspects of epistemic rationality, contingently involve for almost everyone at least some degree of sympathy towards them. Some people can, of course, become aware of the suffering of others and not care about it or even be glad. Such attitudes are frequently the result of conscious or subconscious errors about the attitudes of others towards oneself. A person who became epistemically rational would discover the influence of such errors on his attitude and even when the error-based attitudes lingered, he would try to discount them in making his decisions.[30] Of course we confront a great deal of real malice, hostility and envy in the world; but even here epistemic rationality can have a softening effect if, as Ayer and others have held, it is logically impossible that anyone should be ultimately responsible for his actions and character and therefore that no one deserves the torments of hell (or any other torments) if he is bad any more than if he is good. Still, there may well be some people who would, even if they were epistemically rational, more or less totally lack sympathy for others; if so, they would, on my theory, have no obligation to make sacrifices for them. If, on the other hand, "obligation" is defined to include benevolence, even such people would have an obligation to make sacrifices for others; but with "obligation" defined this way, these people would have no motivating reason to do what they were obligated to do, so nothing would really have been gained.

It might be thought that my sort of utilitarianism without supererogation would result in egoistic public policies (including policies regarding future generations) rather than the altruistic policies prescribed by traditional utilitarianism. Surprisingly, it would not. One of the main strengths of the view is that it would not only require us to favor traditional utilitarian public policies but would give us a strong motivating reason for doing so, without having to assume that we are fully benevolent or even that we would become fully benevolent if we were epistemically rational. The demands for true personal sacrifice in the private sphere would be much less great with my system. But this is not particularly worrisome because, even if one were restricted to nothing more than sophisticated egoistic considerations, a reasonably high degree of morality in the private sphere could still be justified. Furthermore, I suspect that for most people the difference in the private area, between the demands of my system and the demands of traditional utilitarianism, could be largely a matter of supererogatory demands.

But how can this theory justify a traditional utilitarian position on matters of public policy (or, to be strictly accurate, something extremely close to it)? When a public policy that would have the best results for mankind would require personal sacrifice from one—in the form of higher taxes, say—almost invariably the public gain would be immensely greater than one's own sacrifice. Consequently, unless one were extremely egoistic and would remain so even if one were epistemically rational, one would have an obligation on this theory to favor the policy in spite of the higher taxes one would have to pay. For example, suppose that it's a matter of Canada giving wheat to India where following the altruistic public policy would require a dollar from you as well as a dollar from each of the twenty million other Canadians, and that spending the money on India would do roughly twice as much good there as spending it at home. The sacrifice/gain ratio in this case would be roughly one to twenty million: in having the higher taxes imposed, an average taxpayer would lose only a twenty-millionth of what mankind would gain. With a ratio like this one would have to be extremely selfish and one's selfishness would have to be firmly entrenched against the effects of epistemic rationality for one not to have an obligation on my theory to favor the altruistic policy in spite of the higher taxes one would have to pay.

Voting is one of the main ways in which an ordinary citizen can support or fail to support a public policy. The chance that one's vote will prove decisive is extremely low but that does not affect the sacrifice/gain ratio because the chance of one's vote causing a sacrifice to be imposed on oneself would be exactly as low as the chance of that vote leading to a gain for mankind. Sumner and Anglin have objected that even if one's vote in a case like the wheat to India example is decisive, the gain to mankind for which one is responsible should be determined by dividing the total gain by the number of people voting for the policy, that my theory should only count the gain for which one individual is responsible in determining the sacrifice/gain ratio, and that this would yield a ratio that most people would find inadequate to merit their sacrifice. This criticism clearly assumes not only that what a utilitatian should care about is the amount of goodness or badness for which he is responsible but that if a number of people are equally responsible for a given outcome, each one is responsible for a fraction of that outcome equal to one over the number of people involved. Suppose you are faced with two alternatives: either you must, by yourself, confine a prisoner unjustly for two hours or else you must cooperate with 9,999 other people in confining him unjustly for 10,000 hours; and that, in the second case, although your contribution would be no greater than that of anyone else, it would still be essential. In my critics' view, utilitarianism would tell you to take the second alternative because it would only make you responsible for 1/10,000 × 10,000 hours of confinement; where the first alternative would make you responsible for 1/1 × 2 hours of confinement. But this clearly is altogether alien to the spirit of utilitarianism. Furthermore, although utilitarianism is commonly described as holding that we should always do the thing that will have the best consequences, this interpretation fails also, I believe, to capture the true spirit of the doctrine. Surely Henry Sidgwick (to my mind the paradigm of the utilitarian) wouldn't have wanted us to leave out of our calculation events which, although they are not properly speaking *consequences* of our actions, would not have occurred if we had acted differently. Surely what we are to do if we want to act morally is to consider the various states of the world that could occur depending on what we decide to do and to choose the best of them. Put another way, what the utilitarian wants an agent to do is to pick the best of all contingently possible worlds available to him.

One of the main objections to an obligation theory is that it can't consistently give as a reason for not preventing the existence of future generations, that it is *prima facie* wrong to prevent the existence of happy people, without claiming as well that couples likely to have happy children usually have an obligation to have them. Sumner attempts to answer this by arguing that such couples could usually spend the time they would devote to rearing children in other ways which were at least equally beneficial to mankind, so that in terms of traditional utilitarianism they would not have an obligation to have children. But if many of these couples could in fact be *more* useful to mankind by *not* having children, a traditional utilitarian would be forced to say that they have an obligation not to have children; and this is counterintuitive. My modification of utilitarianism gets me out of this awkard corner: it allows me to hold that it is usually beyond the call of duty—i.e., supererogatory—to benefit humanity either by having children you don't want or by not having children you do want. It would normally be commendable rather than obligatory to place the interest of society above your own interests in this sort of decision.

My meta-ethical theory has an enormous advantage in that whenever other theories and mine result in different prescriptions, the other theories tell you to do something that you would choose to do only if you were in some way epistemically irrational. And, unlike many subjectivist theories, my ideal subjectivist theory allows ample room for the criticism of ethical judgments: it is easy to make mistakes about what you would choose to do if you were epistemically rational. However, it does allow for ultimate irresolvable moral disagreements, particularly on the sacrifice/gain ratio. One way to avoid this would be to set the ratio at a level such that it would not be too demanding for any epistemically rational person except a few whose selfishness was both extreme and immune to the effects of epistemic rationality. If the standard were set in this way, almost everyone would either be willing to make the required sacrifices or would only be unwilling because he was not epistemically rational. This alteration has two advantages: in the same circumstances, everyone would have the same obligations, and almost everyone could be given effective motivating reasons for doing at least as much for others as they had an obligation to do. Furthermore, optimific actions would still always be morally acceptable; the theory would still come up with much the same demands as traditional utilitarianism in public matters; and prudential egoistic reasons could still be provided for moral behavior in private matters. There is the disadvantage, however, that there would no longer be the guarantee that you ought to do the thing that you would choose to do if you were epistemically rational. Except for exceptionally selfish persons, the altered theory would never demand greater sacrifices than one would be willing to make, but it would frequently require less sacrifice for the welfare of others than one would be willing to make if one were epistemically rational.

There is some similarity here to Hare's theory that ethical judgments are universal commands. Consider the matter of epistemic rationality: although Hare can't say that ethical judgments are properly speaking *mistaken*, he would presumably be prepared to say that if you issue a command that you would not have issued if you were epistemically rational, your command would be subject to criticism. Here, I think we are reasonably close. We both take obligation to be ultimately a function of attitude. But Hare's theory leads him into difficulty over supererogation. Complete benevolence is built into his theory: in order to make a satisfactory moral judgment, the interests of everyone affected must be considered, and the interests of others are to be counted as heavily as one's own.[31] Consequently, his theory is bound (like an ideal observer theory) to require supererogatory good deeds.

As Hare recognizes himself,[32] it is difficult to accept his meta-ethical view without supposing that we ought to behave like traditional utilitarians; and of course traditional utilitarians require supererogatory good deeds.[33]

Some readers may object that even if there is a broad sense of "obligation" in terms of which obligations are a function of what you would choose to do in an epistemically ideal state, still whenever there is a conflict between obligations in this broad sense and obligations in a narrow sense (where they are purely objective), the latter takes precedence. If this were so it could be argued that, in the case of any obligation to add happy extra people, there would almost always be some purely objective obligation that would take precedence over it.

I have three objections to this:

1. There *are* no purely objective obligations. Factual considerations alone, independently of one's attitudes (including one's attitudes in an epistemically ideal state) cannot force one to accept an ethical judgment. Searle has offered what is perhaps the most plausible attempt to refute this claim.[34] He holds that (a) one can be forced by the facts to admit that a person has made a promise; and (b) that once one has made this admission, it is inconsistent to deny that he has at least a *prima facie* obligation to keep his promise. Though I agree with (b) I have argued elsewhere[35] that (a) is mistaken. To say that a person has made a promise is (1) to make the factual assertion that he has said certain words in a certain sort of situation and (2) to make the ethical presupposition that there is an institution that enables us to acquire obligations by saying such words in such situations. Because (2), the ethical part, is a presupposition, one can't challenge it by saying that that person didn't make the promise: to say that is to deny the objective part of the assertion which may well be correct. But one can admit the objective part without admitting that there is even a *prima facie* obligation if one is prepared to deny that the institution does anything more than make people think that they have acquired obligations. Such a denial would be an evaluation of the institution. Searle is prepared to say that evaluations may be purely objective but he can't use that claim as a premise in his argument, without circularity, because it is by that argument that he hopes to convince us that evaluations can be purely objective.

2. If ethical judgments and/or evaluations were purely objective, they

would simply be *shorthand* ways of conveying factual information; as such, they would deserve no more respect in decision-making than judgments that presented the same information using more words. For example, if "right" happened to mean "conducive to the maximization of the gross national product," that would not provide a reason for altering our attitude towards that curious objective.

3. Suppose that I admit that there are objective obligations and that my objective obligations conflict with what I would choose to do if I were epistemically rational. I can't think of any effective rational means of persuading me to be "objectively" moral so long as I am firmly convinced that I would not choose to be "objectively" moral if I were epistemically rational. In fact, it is an analytic truth that if I were epistemically rational, *any* attempt to persuade me to give precedence to "objectively" moral considerations would be bound to fail. Only if I were *not* epistemically rational, could I be persuaded to do something that I wouldn't do if I were epistemically rational. Someone trying to persuade me would be in a difficult position, to say the least, if he had to admit at the outset that he could only succeed if I were epistemically at fault. He would be rather like a car salesman who had to admit at the outset that if one knew all the relevant facts, one would buy his competitor's car.

What I've been trying to accomplish by rather a complicated route in this section is this: I have argued that there is a broad sense of "obligation" such that if one is glad that he has made a particular sacrifice (in my example, in order to create a happy race of people) and if one is given knowledge by acquaintance of the outcome of one's action (in my case, with those happy people), one would be prepared to do the same thing over again; if one's attitude didn't reflect logical confusion or factual ignorance, one would have had an *obligation* to have made the sacrifice in order to bring about that consequence (i.e., to have created that race of happy people). Suppose now that I am wrong and that there is no such sense of "obligation"–that I have, in effect, simply given a stipulative definition. It would still hold that one would have to be epistemically irrational not to do what one had an obligation to do in my stipulated sense; one would therefore have a strong reason for doing it rather than anything else that one might be obligated to do, given some other sense of "obligation." Thus if my original hypothesis as to how most of us would react to seeing the consequences of creating a happy new race is correct and if our reactions do not reflect epistemic irrationality, most of us would have a strong reason for creating such a race. We would, of course, have an equally strong reason for *not preventing* the existence of such a race or for not preventing future generations if they would be equally happy. They won't be, but so long at least as we think that they will have more happiness than unhappiness we have *some reason* for not preventing their existence. But this is exactly what those who oppose the obligation view wish to deny.[36]

## *Notes*

1. A third objection (which I don't take up here) is that the obligation theory is incompatible with the commonly held view that normally it is morally permissible for couples either to have children or not as they like. In §10, I develop a meta-ethical position designed to support the obligation theory. This position requires a revision in traditional utilitarianism, a revision which allows me to hold that although we have an obligation to preserve mankind, typical couples have neither an obligation to have children nor not to have them.

2. Rawls is the main philosopher whose name has been associated with average utilitarianism. He is not an average utilitarian himself, but he does regard it as decidedly preferable to classical utilitarianism. (*A Theory of Justice*, Cambridge, Mass.: Belknap/Harvard University Press, 1971, pp. 161-165.)

3. Some philosophers claim that even rough cardinal comparisons of pleasure and pain are either meaningless or totally unjustifiable. But this would prevent us from saying many things that are (I think) obviously true. Take the following. "Some prisoners who had at least some pleasure during their stay at Dachau still had far more pain than pleasure while they were there." This judgment clearly presupposes cardinal comparisons of pleasure and pain but we can nonetheless be morally certain that it is correct.

Or suppose that Bertha has a mild headache from 9 A.M. till 9 P.M. while her husband Sam is perfectly comfortable from 9 A.M. until 8 P.M. when he is picked up by the secret police and tortured for an hour. We would all suppose that Sam suffered much more pain than Bertha during the twelve hours, something we are clearly not entitled to suppose unless we believe that Sam's pain from the torture was more than twelve times as severe as Bertha's mild headache pain.

Two other points should be made: (1) It is often the case that my opponents must also assume in their objections–this is true, e.g., of the repugnant conclusion–that cardinal comparisons of utility and disutility are possible at least in theory. (2) If the notion of a life that is neutral in that it contains equal amounts of pleasure and pain (or some other utilities and disutilities) is found objectionable, a stretch of a person's life could be described as neutral iff he would, if he were epistemically rational, be indifferent between living through it again or being unconscious during that stretch of time.

4. Not only is extra population likely to lower the total amount of happiness both for those now alive and for future generations (if there are any), but it could lead to the destruction of all mankind through the more dangerous forms of pollution or through a nuclear war brought on by competition for increasingly scarce resources.

5. Mary Warren contends ("Do Potential People Have Moral Rights?" in this volume) that not only do we not have any obligations relating to possible persons who have not yet been conceived but that even after conception, we have no obligations to the fetus. She claims that although the fetus has the potential for having experiences, this is not enough to give us even a *prima facie* obligation to help realize this potential, or even a *prima facie* obligation to refrain from abortion, i.e., from preventing its realization. It has been argued against her view that an unconscious person also has only a potential for having experiences but that in the case of an unconscious person this is enough to give us *prima facie* obligations towards him and that consequently the same should hold for fetuses when they have only the potential for having experiences.

One possible response to this objection (which I will consider later) is that taken by Engelhardt ("The Ontology of Abortion," *Ethics*, Vol. 84, 1974.), that the crucial moral difference between an unconscious person and a fetus is that the unconscious person has a *history of past experiences* while the fetus does not (what I will call the "history requirement"). Warren argues rather that the crucial difference is that between something which has an "actual and present capacity" for consciousness, and something which has a capacity for consciousness that is not actual and present (what I will call a "plain capacity"). Warren argues that since an unconscious person has a present and actual capacity for consciousness, we may have an obligation to make him, or to allow him to become, conscious; whereas if something–like a fetus–has only a plain capacity for consciousness, we cannot have any such obligation.

The question is what exactly the distinction *is* between these two kinds of capacity. I shall consider a number of possible interpretations of her distinction, none of which will serve her purpose:

(1) The requirement that the capacity be *present* could mean that in order for something to have this "higher" sort of capacity for consciousness, it must be likely that if it is left alone it will become conscious or that it can be made conscious within a short time. But if this is the crucial difference between the two sorts of capacity and if it is accepted that if something lacks the higher sort of capacity we can have no obligation to make it conscious, we get the awkward result that if someone were in a coma from which he could only be roused after a long period of time we would have no obligation to rouse him.

(2) The requirement that the capacity for consciousness be actual could be construed as the requirement that it not merely be a capacity to *acquire* that capacity but that it be that capacity itself. But this also leads to counterintuitive results when it is applied, for example, to a person in a coma.

(3) For something to have a present and actual capacity for consciousness, it must be the case that relatively little needs to be done to make him conscious. This interpretation would again have an unfortunate consequence for someone in a coma: we would have no obligation to bring him out of it if doing so would require a good deal of work.

(4) If something is of the same order of complexity as a human being, it may have a present and actual capacity for consciousness; otherwise not. This would allow us to have an obligation to animate robots provided they were sufficiently complex and it was possible to do so. Warren would clearly find this unacceptable and furthermore, it is hard to see why *complexity* should be morally relevant here.

(5) In order for something to have a present and actual potentiality for consciousness, it must resemble conscious human beings in all physical respects (or this category could be broadened to include animals as well) but to distinguish this from the history requirement, it need never have been conscious. But this would have the unacceptable consequence that if an unconscious creature had a history of consciousness but didn't have the specified physical characteristics, we wouldn't even have a *prima facie* obligation to allow it to become conscious again.

Back to the history requirement. Suppose that we had the alternative of either restoring to life a long-forgotten person—say, the maternal grandfather of the caveman who painted the bison pictures in the Lescaux caves—or of creating someone who has never lived before who would be much happier than the caveman (who would be only moderately happy being restored to life in the contemporary world). Suppose, further, that the expected effects on other people choosing either alternative would be roughly equal. Using the history requirement would force us to say that it would be wrong to create the new person rather than the caveman despite the fact that the new person would be far happier. This, I think, would go against most people's moral intuitions.

I have chosen a long-forgotten person as my example rather than, say, one's own maternal grandfather because our intuitions in the caveman case are not influenced by factors that usually (but need not) accompany a history of consciousness (such as gratitude for good deeds the person might have done, obligations created either by implicit or explicit promises to preserve the person's life, or the obligations which one might naturally feel toward friends or relatives). Considerations such as these are highly relevant, of course, and they bring me in the end relatively close to Warren on the actual rights and wrongs of abortion. Although I think that it is *prima facie* wrong to destroy a fetus, I also believe that far more weighty considerations are needed to justify the destruction of an actual person than to justify an abortion.

6. "A Utilitarian Population Principle," in *Ethics & Population*, edited by Michael Bayles (Cambridge, Mass.: Schenkman, 1976), pp. 81-99.

7. There is still another objection to attempts to save the ontological preference theory by adding the occupants of inevitable slots to the ontologically privileged. Though there is some intuitive appeal in saying that the welfare of inevitable persons is more important than that of possible persons, there is little intuitive appeal in the corresponding claim about the occupants of inevitable slots, particularly when the notion of an inevitable slot is attenuated as it must be to get anything like the right number of occupants of these slots. And there is another matter that I have passed by rather hastily before: the class of persons whose existence is to be regarded as inevitable from the point of view of the population planner should obviously not be made up of those who will exist whatever he does regardless of whether it is morally acceptable or not, but rather of those who will exist regardless of which *morally acceptable* thing he does. Thus the category of inevitable persons is not purely ontological but ethical as well, which muddies the water still more.

8. *Ibid*, p. 89.

9. My objections are addressed to this modification of Singer's principle. His principle clearly needs *some* modification, and this strikes me as the most reasonable move he could make. Singer is aware of the change I have made and has not objected to it.

10. "Utilitarianism: The Classical Principle and the Average Principle," *Canadian Journal of Philosophy*, Volume V, No. 3, November 1975, pp. 409-419.

11. Derek Parfit, "Rights, Interests & Possible People," partially reprinted in Samuel Gorovitz *et al.*, eds., *Moral Problems in Medicine* (Englewood Cliffs, N. J.: Prentice-Hall, 1976), pp. 369-375, at pp. 373-5.

12. The timeless impartiality principle is also of course incompatible with ontological preference theories because they tell us that in adding extra persons we should weigh the welfare of the added persons less heavily than that of the ontologically privileged.

13. Timeless utilitarianism on the other hand only requires that, in adding people, the particular people added should be made as happy as possible. (ii) and (iv) deal with the question of who should be added, once it is granted that someone is going to be added. Timeless utilitarianism ignores this question entirely and bears instead on what should be done once it is decided that some particular person is to be added.

14. One objection to this argument (suggested to me by A. J. Ayer) is that it is always wrong taken in itself to bring about the existence of any group of people regardless of how many of them will be happy if *any* of them will be wretched or perhaps even very unhappy. But this won't do because it entails the absurd conclusion that it would always be wrong *per se* to bring *any* large group of people into existence, even in a world with enormously better prospects for happiness than ours—that it can only be justified as something which, though bad in itself, is unfortunately needed to satisfy the then selfish desires of most people for children.

15. This particular argument for an obligation theory may be confused with others which rely on the claim that there is no plausible principle that can provide a rationale for saying that we have obligations relating to possible wretched people but not relating to possible *happy* people. I think that the following principle would provide such a rationale, and it is not obviously false: *an action is* prima facie *wrong iff it harms someone or someone exists who would have been benefitted by some alternative action*. This principle implicitly denies that it is morally important to bring happy people into existence. A possible

happy person whom you haven't caused to exist *doesn't exist* so your failing to cause him to exist won't be wrong even if it would have been a benefit to him if you had caused him to exist. This is a variation of the principle Parfit attacks with his birth-timing principle (ibid., pp. 373-375).

16. "Repugnant Conclusion," forthcoming in the *Canadian Journal of Philosophy*.

17. "Utilitarianism, Supererogation and Future Generations," forthcoming in the *Canadian Journal of Philosophy*.

18. Bennett's first objection is that we can acount for its being permissible to add a group with some miserable people in it without relying on the counterbalancing effect of the happiness of the happy people in it on the grounds that phasing out mankind even over a 150-year period would "involve ghastly horrors; and the disutilities also include events which, though not intrinsically dreadful, serve to frustrate hopes, abort plans, disappoint expectations, and so on (as when a happy man suffers a disutility by dying quietly in his sleep)." This sort of objection was relevant to the argument I gave in my earlier article ("Utilitarianism: The Classical Principle and the Average Principle"), because I neglected to specify there that the good and bad effects on persons other than those being added were to be roughly equal. (I had meant to take care of that problem by specifying that there was no population problem in the world in question.) But Bennett's objection does not apply to the version of the argument in this paper.

Bennett's last objection is that he has a rule that provides a "clear coherent basis" for the balancing role of the happy people as against the miserable ones, but which does not imply that we have any obligation not to prevent the existence of happy people; namely, that "facts about personal utilities are relevant to moral obligations only through arguments of the form, 'It is obligatory to do *A* because if *A* is not done then there will be people who . . . .' " Clearly, Bennett means to complete his rule by some such expression as "will be worse off than they would have been if *A* had not been done." When so completed, this rule is unacceptable because it violates even the weakest form of Parfit's baby-timing principle. The rule implies that, other things being equal, a prospective mother would have no obligation whatever to make any sacrifice, no matter how small, in the timing of a child's conception, even if this sacrifice would result in a *very* happy baby rather than resulting in another baby who because of birth defects would have a far less happy life, as long as this second possible baby would have a life that was worth living. It has this implication because, given my case, even if she conceives at the less propitious time there will be no person who is less well off than if she had conceived at the more propitious time. The happier baby is the only conceivable candidate, and he or she won't exist.

Bennett might try to avoid this by allowing Parfit's principle as an exception to his rule or, what amounts to the same thing, by filling in the blank in a way compatible with Parfit's principle. But it is difficult to reconcile Parfit's principle with an anti-obligation view. (See §8.)

Besides the fact that Bennett's rule generates counterintuitive consequences, the thing he is attempting to do by means of this rule—balancing the creation of unhappy people with that of happy ones while at the same time not allowing *any* positive value to the creation of happy people—seems basically misguided. Why should the bringing-into-existence of happy people be of great moral importance when they are part of a package along with some unhappy people but *of no moral importance whatever* when they are all by themselves?

Let's imagine that there is one person left in the world (let's call him Z), who shares Bennett's interest in the completion of certain human projects. He has arranged to re-populate the world with test-tube babies but he discovers that although they are likely to complete the projects the rest of humanity has left unfinished, there are more unhappy babies than happy ones. As it stands, Bennett would probably agree that Z had done something for which he is not blameworthy but which nevertheless is objectively wrong. However, he would, I should think, suppose that Z could rectify the situation if he could make enough extra happy babies so that there would be a high enough ratio of happy babies to unhappy ones, and that if it were within his power, Z would have an obligation (even at great sacrifice to himself) to make enough happy babies to achieve that ratio. But let's suppose that after Z had made enough happy babies to reach that ratio, he could go on at relatively little cost to himself (because by now he has the hang of the thing) to make a great many more, even happier, babies. Bennett would have to say that while Z would have a pressing obligation to make the first batch of extra babies, he would have *none whatever* to make any more, no matter how happy they would be and no matter how easy it would be for him to do it; and Bennett would have to account for the difference solely in terms of the existence of the unhappy babies. This seems counterintuitive. It implies that if I want to see how many happy people I have an obligation to bring into existence, the thing to do is not to see how happy they would be or how much sacrifice it would cost me but rather how many unhappy people

I have already brought into existence. And if it is urged that that *is* the right thing to look at if I want to find out at what point creating happy people would be supererogatory rather than obligatory, I must refer my reader to my discussion of this point in "Utilitarianism, Supererogation, and Future Generations" and to that part of §10 dealing with supererogation. Although my account is primarily directed to utilitarians and Bennett is no longer a utilitarian, I suspect that the difference between utilitarianism and his version of consequentialism is, for present purposes, of no real significance.

19. "On Maximizing Happiness", in this volume.

20. To be fair, I should point out that Bennett introduces this notion in a context in which it would be reasonable to expect that it (or similar interests) would be shared by a great many other people so that their combined interests could constitute a powerful reason for preventing the destruction of the human race. Like Kavka, I think that while this is a good reason for not preventing the existence of future generations, another good reason is that it is *prima facie* wrong to prevent the existence of happy people; though, unlike him, I think that arguments *can* be given for that principle. (One of those arguments, incidentally, is not that possible people are in some odd sense waiting in the wings.)

21. The projects which these interests fulfill could have practical application (such as medical theories) or not (such as the completion of some philosophical or mathematical theories).

22. See *Working* by Studs Terkel (New York: Pantheon/Random House, 1972) for an account of how people in a great variety of jobs feel about their work.

23. Even if an interest theory could be made compatible with a version of (2a) that a classical utilitarian would especially want to avoid, this would not, I think, be a serious problem for the classical position. Any theory which assigns intrinsic value to the fulfillment of each and every interest is committed to ascribing it not only to states of consciousness but to physical objects as well, and surely this is a mistake. (This in spite of Nozick's arguments to the contrary in *Anarchy, State & Utopia* [New York: Basic Books, 1974]: Part I, Chapter 3, pp. 42-45.) If on the other hand one ascribes intrinsic value only to the fulfillment of interests directed towards states of consciousness, the best method of measurement would be essentially similar to that I proposed for ideal utilitarianism, a method which offers little support for the extremely optimistic view of existence needed to justify a high ratio in (2a).

27. Singer, *ibid.*

28. It could be objected that if my ethical theory were correct, the grammar of moral discourse should be such that if two people disagree on whether a given action is obligatory, they could conceivably both be right because each is using "obligatory" relative to his own ideal attitude whereas in practice we act as if "obligatory" is not a relativistic term. First, this is only roughly true of actual practice, and secondly, even if the ultimate test for moral judgments is the speaker's own ideal attitudes, so long as they are cognitively ideal attitudes there is more than enough room for mistakes as to what those attitudes would be to account for the impression that all differences in ethical judgments reflect cognitive errors.

I could, however, afford to retreat to a position like Mackie's ("A Refutation of Morals," *The Australasian Journal of Philosophy*, 1946) in terms of which, although the ultimate test for ethical judgments in my version is attitudinal, to say that an action is obligatory is to ascribe a distinctively ethical quality to it, although in fact there are no such qualities. Since all I am concerned with is the question of what the ultimate test is, the difference between my theory and a Mackiean counterpart is not, for my purposes here, of any importance.

29. Although my theory deviates from classical utilitarianism in allowing us to discount the interests of others, the discounting has nothing to do with their ontological status.

30. I am assuming here that a person who has become epistemically rational would want to do what he would choose to do if he had the attitudes that he would have had if he had the same hereditary make-up but had always been epistemically rational.

31. Cf. *Freedom and Reason*, (Oxford: Clarendon Press, 1963), Chapter 6.

32. *Ibid*, Chapter 7.

33. It is possible to construct another sort of universal imperative theory of ethical judgments that could lead to supererogatory demands. Such a theory would stipulate that: (1) the agent be thoroughly egoistic but (2) in order to insure impartiality in making his universal demands, he is supposed to imagine that he is ignorant of his own particular situation; and (3) the agent is supposed to believe (or rather, to *pretend* to believe) that his command will be universally accepted. In these circumstances, the egoistic agent would probably find that he would maximize his own chances for happiness by commanding everyone to be a utilitarian. He would run only a very slight risk of having to make major sacrifices for others because if everyone complied with his command and acted as a good utilitarian, situations would seldom arise in which extreme altruistic behaviour would be required. Thus this sort

of presecriptivism would also seem to lead to traditional utilitarianism and to the supererogation that goes with it.

It might seem that any universal command theory of ethical judgments necessarily leads to problems with supererogation but this is not the case. It could be claimed that obligation-statements are universal commands and that such a command is open to criticism if the agent issues it only because he is in some respect epistemically irrational, is not prepared to obey it, or is not prepared to accept (though not necessarily to *like*) compliance with it on the part of others. If the language were used in this way, one would expect commands in which we would sometimes be required to make sacrifices but only when those others would gain proportionally more than we would lose. (Situations in which one is bound by a promise to help another person are an apparent exception but the effect of the promise would not be to alter the ratio at which one would be required to make sacrifices for others; it would rather be to alter the situation in such a way as to provide one with additional reasons for doing the thing in question. Failing to do so would be likely to have a detrimental effect on one's own reputation and character; it would frustrate the legitimate expectations of the other persons, and it would have a minute effect on the extraordinarily important institution of promising.) This would eliminate supererogatory demands. It also has the consequence that we would not be entitled to expect the complete benevolence from others that we would like: it would commit us to being prepared to accept without protest treatment from others which was only as good as we would be willing to give them in corresponding circumstances.

One trouble with the other two sorts of prescriptivism is that it is difficult to see how one could persuade an epistemically rational person to issue the respective sorts of command unless he were completely benevolent or really believed that everyone else would follow his commands. On this prescriptivist counterpart of my theory, neither of these would be required because the individual is only commanding himself to make those sacrifices that he would choose to make if he were epistemically rational.

34. "How to Derive 'Ought' from 'Is'," *Philosophical Review*, 73, 1964, pp. 49-58.

35. "Facts, Promising and Obligation," *Philosophy*, 50, 1975, pp. 352-355.

36. I am indebted for helpful discussion and criticism to my co-editor Brian Barry and to Jonathan Bennett, John Black, D. G. Brown, Howard Jackson, Peter Singer, Brian Stouffel, and David Zimmerman.

# *Part II*: Assuming That Future Generations Will Exist and That the Future Population Size Is Taken as Given, What Obligations Do We Have to Future Generations?

# Discounting Versus Maximum Sustainable Yield

*MARY B. WILLIAMS*

Scientists[1] recently estimated that "During the last 200 years at least a third of the topsoil on the U.S. croplands has been lost"; another recent scientific study[2] indicates that 70% of U.S. farmland is presently being farmed in a way inconsistent with sustained farming. Other studies[3] indicate that the local varieties and wild relatives of our crop plants are disappearing rapidly under the impact of modern agricultural techniques and the population explosion; the irreversible loss of these gene complexes depletes the genetic resources on which we must draw when our crop plants need the ability to respond to new environmental challenges. These facts, and others like them, reveal a pattern of behavior which, if it is continued, will drastically reduce the earth's ability to provide sustenance and a healthful environment to future generations; if continued long enough it will result in the extinction of *Homo sapiens*.

Do we have an obligation to stop this destructive behavior pattern? In this paper I will try to show that such an obligation does follow from utilitarian theory. A major portion of the paper will be devoted to showing that, for decisions about exploitation of renewable resources, the practice of discounting the interests of future generations is inconsistent with the basic tenet of utilitarianism. There are two reasons for discussing discounting. The first is that discounting is in fact being used in making economic decisions; therefore, if discounting is not morally acceptable, it is important that this fact be made explicit. The second is that if discounting is not morally acceptable, then the distant effects of an action are as important as the immediate effects; consequently the acceptability of a utilitarian method for determining subjective obligation will depend strongly on the acceptability of its method for treating distant effect. The method implicitly suggested by G. E. Moore[4] and J. J. C. Smart[5] depends strongly on the assumption that distant events are only negligibly affected by present actions. I will argue that certain types of action on renewable resources have non-negligible distant effects, so that subjective obligations with respect to such actions cannot be determined by a method based on the negligibility assumption. I will then develop an alternative way of treating the interests of future generations which transforms the problem of estimating all future consequences of an action on renewable resources into a problem of discovering all its contemporary consequences; this transformation allows me to show that utilitarianism implies an obligation for each generation to consume no more of renewable resources than their maximum sustainable yield.

## *Introduction to the Biological Concepts*

The facts contained in the first paragraph show examples of destructive utilization of interest-bearing resources. These two concepts are central to the argument of my paper and must be explained. Interest-bearing resources are those resources like crop species, fish species, draft animal species, topsoil, genetic variation, etc. which are instrumental in changing energy (ultimately solar energy) into energy available for consumption (as food, shelter, clothing, etc.) and which are such that their capacity to supply energy for future consumption is not decreased by utilization of some of the energy they supply. (Organisms tend to produce more offspring than can survive; the excess offspring can be utilized without damaging future productivity, so we can reap the interest without disturbing the capital.) Interest-bearing resources can be contrasted with exhaustible resources like fossil fuels, whose ability to supply energy for future consumption is decreased by every unit of energy consumed. Interest-bearing resources renew themselves and provide a bonus for us; they are usually called "renewable" resources, but in this paper I want to direct more attention to the bonus provided for us.

Destructive utilization of an interest-bearing resource is utilization which results in a lowered capacity to provide energy for future consumption. Destructive utilization may be direct, as when whalers lower the productivity of their resources by catching too many whales, or when farmers lower the intrinsic productivity of their soil by poor soil conservation techniques. Destructive utilization may also be indirect, as when the productivity of a lake is reduced by industries that use it as a place to dump poisonous wastes, or when the productivity of prime farmland is reduced by developers who build surburban housing on it. The effects of such destruction may be irreversible, as when a species is made extinct; or they may be reversible at some cost, as when the closing of a fishery allows an overfished species to recover. In a later section I will discuss some of the biological facts which allow us to decide whether a given instance of utilization is an instance of destructive utilization; at this point we only need to have a intuitive grasp of the concept.

## *Discounting and Utilitarian Theory*

The version of utilitarianism that I will use in this paper is total utilitarianism, in which the principle of utility mandates the maximization of the total utility, summed over all (past, present, and future) people. I will not choose a specific interpretation of utility; instead I will assume that for every interpretation of utility there is a direct functional relationship between utility and consumable energy. This is not an assumption that the utility of a particular act can be measured by the energy it consumes (i.e., it is not an assumption that energy is the ultimate coin of the utilitarian realm); it is merely an assumption that, other things being equal, more consumable energy provides more opportunity for the production of utility, and that more opportunity for the production of utility will be translated into more production of utility. Underlying this assumption is an assumption that the people to whom the energy is available will behave as utilitarians and will distribute the available energy in such a way as to maximize utility. (Thus I am leaving for those people problems such as that of deciding how to deal with interpersonal comparisons, how to choose among distributions with the same utility, etc.) These assumptions allow the problem of utility maximization to be replaced, in an important class of practical situations, by a problem of energy maximization. In this section I will argue that energy maximization (and thus potential utility maximization) forbids the intuitively appealing practice of discounting the interests of future generations.

It is first necessary to make clear the intended meaning of "discounting the interests of future generations." A utilitarian calculus discounts the interests of those living in year $Y$ if it eithers ignores some consequences of action $A$ or, when $(x_1, x_2, \ldots, x_n)$ are the utilities of a set of mutually exclusive and exhaustive consequences of action $A$ over the year $Y$ of all possible worlds, the calculus replaces these utilities with $(r_1x_1, r_2x_2, \ldots, r_nx_n)$ and

$$\sum_{i=1}^{n} r_i \neq 1.$$

(If $r_i$ is the probability of the $i$th consequence, this sum is equal to 1, so a calculus using probabilities does not discount as long as it ignores possible consequences.) I will argue that adjoining to a total utilitarian theory the assertion "This method of determining what action to take ought to be used" makes the resulting theory inconsistent if there is a year $Y$ in the future such that the method discounts the interests of those living in that year.

Assumptions that apparently involve discounting appear at the very beginning of utilitarian thought, in Bentham's hedonic calculus. Two of the seven circumstances which Bentham said affected the value of a pleasure or pain seem to have implications for this problem; according to Bentham[6] the value

> will be greater or less, according to . . .
>
> . . .
>
> 3. Its certainity or uncertainity.
> 4. Its propinquity or remoteness.

Bentham gives an example of a landed estate whose value to an individual rises or falls according to

> the certainty or uncertainty of its coming into possession; and the nearness or remoteness of the time at which, if at all, it is to come into possession.

As we can see from this example, Bentham's lesser value of a remote pleasure is essentially the same as the economist's discounted present value of a future payment; thus we say that the utilitarian is discounting future pleasures. The economist's discounting is justified[7] on the grounds that if he were given today $p$, the (discounted) present value of a future payment $P$, and he invested it at compound interest $d$, then at the time $t$ when the payment $P$ was due he would have amount $P = pe^{dt}$. Since a landed estate has direct monetary value, Bentham may be discussing exactly the same phenomenon as the economist; but he is using the example to illustrate a claim that is supposed to be true of all pleasures. I contend that the utilitarian is not free to use the economist's present value of future payments in his utilitarian calculus because its incorporation into his system will render the utilitarian system inconsistent.

Suppose the landed estate is to come into the man's possession at a certain fixed point in time, so that he can calculate the present value of this future payment; and suppose he sells his claim to it at this discounted value and spends the money in riotous living. The total amount of pleasure in his life is less than it would have been if he had waited, sold it for its full value, and spent the proceeds on riotous living; but this is not inconsistent with the utilitarian command to maximize pleasure, since the utilitarian calculates over all affected individuals, and in this case others received the pleasure lost by the seller. However, suppose that the man had one cow, which he slaughtered for a gluttonous feast; the cow would otherwise have provided a steady supply of milk and calves. For the economist, the cow represents the present value of the future cow-plus-milk-plus-calves. ("Discounting the value of future payments is simply the reverse process of compounding the interest on present payments."[8]) The man has thus chosen to take the discounted value of the future cow-plus-milk-plus-calves. This situation differs significantly from the estate situation in that the pleasure he has lost (the milk plus the calves) has not passed on to someone else; there is less total pleasure in the system as a result of his decision. Thus, in a situation in which future values can actually be removed from the system, rather than simply transferred to someone else in the system, a decision technique based on discounted future values is inconsistent with the mandate to maximize total utility. Clearly, the destructive utilization of interest-bearing resources is a situation of this sort and is therefore forbidden by the utility principle.

The demonstration that a policy of such discounting is inconsistent with utility maximization probably won't cause much distress among philosophers; few utilitarians have been explicitly advocating its use, although I suspect that the assumption that it was justifiable has colored the thinking of many. But among economists, who apply utilitarian theory, its use is standard even in situations involving interest-bearing resources. In his book on the optimal management of renewable resources, Colin Clark states[9]:

> The standard device used to handle questions of intertemporal economic benefits is *time discounting*. Although there is considerable controversy as to the social justifiability of this concept (Solow, 1974), time discounting is normal practice in business management.

Both Clark[10] and Fife[11] have shown that under certain not uncommon conditions a policy of maximization of the present value of harvests would result in extinction of the harvested species; that is, a harvesting policy which is in the long-term economic interests of the harvester may result in the loss of a species which could otherwise have provided a continuing supply of energy for future generations. Therefore this situation gives a clear example of the practical need for a philosophical analysis of our responsibilities to future generations.

Let us now look at the other circumstances mentioned by Bentham which might justify our counting the pleasures of future generations less than our pleasures—namely, their certainty or uncertainty. It will be useful to separate the uncertainty caused by the possibility of death before the future pleasure is available from the uncertainty caused by the possibility that something unexpected will prevent the expected pleasure from being available.

Consider, first, the possibility of death. It certainly seems to be utility maximizing for an individual to discount future pleasures on this ground, but it does not follow from this that it will be utility maximizing for society to do so. Mueller[12] has examined the relationship between the individual discount rate and the social discount rate; assuming that society (or *Homo sapiens*) does not die, he shows that this factor makes the appropriate social discount rate significantly different from the individual discount rate. But a nuclear war may make *Homo sapiens* extinct; surely the possibility of extinction should be counted in arriving at the social discount rate. Just as a man may rationally slaughter his cow because of the possibility that he will die before he could enjoy more utility in the form of milk and calves, so, it seems, a society may, rationally, destructively utilize some portion of its interest-bearing resources because of the possibility of extinction. A simple calculation will reveal the situations in which destructive utilization is consistent with utility maximization. Suppose a resource with destruction utility $B$ produces each year amount $rB$ of non-destructively harvestable utility. (For a species in which we harvest whole organisms, $r$ is the growth rate.) Then the number of years that it takes to produce utility equal to the destruction utility is $B/rB$, which is equal to $1/r$. To be concrete, consider the whale: Growth rates for a whale population may be as low as 5% per year; 1/.05 is equal to 20, so every 20 years such a population produces as much harvestable utility as would have been gained by destructive utilization of the entire population. Therefore, if the population were destructively utilized at time $t$, the whale-derived utility available between time $t$ and time $t + 21$ is $B$; if the population were non-destructively harvested between time $t$ and time $t + 21$, the utility derived from it would be $B + .05B$. So the destructive utilization of a whale population is consistent with utility maximization only if there is a probability of 1 that *Homo sapiens* will become extinct within 20 years.

Notice that the amount of destructive utilization does not figure in this conclusion; the result is the same regardless of the size of $B$. (The destructive utilization of one whale will reduce the 20 year productivity by the equivalent of one whale, so even this small amount of destruction would be inconsistent with utility maximization under the same conditions as the destruction of a population.) I think this is a counter-intuitive result; our intuition leads us to expect that a tiny probability of extinction would justify a tiny amount of destructive utilization. But we find that the only relevant factors are the growth rate of the resource and the propinquity and certainty of extinction. Unless extinction is very near and certain, or the interest rate of the resource is almost zero, *no* destructive utilization can be justified on the grounds of possible extinction.

But, you might argue, that reasoning is based on an implicit assumption that society's ability to utilize resources is unlimited; if society cannot utilize more than, e.g., double its normal consumption, then the extra utility available because a particular resource unit was spared may not be utilizable; and the utility principle would mandate that in the face of certain and near extinction this society should double its consumption as early as necessary to maximize total consumption, even by destructively utilizing renewable resources. That is true, but this does not seem to be our situation: under most extinction scenarios (e.g., the sun blowing up, invasion from space, nuclear war), the more resources there are available at the crucial time, the more likely is *Homo sapiens* to survive. Thus we see that, unless extinction is a clear and present *certainty*, the possibility of not becoming extinct prevents a utility maximizing society from discounting for possible extinction.

The remaining possible justification for destructive utilization of interest-bearing resources is the possibility that something will prevent the expected pleasure from being available. As a first approximation, this might be expressed as "We know the benefits to us, but the benefits to them are only probable." But this lack of knowledge cuts both ways: the species we want to utilize destructively may indeed be destroyed anyway by a deadly virus; on the other hand, it may provide a cure for cancer (as that pestiferous mold penicillium provided a cure for the dread diseases of the nineteenth century). In general, it is clear that the benefits to them may be greater than we envisage just as easily as less than we envisage. Therefore, although we must multiply the benefits we envisage by their probability, we must add to the result terms representing the possible unexpected benefits and harms. If our utility calculation contains all of the possible results of the action, together with an unbiased estimate of their probability, then uncertainty as to whether the expected pleasure will be available does not discount the interests of future generations.

But our utility calculations always contain a residue of possible consequences which are unforeseeable or whose utilities or probabilities cannot be estimated. Do the methods suggested for dealing with these unevaluable consequences discount the interests of future generations? G. E. Moore's suggestion is based on the following assumption[13]:

> We must assume, then, that if the effects of one action are generally better than those of another, so far forward in the future as we are able to foresee any probable difference in their effects at all, then the total effect upon the Universe of the former action is also generally better.

If *A* is the action whose foreseeable results are of greater utility, then this assumption would mandate the appropriate action whenever the actual value of the unevaluable consequences of *A* is no worse than the actual value of the unevaluable consequences of the alternative to *A*. Moore (and later, J. J. C. Smart[14]) argued for this assumption on the grounds that the distant consequences of an action are sufficiently small as to be negligible; that is, they argued that the actual values of both sets of unevaluable consequences are close enought to zero that their addition to the sum would make no difference in the result. Does this argument hold in the biological situations with which we are concerned?

There are three relevant biological properties. The first is the existence and ubiquity of homeostatic mechanisms. These mechanisms tend to damp down the effect of any input that is small relative to the size of the system; they would thus support the possibility that the distant effects will be negligible. But if the input is large enough to break down the homeostatic mechanisms, then the second property, that the death of a biological system is irreversible, will become important. And the third property, that biological systems live in an interdependent relationship with other biological systems, may cause the effect of the breakdown of one system to be magnified as it spreads through the interdependent systems. (Just as the kingdom was lost for the want of a horseshoe nail, so an ecosystem may be lost for the want of an apparently insignificant species.) In the latter two cases, the consequences are probably not negligible. The non-negligibility is made more likely if *A* is an unprecedented action, since this will greatly increase the probability of a significant unevaluable consequence. Actions of a type that has occurred frequently have fewer unevaluable consequences; if they have occurred frequently enough, the biological system will have adjusted to them so that whatever effects they have are less serious. Thus, although the assumption that distant consequences can be neglected was not made in order to justify discounting the interests of distant generations, the effect, in a significant number of biological situations, of acting on it is to make present utilities count more heavily than future utilities. And this is inconsistent with utilitarianism.

But if distant consequences cannot be assumed to be negligible, how should we put them into our utilitarian calculations? We can, of course, use the considerations outlined above to estimate the probable damage and enter it into the calculation, but it is virtually impossible to make such estimates. Fortunately, in the case of interest-bearing resources, the problem of estimating the utility of all effects into the distant future can be reduced to the problem of maximizing present sustainable yield. The next section will show this.

## *Maximum Sustainable Yield*

In the preceding section, I have argued that utilitarian theory forbids destructive utilization. In this section, I will argue that utilitarian theory mandates maximum sustainable yield. The argument requires a knowledge of the relevant biology, so I will sketch the theory underlying the concept of maximum sustainable yield.[15]

Consider a population of organisms which has just migrated into a new, favorable environment. At first, the growth rate of the population will be large and constant; the organisms will be producing as many offspring as their biology allows, and most of these offspring will survive. Denote this intrinsic growth rate of the population by $r$. As the population size increases, members of the population will begin competing with each other for the same resources, and the growth rate will slow down; some of those born will be unable to survive to adulthood, and others will be small and unhealthy because of malnutrition. As the population increases still further, it comes closer and closer to the environmental carrying capacity, $K$, for that population; the growth rate gets progressively lower as the competition gets fiercer. When the population size reaches $K$, no new organisms can survive to adulthood unless an existing member of the population dies; at this point the growth rate of the population, $F(x)$, is zero ($x$ represents population size). The simplest example of a growth rate function which models this behavior is $F(x) = rx(1 - x/K)$. Figure 1 is a graph of this function; figure 2 is a graph showing how the size of our immigrant population would grow if this were its growth rate function.

Now let us consider a population, e.g., of fish, that we wish to harvest. Can we harvest an amount $h$ without impairing the productivity of the population? Is there a maximum amount which can be harvested? Clearly, the amount that we can harvest at a given population size without driving the population size down is determined by the rate

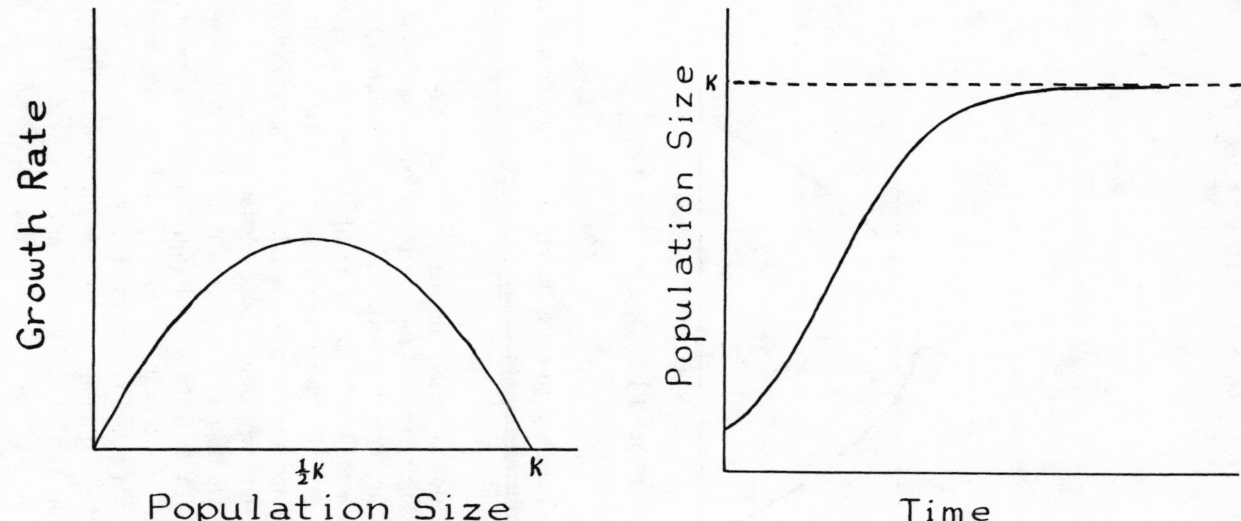


*Figure 1.* Curve showing how the rate at which a population grows is dependent on the size of the population. Notice that, beyond a certain point, the rate of growth decreases as population size increases.

*Figure 2.* Curve showing how the size of an immigrant population will increase until it reaches its environmental carrying capacity.

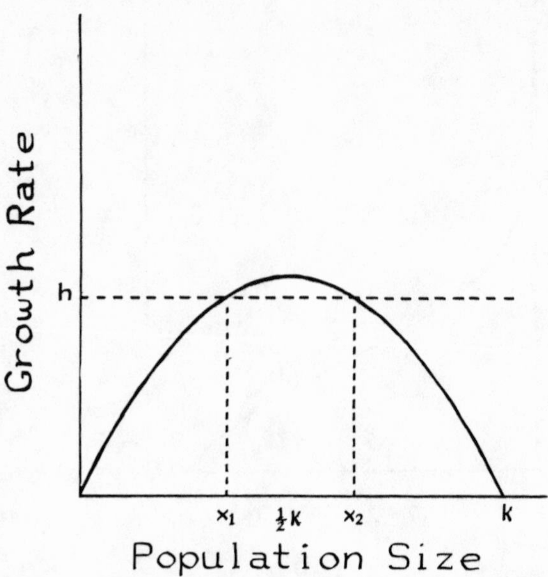


*Figure 3.* Curve allowing us to assess the effect on a population with this growth curve of harvesting at rate *h*.

at which the population can replace the harvested organisms—that is, by the growth rate. Figure 3 shows the effect of a harvest rate which is less than the maximum growth rate. It shows that: if the original population size is below the smaller size ($x_1$) with that growth rate, then harvesting at that rate will drive the population to extinction; if the original population size is between the two sizes with that growth rate, harvesting at that rate will allow the population to increase until it reaches the larger size ($x_2$) with that growth rate, and will cause the population to stabilize at that size. Clearly, there exists a maximum sustainable yield; it is equal to the maximum growth rate. The population has this maximum growth rate at size ½*K*.

Now consider the relationship between maximum sustainable yield and destructive utilization. If the population size is greater than ½*K*, then a harvest rate large enough to drive the size down to ½*K* is not destructive utilization, since the population produces more as its size moves toward ½*K*. If the size is not greater than ½*K*, then a harvest rate that drives the size down is destructive utilization. I have argued above that destructive utilization is inconsistent with energy maximization; for the same reason, any policy other than a policy of maximum sustainable yield is inconsistent with energy maximization. Thus, a maximum sustainable yield policy maximizes total energy.

Therefore, for a resource with this type of growth function, a first approximation to the policy which maximizes total utility is: If the population size is below ½*K*, do not harvest until it reaches ½*K*, and when it reaches ½*K* set the harvest rate equal to the maximum growth rate. If the population size is above or equal to ½*K*, set the harvest rate at the maximum growth rate plus the excess above ½*K*, and set the subsequent harvest rate at the maximum growth rate. Unfortunately, this is only a first approximation to the utility maximization policy. Because the costs of exploitation, as well as the benefits, must be considered in the utilitarian calculation, a better approximation to the desired policy will contain the costs of exploiting the resource. Because preventing harvest of the resource until it reaches ½*K* may cost more in economic dislocation, etc. than is gained by the speed of the increase to ½*K*, a better approximation would take these factors into account. Because the interdependence of some harvestable resources will force us to use a multi-species model rather than the single species model presented above, a better approximation would use such a multi-species model. Other complicating factors will necessitate further revisions of the policy.

Finding the changes in the policy necessary to provide these better approximations will be an extremely difficult practical problem. But in each case the necessary data are data about the contemporary world. The obligation to consider the effects on all subsequent generations has been replaced by an obligation to maximize sustainable yield in the present generation. A policy of taking less than the maximum sustainable yield in order to increase the population size beyond ½*K* is clearly counterproductive; such a policy not only decreases the present harvest, it decreases the future productivity and thus decreases total production. So for these situations, the problem that, under a utilitarian theory, the present generation might have to sacrifice heavily because there are so many more future people does not arise; there are many more future people, but there are many more future cows and whales, too. There is no utility maximizing way to give distant generations a better heritage of interesting-bearing resources than by giving the next generation a heritage of interest-bearing resources which are all at their maximum sustainable yield.

### *Problems*

1. It must be admitted that this policy does not completely absolve us of the responsibility of considering unevaluable future consequences; these still exist. However, it does provide a powerful tool for those wishing to maximize total utility.

2. For those whose ethical system contains both the utilitarian principle and a principle of justice, the following may cause a problem: Because generations previous to ours have practiced destructive utilization, the generation which first institutes a maximum sustainable yield policy will bear an unfair burden as it decreases harvesting in order to bring species up to their maximum sustainable yield. (It might be appropriate to compensate that generation with more than its share of exhaustible resources.) In general, however, a maximum sustainable yield policy seems to mandate a just distribution over the generations.

3. The analysis in the previous section was of one type of interest-bearing resource–species. Its applicability to resources such as topsoil and genetic variation must be worked out.

4. The continued ability of a species to maintain its maximum sustainable yield is dependent on its continued ability to meet new environmental challenges; this is dependent on its genetic variation. Consideration of this problem forces us to realize that we may have to expand the meaning of the word "sustainable"; the biological model we are using implicitly defines "sustainable" as "sustainable under present conditions"; we may need a biological model which includes factors of long-term sustainability.

5. Economic factors may also dictate the need for a model which ensures long-term sustainability rather than year-to-year sustainability. It could, for example, be more cost-efficient to build a new set of the machines used in exploiting a particular resource, operate it at a harvest level above the maximum sustainable yield until the machines are worn out, and then allow the resource to build back to ½*K* before building new machines.

6. Golding[16] has objected that, since people in the far distant future will be unlike us in unpredictable ways, we do not know what to desire for them. This is vitiated by the calculation given earlier, which shows that, for whales, our policy of maximum sustainable yield would be mandated even if we could foresee the relevant desires of people only 21 years in the future; for most interest-bearing resources (whose growth rate is larger than the growth rate of whales), we would need to foresee less than 21 years. In those cases in which it would be necessary to foresee a significant distance, it seems, in the absence of reason to think that desires or needs will change in a particular direction, reasonable to assume that the *best estimate* of future desires and needs is derived from the assumption that their needs and desires will be pretty much like ours.

## *Conclusion*

The obligation to follow this policy does not exhaust our obligations concerning future generations; in particular, it does not cover whatever obligations we have concerning non-interest-bearing (exhaustible) resources. Nor does this policy tell us how to choose among the possible different ways of getting the same total yield of energy in a multi-species system. Nor does this policy provide complete escape from practical difficulties; the difficulties of determining the maximum sustainable yield of an ecosystem will be formidable. However, this policy does provide guidance about a significant set of actions affecting future generations; by changing the problem from one of predicting all future consequences of an action to one of discovering facts about our contemporary ecosystem, it significantly reduces the difficulty of finding reasonably good answers to the problem.

The maximum sustainable yield policy has been presented in this paper as derivable from total utilitarian theory; it may also be derivable from other moral theories. Moral philosophers who claim that obligations can refer only to existing persons may find that, since a maximum sustainable yield policy can be justified by its effect on the next generation, their theory gives the same future-protecting effect as utilitarian theory. Such derivation from other major moral theories would greatly strengthen the claim that our social institutions should be changed to ensure a maximum sustainable yield policy.

In summary, I have argued that utilitarian theory mandates a specific policy with respect to renewable resources. The biological structure of renewable resources allows us to transform the theoretically intractable problem of estimating the distant consequences of an action on renewable resources into a scientifically difficult but theoretically tractable problem of estimating its contemporary consequences. This transformation is accomplished not by using the dubious (and in some cases obviously false) assumption that the distant consequences are negligible but rather by using well-established biological theory to show that no policy we could follow would give distant generations a heritage of renewable resources with more expected utility than a maximum sustainable yield policy.

*Notes*

1. Pimentel, D. *et al.*, "Land Degradation: Effects on Food and Energy Resources," *Science*, 194: 149-155, 1976.
2. Brink, R. A. *et al.*, "Soil Deterioration and the Growing World Demand for Food," *Science*, 197: 625-630, 1977.
3. Frankel, O. H. and Hawkes, J. G., "Genetic Resources–The Past Ten Years and the Next," pp. 1-11, in *Crop Genetic Resources for Today and Tomorrow*, edited by Frankel, O. H. and Hawkes, J. G., Cambridge University Press, 1975.
4. Moore, G. E., *Principia Ethica*, Cambridge University Press, 1971, pp. 152-154.
5. Smart, J. J. C. and Williams, B., *Utilitarianism: For and Against*, Cambridge University Press, 1973, p. 33.
6. Bentham, J., "An Introduction to the Principles of Morals and Legislation," reprinted in *The Utilitarians*, Bentham, J. and Mill, J. S., Anchor Books 1973, Chapter IV.
7. Clark, Colin, *Mathematical Bioeconomics: The Optimal Management of Renewable Resources*, John Wiley and Sons, 1976, p. 69.
8. Clark, *loc. cit.*
9. Clark, *op. cit*, p. 31. The reference within the quotation is to Solow, R. M., "The Economics of Resources or the Resources of Economics," *American Economic Review*, 64, 1974, 1-14.
10. Clark, Colin, "The Economics of Overexploitation," *Science*, 181: 630-634, 1974 (reprinted in *Managing the Commons*, edited by G. Hardin and J. Baden, W. H. Freeman, 1977).

11. Fife, Daniel, "Killing the Goose," *Environment*, 13 (3): 20-27, 1971 (reprinted in *Managing the Commons*, edited by G. Hardin and J. Baden, W. H. Freeman, 1977).

12. Mueller, Dennis C., "Intergenerational Justice and the Social Discount Rate," *Theory and Decision*, 5: 263-273, 1974.

13. Moore, G. E., *op. cit.*, p. 154.

14. Smart, J. J. C., *op. cit.*

15. For a more detailed exposition of the maximum sustainable yield theory, see Clark, *Mathematical Bioeconomics*.

16. Golding, Martin, "Obligations to Future Generations," *Monist*, 56: 85-99, 1972.

# The Futurity Problem

*GREGORY KAVKA*

Whether we should allow population and industry to grow essentially unchecked, as we have in the past, is currently the subject of an active debate within the scientific and intellectual community. Pessimists, such as the authors of the Club of Rome Report, *The Limits to Growth*,[1] warn that this would lead—perhaps within a few generations—to extreme shortages of food, clean air, fossil fuels, and other resources needed to sustain human life and civilization. The result would be a cataclysmic decline in population and industrial output, and human death and suffering on an unprecedented scale. On the other hand, optimists, such as Herman Kahn of the Hudson Institute, argue that the modernization of presently underdeveloped countries will produce a natural plateau in world population at a level that the earth's environment and resources can easily support, given probable technological advances.[2] I shall not enter this debate, but shall simply *assume* that the dire warnings of the pessimists, who seem to be in the majority, are credible. If this is so, a serious moral question confronts our generation (i.e. those presently living). Are we morally obligated, in order to prevent impending catastrophe for mankind, to impose strict limits on population growth, pollution, and resource use, at the cost—to many of us—of a significant decrease in our material standard of living and our freedom to have large families?

Answering this question adequately would require solving two difficult problems in moral theory. The first concerns whether (relatively) rich individuals and groups are morally obligated to offer aid to strangers in desperate need, if so doing would impose substantial costs on those rich individuals and groups or on their friends and loved ones. (It is generally acknowledged that rendering aid under such circumstances is praiseworthy and good, but it is by no means obvious whether it is morally required.) Because it concerns the extent to which morality permits one to favor the interests of one's friends (including oneself) over the interests of strangers, I call this the Friends and Strangers Problem. Our second problem concerns whether future people are different, in morally relevant ways, from present people. The following formulation of the problem makes clear its independence from the first problem; putting aside considerations based on special relationships such as love, friendship, or contractual obligation, ought one, in his moral decision making, assign equal weight to the interests of present and future persons? In other words, if we think of "strangers" as those to whom one stands in no such special relationships, are the interests of *future* strangers worthy of equal consideration with those of presently existing strangers? Let us call this the Futurity Problem.

The relationship between these two problems and the question of our obligations to future generations may be explained as follows. Suppose that we are obligated to aid desperately needy strangers who are now alive, even at substantial cost to ourselves and our friends. If the needs and interests of future people are as important, morally speaking, as those of present people, it would apparently follow that we are obligated to make substantial sacrifices, if necessary, to prevent *future* strangers from being desperately needy.[3]

Of our two problems, the Friends and Strangers Problem has received much more attention in the philosophical literature.[4] However, the Futurity Problem is equally interesting and important, and I shall leave the other aside to focus on it. Thus, instead of trying to prove that we are obligated to sacrifice for future generations, I seek only to establish the more modest conditional conclusion that *if* we are obligated to make sacrifices for needy present strangers, then we are also obligated to sacrifice for future ones. We may arrive at this conclusion by considering, and rebutting, three sorts of reasons that might be offered for *not* giving the interests of future people equal consideration with those of present people: the temporal location of future people, our ignorance of them, and the contingency of their existence.

### *I. The Temporal Location of Future People*

The most obvious difference between present and future people is that the latter do not yet exist. Does this difference in temporal location in itself constitute a reason for favoring the interests of present over future persons? It does not seem so. Location in space is not a morally relevant feature of a person, determining his worthiness for consideration or aid. Why should location in time be any different? Further, it is part of our general conception of the rational person that he assign the same importance to the satisfaction of a desire whether he has it now, or knows he will have it in the future.[5] Since rational prudence (which concerns the satisfaction of desires) sees no intrinsic importance in the temporal location of a desire, it would seem that rational morality (which concerns the well-being of people) should attach no intrinsic importance to the temporal location of people.

Now, of course, temporal location does make a difference to morality—when that location is in the *past*. For surely, it would be absurd to give equal weight to the desires of living and dead persons. This, however, may be admitted without affecting the claim of equal status for *future* people. There are two main reasons for favoring the desires of the living over those of the dead. First, nearly all of the desires of the dead concerned matters in their own lifetimes that are now past and cannot be changed. Second, consider those desires of persons now dead that were directed toward future states of affairs that living people might still bring about. Since the persons having had those desires will not be present to experience satisfaction in their fulfillment or disappointment in their non-fulfillment, it is reasonable to downgrade the importance of these desires (and perhaps ignore them altogether) in our moral decision making. Now, it is clear that neither of these two reasons applies to the desires of future people. We *are* in a position to act to make it more likely that many of the desires of future people will be satisfied, and future people *will be* around to experience the fulfillment or non-fulfillment of their desires. Again, the analogy to rational prudence is instructive. We regard it as rational for a person to give equal weight to his present and (known) future desires, even though we would regard it as silly for him to give equal weight to past desires. It may be concluded that while there are sound reasons, when deciding *whose* desires to satisfy, to favor present over *past* people, the difference in their temporal location does not constitute a reason for favoring present over *future* people.

### *II. Our Ignorance of Future People*

While the temporal location of future people is, in itself, not a reason for discounting their interests, other factors resulting from their temporal location might be. In particular, it could be argued that our *ignorance* of future people renders us less able to promote their interests than those of present people. For future people are not around to tell us what their desires are (or will be). Also, our ability to shape future events generally decreases as they become temporally more distant, so it may be thought that we would be less able to satisfy the desires of future than of present people, even if we knew in detail what those desires will be.

Does this relative ignorance of what future people will want, and how to get it for them, justify us in paying less attention to their interests in decision making? I am doubtful that it does to any substantial degree. For we do know with a high degree of certainty the basic biological and economic needs of future generations–enough food to eat, air to breathe, space to move in, and fuel to run machines. The satisfaction of these needs will surely be a prerequisite of the satisfaction of most of the other desires and interests of future people, whatever they may be. Further, if the pessimist's warnings are correct, certain burdensome things our generation could do now would substantially promote the satisfaction of these needs and interests. First, our generation could limit population growth, pollution, and the use of non-renewable resources. Second, we could make very heavy investments in research in what may be called the *survival sciences*–agriculture, population control, energy production, war prevention, etc. Third, we could develop and design institutions and organizations to represent the interests of future generations. Their purpose would be to propose social programs to benefit posterity, advise policy makers, pressure legislators to take the interests of posterity into account, and encourage the public to evaluate policies in terms of their effects on future, as well as present, generations.

What I am suggesting is that we view our ignorance of the interests of future people as being analogous to a young adult's ignorance of the desires and interests he will have in old age, say, after retirement. It is unlikely that a young adult will know in detail the goals and desires he will have in forty years: whether, for example, he will wish to spend his time traveling, doing volunteer work, or drinking beer. However, he can believe with a high degree of confidence that his important needs and interests will include good health, adequate food and shelter, and security for his loved ones. And there are definite things he can do now that will make it more likely that these needs will be met: saving or investing a portion of his income, eating properly, exercising regularly, etc. Rational prudence would advise him to do these things, despite his ignorance of the details of the desires he will have when old. Similarly, morality advises us to take steps to insure an adequate supply of resources for future generations, despite our ignorance of the details of the desires that future people will have.

An interesting variant of the argument from ignorance is presented by Martin Golding, in an article titled "Obligations to Future Generations."[6] Golding contends that we should regard future people as members of our moral community, whose interests we should look after, only if we know what to desire for them. But, he claims, we know what to desire for them only to the extent that we can expect them to share our conception of the good life for man. Since this expectation becomes less credible as we consider more distant generations, Golding concludes that we essentially ought to confine our attention to helping "immediate posterity" achieve our shared conception of the good life.

I do not find this argument convincing. For, depending upon how one understands the notion of "a conception of the good life," it seems that the argument either goes against the grain of our deep-seated beliefs about human equality or fails to establish the conclusion that Professor Golding reaches. To see this, let us briefly examine the claim–fundamental to our moral tradition–that all men are equal and are worthy of equal consideration.

When we say that all men are equal, we are asserting that they are alike in certain important respects. Clearly, people are *not* alike, but are widely diverse in their cultural practices, political ideologies, religious beliefs, life-styles, and values. If most or all people *are* alike in significant ways, it is, as I pointed out in an earlier paper,[7] in virtue of their possession of certain very general features: their vulnerability to physical and mental suffering and to death, their capacity for enjoyment (including the enjoyment of complex activities and interactions with others), their self-consciousness, their capacity for long-range purposive planning and action, and their capacity for cooperation and identification with others. These general features are, among other things, what make human beings capable of entering into and benefiting from moral relations with others; they are, as I see it, the valid basis of the claim that all men are equal.

Two aspects of this elucidation of the traditional conception of human equality are worth noting. First, there are not degrees of membership in the human moral community. One is a full and equal member of that community if one possesses a sufficient number of the above features in sufficient degree. (The cut-off point of membership may, of course, be vague and ill-defined.) Second, membership in the human moral community is not dependent upon possessing any particular *substantive* conception of the good life; though those possessing the credentials for membership will doubtless share our *formal* conception of the good life as one in which the individual engages in a variety of complex and cooperative activities with others, in which the desires he regards as important are usually satisfied, and in which the projects he cares most about are generally carried forth to successful completion.

The implications of these observations are these. The features in virtue of which we regard *present* persons of other cultures, nations, political persuasions, and life-styles, as equal with ourselves, are quite general features that will certainly be shared by future people for very many generations. The moral status of such persons and our reasons for promoting their interests are not dependent upon their sharing our substantive conception of the good life. (Admittedly, complications would arise if we had good reason to suppose that their conception of the good life would be the same as our conception of a morally evil or inhuman life; but it is doubtful we have such reasons.) Hence, our ignorance of the degree to which, in fact, future generations will share our substantive conception of the good life does not seem to be a valid reason for favoring present over future strangers, much less a reason for ignoring, in our planning and practices, the well-being of all generations save the next few.

### *III. The Contingency of Future People*

Having rejected the temporal location of future people and our ignorance of them as substantial reasons for downgrading the importance of their interests, we must now deal with the most perplexing and least tractable feature of future people—their contingency. The trouble with future people, we might say, is not that they do not exist *yet*, it is that they might not exist *at all*. Further, what and how many future people will exist depends upon the decisions and actions of present people. To see how this existential dependence of future persons on the decisions of present ones affects the moral relationship between the two, let us consider two analogies.

First, suppose that a moral person realizes that he cannot fulfill both of two promises he has made, though he can fulfill either one. If he cannot obtain release from either promise, he will decide what to do by considering such factors as how much each promisee would be harmed by his failure to keep the promise in question, and how adequately he would be able to compensate each promisee for non-fulfillment. Now imagine that he has this same realization about two promises—one that he has already made and a second that he has been planning to make in the future. It would be wildly wrong-headed for him to proceed, as in the previous case, by weighing such considerations as his ability to compensate each promisee for non-fulfillment. For he has not yet made the second promise and thus has available to him the option, which he clearly ought to adopt, of keeping the first promise and simply not making the second. The contingency of the planned future promise on his own decision gives him strong reasons not to treat that promise on a par with promises he has already made.

A second and somewhat closer analogy to the situation of the present generation with respect to future generations involves a poor couple that has some children and is planning to have more. Should they treat the interests of their prospective children on a par with those of their existing children, by husbanding resources that could be used by the latter? Not if this would cause the existing children to suffer serious deprivation. For in that case, they should simply not have any more children.

These two examples suggest that, under conditions of scarcity, resource distributors have reason to show preference for existing resource consumers (e.g. people or promises) over future resource consumers whose very existence is dependent upon the distributor's decisions and actions. It is important, however, not to misunderstand the nature of these reasons or the kind of preferences they support. Under scarcity, there seems to be reason to meet the needs of existing consumers rather than bringing into existence too many new consumers who will make demands on scarce resources. This does not mean, however, that consumers that one assumes or knows *will exist* are less important or less worthy of receiving resources than those presently existing. To see this, suppose that the parents in our example *know* they will not change their mind about having more children, even if they save no resources to care for them. Under these circumstances, they ought to give their prospective children equal consideration with their present ones.[8]

The implications of these examples with respect to our relationship to future generations are as follows. Suppose, following the pessimists, that we (i.e. those presently living) cannot (i) consume as much as we want and could, and (ii) have as many children as we want and could, and (iii) still leave sufficient resources to take care of the needs of future people. Then, we must either consume less or produce fewer children, if we are to leave enough for future generations. Now, our examples do not indicate that the contingency of future people in any way warrants our abandoning the goal of conserving resources adequate to the needs of future people. What they do suggest is that producing *fewer* future people (than we could), so as to allow us both to provide for the needs of those future people who are produced and still to consume what we want, would be a morally viable option.

A different face of the contingency issue appears when we consider situations *not* involving great scarcity. Suppose that a happy childless couple is deciding whether to have a child. Imagine that they know that each would be somewhat less happy in the long run if they had the child, but that the child would be a happy one, and that its happiness would greatly exceed the loss of happiness they would suffer as a result of having it. If we proceed to evaluate each of their alternatives–having and not having a child–in terms of the happiness of the people that would be affected by it, an odd result emerges. Whichever act they choose turns out to be the better one! For suppose that they have the child. This is better because the child's happiness more than makes up for the small loss in happiness they each suffer. But if they do not have the child, this also turns out to be better. For they have benefited (i.e. done better for themselves than if they had produced the child), and *no one* has been adversely affected.[9]

The oddity, that of each of two alternatives seeming better than the other, arises out of the contingency of the child's existence on the decision in question. Because of this contingency, the act of not having the child is evaluated in terms of its effects on the parents alone, while the act of having the child must be evaluated in terms of its effects on a different set of people–the parents *and* the child. This produces the odd result of each act being better than the other, when evaluated by what seems to be the same criterion: the happiness of those affected. This oddity can be avoided only by making the controversial move of treating non-existence as a harm or opportunity-cost suffered by the non-existent child.[10]

This puzzling aspect of the contingency issue relates to an important theoretical question about our moral relationship to posterity. It was suggested above that limiting the size of the next generation to allow more consumption in this generation would not be an objectionable policy. But suppose this policy were carried to its farthest extreme. Suppose, that is, that everyone now living voluntarily agreed to forego the pleasures of childbearing and agreed to undergo sterilization, so that they could live out their lives consuming and polluting to their heart's content without worrying about the effects on future generations. (This would be in some ways analogous to the parents in our last example foregoing having a child, so they could be as happy as possible.) Would there be anything morally wrong about our generation (or some later generation) doing this? Or, to put the matter somewhat differently, does a moral person have any reason to care that the human race survive?

Note that this question has interest aside from its implications concerning the purely imaginary possibility that people will unanimously decide not to reproduce. For some pessimists fear that if we do not control the growth of population and pollution, the very existence of the human species, as well as the existence of modern civilization, will be endangered. Hence, whether we, as moral persons, have reason to care that mankind survive, is a question that bears on our attitudes toward uncontrolled growth. It is this question that I wish to consider next.

## *IV. The Survival of the Human Species*

Setting aside their particular desires to have and raise children, why shouldn't present people simply refrain from producing future people, so that they can live out their lives consuming and polluting at will? No doubt the cessation of reproduction would force serious readjustments in the economy. And if carried through to the bitter end, such a program would lead to the last people alive suffering from severe loneliness and a shortage of services. But, such considerations aside, would it be morally wrong for present people to act collectively in this way if they freely chose to do so? One might be tempted to object to such action on the grounds that it would be unfair to future generations.[11] But this objection flounders in the face of the fact that if the action were successfully carried out, there would *be* no future generations to have been treated unfairly by it. Leaving fairness aside, the central question becomes whether we, as moral persons, have any reason to care about the survival of our species. Some philosophers, e.g. Jan Narveson,[12] suggest we do not. I should like to set out my reasons for thinking that we do.

It is generally acknowledged that human life has value, and hence the lives of existing people are, with rare exceptions, worth preserving. If we dare to venture the question of *why* human life is valuable and worth preserving, the answers we receive—religious answers aside—are likely to fall into three categories. First, there are answers that explain the value of life in terms of the pleasures contained therein. Second, it may be held that certain human experiences or relationships (e.g. loving another person) are valuable in themselves, beyond the pleasures they contain, and it is the having of such experiences (or the possibility of having them) that makes human life valuable. Third, it may be thought that the value of human life is to be found in the human capacity for accomplishment, the fact that human beings set and achieve goals, and exercise and develop various complex capacities. What is of interest here is that, whichever of these views of the value of human life (or combination of such views) one adopts, it turns out that the lives of future people would almost certainly possess the properties that make the lives of present people valuable, and hence would be valuable themselves. This seems to be a reason for creating such lives; that is, for bringing future people into existence.

Now this last claim is presumably what my opponents would deny. They would contend that the fact that one state of affairs contains more equally valuable elements than another, does not constitute *any* reason to bring the former rather than the latter about. This contention is sometimes expressed using the following example. Imagine God deciding between creating a universe with one planet occupied by *n* happy people, and a universe with two planets, *each* occupied by *n* people just as happy as those in the first universe. Does the fact that there are twice as many happy people in the latter universe constitute a reason for God preferring to create it? My opponents would say, No. Notice that our problem concerning future generations is quite analogous to this one, the difference being that the extra equally happy people are located in later generations rather than on another planet. Now I confess to being one of those who strongly feels it would be better for God to create the greater number of equally happy planets (or generations).[13] I doubt, however, that this point can be argued. The preference for *more* happy people seems to rest on a basic intuition, comparable perhaps with Mill's intuition that some pleasures are more choiceworthy than others of equal intensity. I hope and expect that others share this intuition, but I cannot prove it to be a valid one.

There is, however, an argument for preserving our species that does not depend upon this basic intuition, though it depends on others perhaps equally controversial. This concerns certain collective enterprises of man, the shared accomplishments of our species. There are few of us who have not at some time or other been awed and inspired by mankind's intellectual, artistic, scientific, or technological accomplishments. Implicit in this attitude of awe is the view that these achievements are marvelous, valuable, and worthy of admiration for reasons that transcend their usefulness to us. If this attitude is not misguided, the accomplishments of mankind in the intellectual, artistic, and scientific spheres, and the likelihood of continued progress in these fields, give us a substantial reason to wish the race to survive. For if the life of our species ends, so will these collective enterprises; while if it continues, spectacular accomplishments in such fields of endeavor are highly probable. One suspects that at least some of those who are indifferent to whether happy people will exist in the future, will not be indifferent to the continuation and progress of these admirable human enterprises, and will regard their development as a reason for wanting mankind to go on.

The notion that our species should be preserved gains additional support from an analogy that can be constructed between the life of the species and the life of an individual. Imagine an individual choosing between two strategies for living. First, living to the fullest for a few years, consuming and creating at a rapid rate but dying soon as a result. Second, consuming and creating at a moderate pace in the near future and living a long life of progressively greater accomplishments, with total accomplishments far surpassing those that could be attained in a short life. Choosing the short life in such circumstances would be analogous to our generation's cutting out reproduction in favor of unlimited present consumption. Choosing the long life would be analogous to our generation's limiting consumption and growth so that the species can survive and progress for a very long time. In the individual case, we are strongly inclined to approve the choice of the longer life, to have greater respect for the individual making that choice than for the individual who chooses the short but sweet life. This suggests, by analogy, that we should prefer a longer life of increasing accomplishment for mankind, to having human history cut short to facilitate present consumption.

This analogy between individual and species life also helps us see what is wrong with an objection that has been raised against caring about the survival of the species.[14] The objection is based on the prediction that the expanding sun will swallow up the earth within twelve billion years or so. It is, in effect, claimed that, since our species will ultimately be extinguished anyway, we have no reason to act to prolong its existence. To see that this claim is fallacious, it is sufficient to note that each of us knows that he, individually, is mortal. It hardly follows that one has no reason to prolong his own life, especially if, as in the case of the species, one has reason to suppose that one's accomplishments will grow in magnitude with age.

A final implication of the analogy between individual and species life is that our desire for the survival of the species should not be *unconditional*. If a person recognizes that his continued existence would uncontrollably result in his moral, intellectual, and physical degeneration, he has good reason to wish for an early death, even to commit suicide. Similarly, if we knew that future generations would inevitably descend into bestiality or a Hobbesian war of all against all, it might be reasonable for us to put an end to the species deliberately. Fortunately, we do not know this. Such a future for our species could come about as a result of extreme scarcity brought on by uncontrolled population growth and pollution, or as a result of large scale nuclear war. But if we had the will and means to end reproduction deliberately, we would, *ipso facto*, be in a position to alleviate the former danger. And the threat of nuclear war, while hardly negligible, is not so imminent and certain as to make voluntary suicide of the species a preferable alternative to living under that threat.

To summarize, there seem to be two main sorts of reasons, that moral persons will appreciate, for wanting the human species to survive. First, human life has value and is generally a good thing to those possessing it. Second, the continuation of our species will very likely mean the continuation of its collective artistic, intellectual, and scientific accomplishments. Further, certain features of the analogy between the life of an individual and the life of the species suggest the reasonableness of the preference for continuation over termination of the species. Taken together, these considerations suggest that a moral person should not be indifferent to mankind's survival.

## *V. Aid Between Nations and Generations*

In this concluding section, I should like to consider briefly the implications of our discussion of the Futurity Problem with respect to two issues: the form in which rich countries give aid to very poor ones, and the distribution of resources between generations. To take the aid question first, let us suppose that a rich nation has decided to give a fixed quantity of aid to a very poor and overpopulated nation with many starving people in it. (The question of how large this quantity of aid ought to be falls under the Friends and Strangers Problem and will not be taken up here.) Should the aid be given (i) in the form of food or (ii) in the form of birth control devices, machinery, help in governmental and educational planning, etc?

It seems obvious at first that the aid ought to be in the form of food to save people from starvation. But then, it will be pointed out, some forms of aid (e.g. food aid) tend to accelerate population growth while other forms (e.g. birth control and education) tend to inhibit population growth. Thus, giving aid in the form of food could be expected to result in more starving people in the country in the long run than if the aid were given in other forms.[15] Granting this, however, our temptation to feel that the aid ought to be given in the form of food remains strong. This is partly the result of hoping that technological discoveries in birth control or food production will obviate scarcity problems in time to keep later generations of the country's citizens from starving. But suppose we take this factor into account? Suppose we discount the needs of future generations in the country by a fraction representing the probability of such technological developments, and suppose it still appears that food aid will result in more starving people in the long run? One may continue to feel that food aid should be given. After all, these presently starving people definitely exist, they exist *now*, and we know that they are hungry. If, however, the arguments of the first three sections of this paper are correct, this feeling is unwarranted. The needs of future people deserve equal consideration with those of present ones. Hence, it is not unreasonable to prefer, on moral grounds, that a fixed quantity of aid be given in population growth inhibiting (rather than inducing) form, even if this would allow some people to starve that might have been saved. This is so, because it is as important to prevent persons who will be born later from starving as it is to prevent persons who exist now from starving.[16]

Let us turn from the issue of aid between countries to the more general one of aid between generations. The question to be considered is: How much of the earth's resources may any given generation use up and how much should it preserve for use by later generations? Of course, we cannot determine the *obligations* of our generation to save resources for later generations without solving the Friends and Strangers Problem. For most of our friends (i.e. those to whom we stand in special relationships, including ourselves) are in our own generation; hence, morality may allow us to show, in our actions, a bias in favor of our own generation. We can, however, explicitly set aside considerations based on special relationships; we can ask what ideal standard of generational resource use follows from the view, defended above, that the interests of future persons are worthy of equal consideration with those of present persons.

John Locke supposes that men in the state of nature are moral equals and that God has given to them, in common, the use of the earth and its resources. He claims that, under these conditions, an individual may fairly appropriate land for his own use–without belying the equal status of his fellows–provided that he (i) uses rather than wastes what he appropriates and (ii) leaves "enough and as good for others."[17] Locke justifies the latter condition on the ground that one who appropriates a resource but leaves enough and as good for others, leaves others as well off as they were prior to the appropriation. Hence, they are not injured by his act and have no complaint against him.[18] Given that present and future persons are moral equals with equal claim to the earth and its resources, Locke's analysis can be extended to apply to the problem of generational resource use. Accordingly, we say that a generation may use the earth's resources provided that it (i) does not waste them (i.e. uses them to satisfy human interests) and (ii) leaves "enough and as good" for future generations. In the spirit of the justification Locke offers for his second condition, I interpret this to mean that, in this context, the generation in question leaves the next generation at least as well off, with respect to usable resources, as it was left by its ancestors. (In which case, later generations cannot be said to have been injured by this generation's use of resources.) Since it is individuals, and not generations *per se*, that are regarded as equal, I understand the relevant measure of usable resources to be relativized to population. This means that if a given generation insists on having more than one descendant per capita, it is to aim at leaving proportionally more total resources.

It might at first appear impossible that any generation live up to the Lockean standard. For questions of waste aside, how could a generation use *any* resources at all and leave even an equal number of descendants with as many resources as they themselves inherited? The question is readily answered by noting that some physical resources are renewable or reusable, and that knowledge–especially scientific and technological knowledge–is a usable resource that grows without being depleted and enables us to increase the output of the earth's physical resources. Thus, what the Lockean standard recommends is that each generation use the earth's physical resources only to the extent that technology allows for the recycling or depletion of such resources without net loss in their output capacity. Aside from its equity, perhaps the most attractive feature of this standard is the following. If all succeeding generations abided by it, mankind could go on living on earth indefinitely, with living standards improving substantially from generation to generation, once world population were stabilized. Or, to put the point somewhat differently, the Lockean standard prescribes a world in which the fixed natural capital supplied by our planet is essentially preserved, and men live off the ever increasing interest generated by expanding technology.

Is the Lockean standard unfair to our generation? It appears so when we consider that vast investments to speed development in poor countries may have to be made soon, if those countries are to be eased throught the demographic transition in time to stabilize world population at supportable levels. Won't our generation then have to use more than our share of resources to deal with the threat to later generations of disastrous overpopulation? Perhaps so. But this special use of resources can be accomodated to the general framework of the Lockean standard in either of two ways. First, by treating the case of our generation as special, so that our task is one of creating initial conditions in which future generations may attain compliance with the Lockean standard without excessive sacrifice. Second, by treating the pronatal practices, institutions, and attitudes that we have inherited from our ancestors as a special kind of *negative* resource, so that our extra use of other resources would be balanced out if we eradicated this negative resource; we would be leaving our decendants as well off as we were left, all things considered.

I close with a brief summary of my conclusions. The temporal location of future people and our comparative ignorance of their interests do not justify failing to treat their interests on a par with those of present people. While the *contingency* of future people *does* justify granting priority to the needs of existing people, it does so only in the sense of warranting population limitation as a means of limiting the total needs of future generations. However, population limitation carried to the utmost extreme, i.e. the end of the species by collective decision not to reproduce, would not be morally justified. Granting the equality of present and future people, it follows that it is not morally wrong for rich nations to consider the population-related effects of various forms of aid in determining how to help poor overpopulated nations. Finally, the equal moral status of present and future persons suggests that our generation should, ideally, aim collectively at leaving our descendants a planet as rich in usable per capita resources as that we have inherited from our ancestors.[19]

## *Notes*

1. Donella and Dennis Meadows, Jorgen Randers, and William Behrens III, *The Limits to Growth* (New York: Universe Books, 1972).

2. Herman Kahn, William Brown, and Leon Martel, *The Next 200 Years* (New York: William Morrow, 1976).

3. This would be so even if the amount of aid needed by present strangers alone were more than the maximum we (relatively rich people) are obligated to give. For, in that case, we should use a portion of our aid for the benefit of future strangers, even though this would mean failing to meet the needs of some present strangers we could otherwise have helped. See the opening paragraphs of Section *V*, below.

4. See, e.g., the essays in William Aiken and Hugh La Follette, eds., *World Hunger and Moral Obligation* (Englewood Cliffs, N.J.: Prentice-Hall, 1977).

5. I assume the rationality of discounting one's *expected* future desires to take account of the possibilities that one's expectations are wrong or that one will die in the interim. Similarly, we should discount the interests of any expected future generation by the probability that the human race will die out prior to that generation. The implications of our uncertainty about what future generations will want are discussed in Section *II*, below.

6. Martin Golding, "Obligations to Future Generations," *Monist* 56 (1972): 97-98.

7. "Equality in Education," in John M. McDermott, ed., *Indeterminacy in Education* (Berkeley: McCutchan, 1976).

8. They should, of course, take account of the possibility that they will be unable to produce more children, and discount the interests of their prospective children accordingly.

9. It should be emphasized that the problem discussed here is *not* the same as the average versus total utility problem. This can readily be seen if we let $x$ be the total happiness of the two parents if they do not have the child, $x - y$ be their total happiness if they do have it, and $z$ be

the child's happiness (if it exists). If $z > y + \frac{1}{2}x$, both total and average happiness would be maximized by the production of the child. Yet, if they do not have the child, the parents have still maximized utility for those affected by their act.

10. I make this move, in a special context and for a limited purpose, in my "Rawls on Average and Total Utility," *Philosophical Studies* 27 (1975): 241.

11. Mistakenly, I did not resist a similar temptation in "Rawls on Average and Total Utility," 250.

12. Jan Narveson, "Utilitarianism and New Generations," *Mind* 76 (1967): 62-72.

13. I do not endorse the stronger claim that God would be obligated to create the greatest possible number of happy people (generations). For it is likely there is no limit on the number of happy people (generations) an omnipotent being could create. Cf. Robert M. Adams, "Must God Create the Best," *Philosophical Review* 81 (1972): 317.

14. This objection is cited, but not endorsed, by Robert Heilbroner in "What Has Posterity Ever Done for Me?," a postscript to his *An Inquiry Into the Human Prospect* (New York: W.W. Norton, 1975).

15. An argument of this form is pressed in Garrett Hardin, "Lifeboat Ethics: The Case Against Helping the Poor," in *World Hunger and Moral Obligation*, pp. 15-17.

16. Cf. the excellent discussion of the closely related "statistical lives" problem in Charles Fried, *An Anatomy of Values* (Cambridge, Mass: Harvard University Press, 1970), Chap. 12.

17. John Locke, *Two Treatises of Government*, ed. by Peter Laslett (New York: New American Library, 1965), Second Treatise, secs. 4, 26-27, pp. 309, 328-329.

18. Locke, Sec. 33, p. 333.

19. This is a slightly revised version of a paper read on December 2, 1977, at the conference on Obligations to Future Generations at the University of Delaware. I am indebted to Virginia Warren and Joseph Runzo for helpful comments.

# Circumstances of Justice and Future Generations

*BRIAN BARRY*

## *I*

In this paper, I do not intend to raise questions concerning population policy, of the kind that are discussed elsewhere in this volume. Nor do I propose to ask whether we have an obligation to ensure that there will be future generations at all. I have come to believe that the value of continued human existence has to be a premise of other arguments that invoke the interests of actual (present or future) human beings. It cannot be derived from any such argument, and I do not think that anything is gained by invoking the supposed interest of potential persons in becoming actual.[1]

The question to be addressed here is as follows: assuming that there will be people in the future, can it be said that we should be behaving unjustly if we neglected their interests in deciding how much to use up finite resources, how far to damage the environment in ways that are irreversible or at any rate extremely expensive to reverse, and how much to invest in capital goods or research and development of new technologies (e.g. into non-exhaustible energy sources)? Naturally, the interests of those currently alive may well set some limits to the amount of resource depletion, environmental damage and lack of investment that can occur without injustice. But suppose (as seems quite likely) that these limits would be more stringent if the interests of future generations were taken into account. Does justice require us to stay within those stricter limits?

It may be asked why we should bother to pose the question in terms of justice, and I have found this question is often raised. For it seems clear that reference to the virtue of humanity would lead to the conclusion that we ought not totally to ignore the interests of future generations. I accept the conclusion but I will go on to observe that the same might equally well be said of relations between contemporaries. Why, then, would people attach importance to attempts to stake out claims based on justice, if there were nothing to be lost by falling back on claims based on humanity?

The answer is, I take it, twofold. First, although it is true that justice and humanity both exclude a total disregard for the interests of others, that does not make them by any means equivalent in general. Humanity requires that we respond to others' needs whereas justice requires that we give them their due. If something is due you, you do not have to show that you need it or that you will make better use of it than other possible claimants. Justice and humanity thus diverge in content.

Second, claims based on justice are commonly regarded as having a higher priority than claims based on considerations of humanity. An extreme but not I think atypical view is the one expressed by John Rawls: that the claims of justice have absolute priority over any others. "Each person possesses an inviolability founded on justice that even the welfare of society as a whole cannot override."[2] The implications of this within Rawls's own theory can be seen by noting that (for reasons I shall discuss later) Rawls says that animals are "outside the scope of the theory of justice." Although "duties of compassion and humanity" apply to animals,[3] the overriding priority of justice would presumably entail that we would never be right in moving to protect the interests of animals if this entailed committing an injustice against human beings.

If future generations were held to be likewise "outside the scope of the theory of justice" their claims would be reduced to the same residual status as the claims of animals are granted by Rawls. As I shall argue below, Hume's theory of the circumstances of justice does quite clearly entail that animals and future generations are outside the scope of justice, and for exactly the same reasons.

It is not necessary to go all the way with Rawls in order to regard claims based on justice as more pressing than claims based on humanity. In contemporary political debate, the most striking illustration of the importance that is attached to making out a case for aid in terms of justice rather than relying on humanity can be found in the sphere of relations between rich and poor countries. With perhaps as many as a billion people suffering more or less severely from malnutrition, and an estimated thirty-five thousand children under the age of five dying each day from a combination of under-nourishment and infectious diseases,[4] the case on humanitarian grounds for the rich countries to provide aid out of their superfluity is clear enough. But advocates of aid do not content themselves with pointing out the case based on considerations of humanity, which is so simple and straightforward, but try to construct arguments to the effect that the present distribution between rich and poor countries is a reflection of injustice. These arguments, which take various forms, have in common that they are complex and difficult if not impossible to verify because they appeal to counterfactuals–what the pattern of distribution would be in the absence of various features of the world as it actually has developed and is now.[5]

The humanitarian case, which depends on no elaborate chain of argument or resort to counterfactuals, and requires no more than the establishment of the facts of preventable suffering, has nevertheless been remarkable for its lack of success in bringing about worldwide redistribution. In the current recession among the industrialized countries, indeed, it has been noteworthy that the already exiguous aid to poor countries has been one of the first victims of government belt-tightening. It is therefore highly understandable that advocates of aid to poor countries should despair of humanitarian appeals and hope that a claim based on justice, if it could be made out, would have more impact.

In the final section of this paper, I shall propose a relatively simple principle of justice which would at once underwrite the claims of poor countries and of future generations to certain kinds of consideration. Before this, however, I shall investigate the notion that the circumstances of justice are absent in relations between one generation and its successors, this having the implication that justice and injustice cannot properly be predicated of those relations.

## *II*

The actual term "circumstances of justice" is drawn from *A Theory of Justice*,[6] but Rawls there refers us to Hume, remarking that "Hume's account of them is especially perspicuous" and that his own statement of them "adds nothing essential to [Hume's] much fuller discussion."[7] In spite of the intense scrutiny to which almost every aspect of Rawls's theory has been subjected, I do not know of any critic who has challenged Rawls's incorporation by reference of Hume's discussion, in the *Treatise* and the *Enquiry*, of the circumstances of justice. Moreover, I get the impression that the Hume/Rawls doctrine of the circumstances of justice may be well on the way to becoming part of the conventional wisdom. Since I, at any rate, have only recently come to realize how insidious is the doctrine, I am prepared to believe that others may also have let it slide by too easily. I shall therefore try to show, by a detailed examination of Hume's account, that the doctrine of the circumstances of justice, in the form in which Hume puts it forward, is false.

The assertion around which Hume's analysis of justice is organized is that justice is an artificial virtue. What does Hume mean by this? One thing he means is that, putting it in modern jargon, the rules of justice define a social practice. In the absence of some assurance that others will play their part there is no reason for anyone to do his. In an attractive metaphor, he likens the product of benevolence to "a wall built by many hands, which still rises by each stone that is heaped upon it, and receives increase proportional to the diligence and care of each workman."[8] In other words, whether others are benevolent or not benevolent, it will always be an improvement in the state of the world for me to act benevolently. Justice, by contrast, produces its effects in the manner of "a vault, where each individual stone would, of itself, fall to the ground; nor is the whole fabric supported but by the mutual assistance and combination of its corresponding parts."[9] "Whatever is advantageous to two or more persons if all perform their part, but what loses all advantage if only one perform, can arise from no other principle."[10]

This is not, however, the most central or distinctive claim that Hume wants to make in saying that justice is an artificial virtue. What he means is that there is no external standard of justice against which the rules can be assessed. The "vulgar definition of justice" as "a constant and perpetual will of giving every one his due" is mistaken in supposing that it makes sense to think of a "due" that is "independent of justice, and antecedent to it."[11] In the same way that Hobbes denied the possibility of laws being unjust, because the laws define what is just and unjust, so Hume claims that the rules of justice cannot be subjected to criticism on the basis of independent criteria of justice because they define what justice is.

Rules of justice, Hume maintains, arise out of and are sustained by mutual interest that people have in securing stability of possessions. "It is self-love which is their real origin; and as the self-love of one person is naturally contrary to that of another, these several interested passions are obliged to adjust themselves after such a manner as to concur in some system of conduct and behaviour."[12]

Hume's position is substantially the same as that recently and more long-windedly set out by F. A. Hayek in *The Mirage of Social Justice*.[13] Rules of justice (which for both authors amount to rules of property) are conventional. To criticize such rules on the basis of some abstract standard of justice (what is people's "due" in some sense not defined by the rules themselves) is absurd. But this is not to say that there is no basis on which proposed rules of justice can be criticized. Since the rules exist because it is to everyone's advantage that they should, we can criticize alternatives to the existing rules on the grounds that everyone would lose from a change to such rules. So, in the *Enquiry*, Hume goes out of his way to attack proposals for egalitarian redistribution. The work of modern conservatives like de Jouvenal and Hayek adds little to Hume's arguments: that the lack of incentive would make everyone worse off and that the concentration of political power necessary to carry out the redistribution would be too dangerous to liberty.[14]

Hume's discussion of the circumstances of justice can be understood only in the context of his attempt to show that justice is an artificial virtue in the sense that I have just distinguished:

> Thus the rules of equity or justice depend entirely on the particular state and condition in which men are placed, and owe their origin and existence to that utility which results to the public from their strict and regular observance. Reverse, in any considerable circumstance, the condition of men; produce extreme abundance or extreme necessity; implant in the human breast perfect moderation and humanity, or perfect rapaciousness and malice—by rendering justice totally *useless*, you thereby totally destroy its essence and suspend its obligation upon mankind.
>
> The common situation of society is a medium amidst all these

> extremes. We are naturally partial to ourselves and to our friends; but are capable of learning the advantage resulting from a more equitable conduct. Few enjoyments are given us from the open and liberal hand of nature; but by art, labour, and industry, we can extract them in great abundance. Hence the ideas of property become necessary in all civil society; hence justice derives its usefulness to the public; and hence alone arises its merit and moral obligation.[15]

Rawls accurately summarizes Hume's "curcumstances of justice" as moderate scarcity, moderate selfishness and relative equality.[16] (Only the first two are referred to in the passage quoted.) On the face of it, if these are the circumstances of justice then things look black for future generations. We may be confident that moderate selfishness is here to stay but we cannot be sure of moderate scarcity (maybe at some time in the future the whole human race will be destitute) and the lack of equality between us and our successors is guaranteed by "time's arrow," which enables us to affect our successors while depriving them of the ability to affect us. A lot therefore hangs on the question whether the doctrine of the circumstances of justice is true or not, and it is that question which I now take up, subjecting each of the alleged conditions to scrutiny in turn.

## *III*

The condition described by Rawls as "moderate scarcity" is analysed by Hume in terms of an upper and a lower bound on the generosity of nature in supplying men's wants. The upper bound is that, if everything human beings wanted were as freely available as air normally is (the mythical "golden age" of the classical poets), the "cautious, jealous virtue of justice" would never have become established. "Justice in that case, being totally useless, would be an idle ceremonial, and could never possibly have place in the catalogue of virtues."[17]

In accordance with his overall argument, Hume emphasizes that the reason why the virtue of justice would have no place is that it would be "totally useless." He thus takes the fact that justice is inconsistent with unlimited abundance to be a support for the view that justice is founded on utility. But, as David Miller has pointed out, this is not a valid move. "It proves only that the belief in justice arises from a society of moderate scarcity, not that men have their belief because they see it is in the public interest to have rules of property."[18]

More specifically, the fact that there would be no room for justice in a "golden age" is simply the consequence of the fact that the subject-matter of justice is the distribution of things that are in short supply. So if nothing were in short supply (relative to total demand) the concept of distributive justice would have no application. Equally, if there were no scarcity there could be no virtue of generosity (nobody is praised for being open-handed with air) and no virtue of frugality (nobody is praised for its careful husbanding). Yet these virtues are, for Hume, natural virtues. This shows that nothing follows about justice being an artificial virtue from the fact that its application presupposes scarcity.

The upshot of this discussion is, then, that we can accept Hume's assertion that justice would have no place if nature were sufficiently abundant in providing for men's wants. But we have no reason for accepting Hume's formulation of it, that the question is one of the "usefulness" of justice. It is perfectly open to us to say that there are non-conventional criteria of justice but that they have no application in the absence of scarcity.

## IV

Hume's assertion of a lower bound to the generosity of nature as a circumstance of justice, which Rawls also accepts, seems to me to be without foundation:

> Suppose a society to fall into such a want of all common necessaries that the utmost frugality and industry cannot preserve the greater number from perishing, and the whole from extreme misery; it will readily, I believe, be admitted that the strict laws of justice are suspended in such a pressing emergency, and give place to the stronger motives of necessity and self-preservation.... The public, even in less urgent necessities, opens granaries without the consent of proprietors, as justly supposing that the authority of magistracy may, consistent with equity, extend so far; but were any number of men to assemble, without the tie of laws or civil jurisdiction, would

an equal partition of bread in a famine, though effected by power and even violence, be regarded as criminal or injurious?[19]

Let us concede Hume's statement of the case: that the normal rules governing distribution would be properly suspended in situations like those depicted above. Does this support the implication that Hume wishes to draw, that justice is an artificial virtue? I think not. One line of argument is as follows: "If justice and the public interest are actually independent values, there may be circumstances in which the public interest is allowed to override justice." Thus, in the granary case, people "do not wholly cease to respect the claims of ownership, but rather allow these claims to be overriden by considerations of humanity and the public interest."[20]

Consider the case of a country threatened by an invasion in which there is reason to fear that some section of the population (identified by ethnic background, membership of a political movement, etc.) contains potential fifth columnists. Suppose that all the members of this group are interned for the duration of the war. This would clearly be unjust in that it imposes a serious penalty on some people not for anything they have done but for what they might do, and, over and above that, does not consider individual cases but makes membership of a certain class the basis of internment. Yet such a policy might be, in sufficiently extreme circumstances, defensible in terms of the overriding value of national survival.

Hume's granary case might be like this: the taking of the grain from its owners is unjust but nevertheless morally acceptable because of the overriding importance of preventing starvation. Certainly, nothing Hume says goes to show that that is not a correct analysis of the situation. It may perhaps seem rather trivial to ask whether the laws of justice are "suspended," as Hume says, or "overridden," as David Miller suggests, since in either case the rules of justice are conceded not to apply in a situation of extreme scarcity. But, unless we give Hume the answer he wants, he cannot use the case to support his claim that the rules of justice are a conventional device for securing the public interest by indirect means.

However, I am not prepared to concede that the case is as Hume states it. I see no reason why it should be accepted that criteria of justice are out of place in conditions of extreme scarcity. Hume himself, be it noted, speaks of "an *equal* partition of bread in a famine."[21] Might not an unequal partition (or, more precisely, an unequal partition in which the departures from equality were not based on conditions such as pregnancy, sickness, heavy manual labor etc.) be criticized as unjust?

It seems to me that the justice (or, perhaps more naturally, fairness) of a rationing scheme is something that can always be intelligibly queried. Perhaps even more plainly, the application of the scheme can be brought before the bar of fairness: is it being administered impartially, or are some people getting specially favourable treatment?

Experience suggests, indeed, that any system of rationing automatically produces public controversy about its fairness. The wartime food rationing scheme in England is a case in point, and in the postwar period the allocation of council housing to applicants (which is usually done by a system of "points") has similarly attracted much controversy conducted largely in terms of fairness.

Even in a wealthy country like the USA, there are limits to the amount of expensive medical treatment (chronic hemodialysis, coronary bypass surgery) that can be carried out, and the supply of donors for transplants limits the number (of, for example, kidney transplants) to well below the number of people that might benefit. The existence of a *de facto* rationing system has led inevitably to questions about the fair way to select people for treatment.[22]

Thus, to illustrate the kinds of problem that immediately present themselves, consider the criteria used by the selection committee in the early days of the Seattle Artificial Kidney Center: "A person 'worthy' of having his life preserved by a scarce, expensive treatment like chronic dialysis was one judged to have qualities such as decency and responsibility. Any history of social deviance, such as a prison record, any suggestion that a person's married life was not intact and scandal-free, were strong contraindications to selection. The preferred candidate was a person who had demonstrated achievement through hard work and success at his job, who went to church, joined groups, and was actively involved in community affairs."[23] This state of affairs induced the caustic remark that "the Pacific Northwest is no place for a Henry David Thoreau with bad kidneys." The authors of this comment, a psychiatrist and a lawyer, went on to say, in terms highly relevant to the present discussion, that "*justice requires that selection be made by a fairer method* than the unbridled consciences, the built-in biases, and the fantasies of omnipotence of a secret committee."[24]

This discussion also shows that the application of criteria of justice extends beyond the relatively benign case of the famine envisaged by Hume to the more extreme case in which "the utmost frugality and industry cannot prevent the greater number from perishing."[25] For, as the pioneer of chronic hemodialysis has said, scarcity and the selection it makes necessary entail "the decision by somebody on some grounds that somebody will not be permitted dialysis or transplant, which says, in effect, he must now die."[26] The question "Who is to be saved?" is one within the scope of justice.

It might be said that none of this shows justice to be a virtue independent of humanity, because the only basis on which one could call one basis for distribution more just than another is that is more humane. When we criticize a rationing scheme as unfair, on this view, we are simply saying that it does not distribute the food (or whatever) in the way that will do the most good. But this seems not to be correct. For there might be a number of ways in which the scarce good might be distributed that would equally well satisfy the demands of humanity and yet we could still say that one was fairer than another. In situations where all can be saved, equal sacrifice is fairer than unequal, whatever a utilitarian calculus might determine.[27] And in a situation where an equal division means that all perish (or far more than would have to if an unequal distribution were introduced) we can still talk about the fairness of the selection process that condemns some to certain death so that the others may survive.[28]

What I am saying can be put another way: if we allow Hume to appropriate the term "justice" for property rules and nothing else, then he is right in claiming that justice may properly be waived in situations of extreme scarcity. For it is unacceptable for some to be permitted excess if others are destitute. But the reason is not only one of humanity, and if Hume insists on equating "rules of justice" with "property rules" we must simply import another word—"fairness" is the obvious candidate—to enable us to say that there are criteria for evaluating a distribution even in conditions of extreme scarcity.

The issue raised here has direct implications for the applicability of the concept of justice to intergenerational relations. For a critic of Rawls has pointed out that, by postulating that the people in the original position know that the circumstances of justice obtain, Rawls is committing himself to the proposition that the circumstances of justice hold in all generations (past, present and future) since the people in the original position do not know what generation they belong to:

> In order to show that the circumstances of justice will obtain for all future generations, we must postulate either that there will be ever-expanding sources of raw materials and energy for us to exploit or that, through population control and technological advances, mankind will achieve homeostasis in this environment. Otherwise the resources will be exhausted no matter how provident we are. And so, barring these optimistic assumptions, justice among all generations is not possible because the circumstances of justice will not obtain. Since there is no good evidence that either of these assumptions will be proven correct, we do not seem justified in supposing that the circumstances of justice among all generations of mankind exist.[29]

But if I am right, there are no grounds for accepting this part of the doctrine of the circumstances of justice. So although the argument is an effective *ad hominem* one against Rawls, it does not tell against the claim that the concept of justice is applicable in all times and places, whatever their circumstances.

## *V*

The third circumstance of justice is moderate selfishness. Again, Hume suggests that the virtue of justice can arise only if the extremes are absent: "if men pursued the public interest naturally, and with a hearty affection, they would have never dreamed of restraining each other by these rules [of justice]; and if they pursued their own interest, without any precaution, they would run headlong into every kind of injustice and violence."[30]

It should be noticed at once that, although Hume wishes, for his own polemical purposes, to extend the "not too much, not too little" formula from scarcity to selfishness, the two extremes that he presents are not really two extremes of selfishness. Hume does, indeed, deny that, as a matter of fact, people are totally selfish. He suggests that, "though it be rare to meet with anyone who loves any single person better than himself, yet it is as rare to meet with one in whom all the kind affections, taken together, do not overbalance all the selfish."[31] But this does not help much in securing social union because "in the original frame of our mind our strongest attention is confined to ourselves; our next is extended to our relations and acquaintance; and it is only the weakest which reaches to strangers and indifferent persons."[32] "Benevolence to strangers" is therefore "too weak" to "render men fit members of society by making them abstain from the possessions of others."[33]

The point is not therefore that justice is inconsistent with total selfishness, for the benevolent sentiments people have are confined to too narrow a circle to make any difference. Justice is, Hume says, founded on mutual self-interest: "itself alone restrains it." The question, is not one of the "wickedness or goodness of human nature" but "the degrees of men's sagacity or folly."[34] The rhetorical "not too much, not too little" device is thus misleading here. The opposite extreme to total benevolence, that makes the virtue of justice inapplicable, is not total self-interest but *unintelligent* self-interest.[35] It is not therefore correct to say that the circumstances of justice, on Hume's account, include some intermediate degree of selfishness. They only exclude total benevolence.

It seems to me that Hume is quite correct in denying that benevolence is a necessary motive for the observance of justice. People who genuinely care a lot about the welfare of (some) others (e.g. those they know) are not always very scrupulous in weighing the claims of those they care about against the claims of others. And conversely people who are punctilious in carrying out the requirements of justice may not be particularly benevolent, as John Aubrey's story about Mathew Hale illustrates: some dining companions in the Middle Temple,

> Having made an end of their Commons, fell unto various Discourse, and what was the meaning of the Text (Rom. v. 7) "For a just man one would dare to die; but for a good man one would willingly die." They askt Mr. Maynard what was the difference between a just man and a good man. He was beginning to eate, and cryed:–Hoh! you have eaten your dinners, and now have leasure to discourse; I have not. He had eate but a Bitt or two when he reply'd:–I'le tell you the difference presently: serjeant Rolle is a just man, and Mathew

> Hale is a good man; and so fell to make an end of his dinner. And there could not be a better interpretation of this Text. For serjeant Rolle was just, but by nature penurious; and his wife made him worse: Mathew Hale was not only just, but wonderfully Charitable and open handed, and did not sound a trumpet neither, as the Hypocrites doe.[36]

What is more questionable, of course, is whether self-interest is an adequate motive for behaving justly, as Hume's theory requires him to maintain. In the closing four paragraphs of the *Enquiry*, Hume allows himself to entertain doubts on that score, considering the possibility that "according to the imperfect way in which human affairs are conducted, a sensible knave, in particular incidents, may think that an act of iniquity or infidelity will make a considerable addition to his fortune, without causing any considerable breach in the social union and confederacy."[37]

Hume's attempt to convert this "sensible knave" to the path of justice is remarkably feeble. One argument is that the best things in life are free: the "natural pleasures" are incomparably preferable to the "feverish, empty amusements of luxury and expense."[38] But while it is true that health is more important than money, most people may still believe that health plus money is better than health without money. In any case, Hume has built his whole theory on the proposition that the desire for more material possessions is an almost universal feature of human nature, and it is a bit late in the day to go back on that. Another argument is that there is always the risk of overreaching oneself and being found out, but this amounts to a recommendation of cautious knavery rather than a reason for not being a knave.

Hume's only serious argument is that "in all ingenuous natures the antipathy to treachery and roguery is too strong to be counterbalanced by any views of profit or pecuniary advantage. Inward peace of mind, consciousness of integrity, a satisfactory review of our own conduct—these are circumstances very requisite to happiness, and will be cherished and cultivated by every honest man who feels the importance of them."[39] The trouble with this is that it is transparently circular: it says in effect that an honest man is an honest man. If a man is not a knave, he will feel uncomfortable if he behaves in a knavish fashion. But what reason has he for not being a knave, or (if it is too late now to change his character) for not wishing he had been brought up as a knave?

No wonder Hume concedes, in introducing this argument, that "if a man think this reasoning [that honesty is not invariably the best policy] much requires an answer, it would be a little difficult to find any which will to him appear satisfactory and convincing."[40] The only form of argument, I conceive, that could be relevant here would be one to the effect that justice is a good thing quite apart from its general long-run tendency to be in everyone's interest. But that form of argument Hume has denied himself by insisting that there are no external and independent criteria of justice. The good of justice, for Hume, simply *is* its long-run tendency to conduce to everyone's interest, so if, in a given case, it does not conduce to someone's interest, there is nothing more to be said to him.

It may be worth noting, incidentally, that the difficulty Hume runs into here is not intrinsically related to the assumption that the person to be convinced is motivated by self-interest. Suppose someone were motivated by the public interest. Hume constantly draws our attention to the fact that "a single act of justice is frequently contrary to *public interest*; and were it to stand alone, without being followed by other acts, may in itself be very prejudicial to society."[41] A truly benevolent person who had the opportunity to behave unjustly on such an occasion with good reason to expect that the usual indirect ill-effects would not supervene could not be argued with.

I do not want to say that in cases of such a kind (the desert island deathbed wish, etc.) it would always be wrong to act contrary to the requirements of justice. But the point is that Hume cannot advance any reason why there should even be a moral problem here. Justice has not value in itself so there is nothing to put in the scales against benevolence. All Hume can say is that if you have been brought up a certain way you will feel bad about it, but presumably a truly benevolent person should seek to overcome such a superstitious feeling or, if he cannot do that, set it against the net benefit to others in deciding what will maximize overall utility.

None of this shows that Hume is incorrect in denying that there are any non-conventional criteria of justice. But it does suggest that the implications were such as even Hume himself ultimately found unpalatable.

## *VI*

The validity of Hume's argument that "limited generosity" is a circumstance of justice depends directly on the truth of his central proposition that justice is an artificial virtue. Suppose that each person "feels no more concern for his own interest than for that of his fellows."[42] Everybody would be a Benthamite utilitarian, counting each individual for one and nobody for more than one. Thus, somebody would always perform a service for me "except the hurt he thereby receives be greater than the benefit accruing to me."[43] If we assume (as Hume appears to) that a utility-maximizing calculus of this kind can yield determinate conclusions, we must expect that there will be universal agreement about what each person ought to do. (The "ought" here is a hypothetical imperative: it prescribes the means for each person of carrying out the purpose that he naturally has of maximizing total utility.) Clearly, if justice is a convention designed to settle disputes by providing a fixed set of rules, the scenario described would leave no room for the application of justice. But if it makes sense to say that such a society would be unjust, it follows that justice cannot be purely conventional.

It seems to me that we could quite intelligibly say that this society's peaceful equilibrium was founded on injustice, and advance is support of that claim the usual arguments against the equation of justice and utility. Utility is maximized when the marginal utility of each good is maximized, and that entails giving more to efficient "pleasure machines."[44] But there is no reason based on justice why those who are naturally fortunate in being able to obtain a lot of pleasure from a given quantity of goods should have that advantage compounded. There is no need to continue. The list of anti-utilitarian arguments is familiar enough.

It might be said that I am overlooking the point that in the society of perfect utilitarians we are imagining, everyone–including those who make the sacrifices to increase net total utility–would be consenting to the arrangements. No doubt consent is relevant to justice: it may be just for me to give you something when it would not be just for you to take it without my permission. But is consent decisive? I think not.

It seems to me to make perfectly good sense to say that someone freely consents to an unjust arrangement, for example because he incorrectly believes that it is required by justice. Suppose in some society it were universally accepted that some people were by birth entitled to economic and social privilege. There would be no conflict over distribution yet we could surely say that this social system was unjust.

When confronted, for example, with the facts of untouchability in India we do not, I believe, have to know whether or not the untouchables themselves accept the legitimating world-view of the *varna* system before reaching the verdict that the operation of the caste system constitutes a paradigm of injustice. I should be inclined, indeed, to go further, and say that, if we found that untouchables did accept their treatment as just, that would be the basis for an even stronger indictment, since it would show that untouchables were suffering not only economic and social deprivation but also from the lack of an inner sense of worth as human beings.

A society of utilitarians would not, of course, be anywhere near as unjust as a caste society. But, if the caste example succeeds in showing that consent is not inconsistent with injustice, the possibility is surely opened up that the sacrifices some people would be called on to make in the cause of maximizing total utility would be unjust even though, in a society of utilitarians, they would be voluntarily accepted.

Suppose, however, that my contention is not granted and it is held that, in the absence of conflicting claims, justice has no application. What then follows? Not that justice is founded on utility, as Hume wishes to maintain. All we have to do is extend the conclusion we reached earlier for the case of unlimited abundance.

We said there that one could quite consistently accept that justice has no application where everybody's wants can be satisfied without effort and without any limit to the extent to which others could satisfy theirs and yet at the same time say that in the absence of these conditions non-conventional criteria of justice come into play. We should now have to add that justice has no application where everybody's *claims* can be simultaneously satisfied. But again we can go on to say that this is quite consistent with affirming that, when the sum total of claims adds up to more than the amount available for distribution, the criteria of justice than become relevant are non-conventional.

## VII

The core of Hume's argument is that rules of justice arise and are maintained only when and so long as they are mutually advantageous to the parties. The third circumstance of justice–equality–in effect identifies the parties. Only those who are in a position to cause trouble unless they are cut in on the deal qualify for a seat at the bargaining table.

Thus, animals are excluded from the scope of justice not because (as has been held before Hume and after him) they lack the power of reasoning but because they cannot cause us trouble if we maltreat them. Of course, an individual animal may in certain special circumstances be able to injure or even kill an individual human being who is maltreating it[45]; but collectively human beings are clearly on top.

Hume's unflinching recognition of the implications of the doctrine of the circumstances of justice poses the issues with admirable clarity:

> Were there a species of creatures intermingled with men, which, though rational, were possessed of such inferior strength, both of body and mind, that they were incapable of all resistance, and could never, upon the highest provocation, make us feel the effects of their resentment, the necessary consequence, I think, is that we should be bound by the laws of humanity to give gentle usage to these creatures, but should not, properly speaking, lie under any restraint of justice with regard to them, nor could they possess any right or property, exclusive of such arbitrary lords. Our intercourse with them could not be called society–which supposes a degree of equality–but absolute command on the one side, and servile obedience on the other. Whatever we covet, they must instantly resign. Our permission is the only tenure by which they hold their possessions; our compassion and kindness the only check by which they curb our lawless will; and as no inconvenience ever results from the exercise of a power so firmly established in nature, the restraints of justice and property, being totally *useless*, would never have place in so unequal a confederacy.[46]

It is an immediate consequence of Hume's position that, if beings from another world were to arrive on earth, with some combination of personal characteristics and technology that made them collectively as superior to us as we are to animals, we could appeal to them to give us "gentle usage" but could make no complaint of injustice, *even among ourselves*, if they declared the whole of the earth their property and proceeded to exploit it (and us) for their own purposes.

But there is no need to resort to science fiction. Hume, himself, in the paragraph following the one quoted above, observes that "the great superiority of civilized Europeans above barbarious Indians tempted us to imagine ourselves on the same footing with regard to them [as men are in regard to animals], and made us throw off all restraints of justice and even of humanity, in our treatment of them."[47]

Here, I think, Hume must be accused of drawing back from the full implications of his doctrine. Why does he say that the European settlers were only "tempted to imagine" themselves above justice? Surely, on his theory, they *were* above justice in relation to the Indians. Right from the start, the European settlers were able to impose their "lawless will" on the Indians; and, although the Indians were not, of course, as helpless as Hume's hypothetical "species of creatures" to cause trouble, they could not (as events proved) long resist any course of action that the Europeans were determined on.[48] Red Cloud, the Sioux Chief, said in a speech in New York in 1870: "All I want is right and just."[49] A follower of Hume would have to say that he was mistaken in thinking that right and just had any place in relations between Indians and whites, given the superiority of the rifle to the bow and arrow.

H. L. A. Hart, having set out (following Hobbes and Hume) "approximate equality" as a feature of the human condition,[50] goes on to note that "neither the law nor the accepted morality of societies need extend their minimal protections and benefits to all within their scope." So that, "though a society to be viable must offer *some* of its members a system of mutual forbearances, it need not, unfortunately, offer them to all." Slave societies, Nazi Germany and contemporary South Africa are offered as illustrations.[51] But Hart also says that "injustice" is the term properly used whenever benefits and burdens are distributed on grounds that are irrelevant, "so 'unjust' would be appropriate for the expression of disapproval of a law which forbade coloured people the public means of transport or the parks" because, "at least in the distribution of such amenities, differences of colour are irrelevant."[52]

This seems to me a correct statement of the case. If I have to say why Hume's theory should be rejected, I "must confess that, if a man think that this reasoning much requires an answer, it would be a little difficult to find any which will to him appear satisfactory and convincing."[53] But I think my problem is less severe than was Hume's in finding an answer to the "sensible knave." Hume's problem was that he really could not, consistently with his own theory, develop an adequate argument against the "sensible knave." Mine is simply that, if someone can read a history of European settlement in Australia and the Americas, or a history of Negro slavery, without admitting that he is reading about a history of monstrous injustice, I doubt if anything I say is likely to convince him. I would have a similar doubt about someone who, asked whether or not South African racial policies are unjust, replied that the answer would depend on an estimate of the whites' ability to hold down the rest of the population indefinitely. I am inclined to think that nobody would give such an answer unless he had already been exposed to the theory of the circumstances of justice, so all I can do is point out that Hume offers no independent grounds for accepting the theory.

This point is worth emphasizing. If we agree with Hume that justice would have no application where any of the circumstances of justice failed to hold, that strengthens his claim that the rules of justice are conventional. But the assumption that the rules of justice are conventional cannot then be used as a premise in the argument that the circumstances of justice are necessary for the rules of justice to apply. We must make up our own minds about that.

The only independent argument that Hume offers is patently unsatisfactory. In the *Treatise* he argues that "all virtuous actions derive their merit only from virtuous motives, and are considered merely as signs of those motives." And he concludes from this that "the virtuous motive must be different from the regard to the virtue of the action."[54] But suppose we agree that a well-intentioned action that, for reasons beyond the control of the actor, fails to have the intended consequences still shows evidence of a virtuous motive; and that an action that accidentally fulfills a duty without that being intended by the actor does not exhibit a virtuous motive. It does not follow, as Hume seems to think here, that there is any incoherence in saying that a type of action is virtuous if a desire to do an action of that type constitutes a virtuous motive. Hume would have been correct if he had said that an action confers merit on the actor only on the basis of the motive it exhibits. But that formulation would make it clear that the desire to do an action of a certain kind (e.g. pay a debt) can be, quite consistently, held to be a virtuous motive.

It seems plausible that Hume himself came to recognize the weakness of the argument from alleged circularity. For he makes no use of it in the *Enquiry* and relies exclusively on the argument from the circumstances of justice. If we reject Hume's claim that justice has no application in the conditions stated, we are bound to reject the doctrine of the circumstances of justice.

I would suggest that the requirement of equality is a dramatic illustration of what is wrong with the theory, and provides sufficient grounds for rejecting the theory from which it is deduced. This is not to say that it is without explanatory power. It may well be that the idea of justice could arise only among approximate equals, and it is still true that justice is more likely to be realized among approximate equals than when injustice can be perpetrated with impunity. But that does not mean that the concept of justice is limited to such contexts.[55]

## *VIII*

If the doctrine of the circumstances of justice is true, it must follow that there can be no place for justice between the generation of those alive at any given time and their successors. For it is clear that, even if we waive the problem about moderate scarcity that has already been mentioned, there can be no getting round the total absence of equality.

In a recent article, the author, D. Clayton Hubin, postulates the correctness of the doctrine and draws that conclusion from it: "Hume, and those following him, require as a condition of justice that members of the society be roughly equal in those abilities which allow one person to dominate another. Rawls, in particular, requires that 'the individuals are roughly similar in physical and mental powers; or at any rate, their capacities are comparable in that no one among them can dominate the rest' (*A Theory of Justice*, p. 127). The idea is that even the strongest must be vulnerable to the weakest. But this assumption does not hold between members of various generations. Members of earlier generations are invulnerable with respect to members of later generations."[56]

However, he maintains that he can "account for much of our duty to provide for future generations in terms of a duty of justice *with regard to future generations* (but not owed to them)."[57] Hubin employs for this purpose a construction modelled on the Rawlsian original position, in which the people know what generation they belong to (information that would be withheld by Rawls) but do not know about their personal characteristics. They are mutually disinterested, but they "know that it is a general psychological fact about people in our society that they care about their offspring to such a degree that they to some extent identify their offsprings' [*sic*] interests with their own."[58]

I do not want at this stage to get mixed up in the question how Rawls's original position relates to the doctrine of the circumstances of justice. I shall address that question in the next section of this paper. (Hubin himself, it should be said, offers no explanation of the move from the circumstances of justice to the original position, apparently not seeing that there is a problem of compatibility.) Fortunately, however, I do not think that anything crucial in his arguments depends upon the construction involving the original position.

Let us formulate the case by saying that we are dealing with a society in which the circumstances of justice hold: there is moderate scarcity; the strength of benevolence, or other "natural" claim-limiting mechanisms, is insufficient to avert conflicting claims; and the society is not divided into powerful and powerless groups, that is to say it is not a colonial society, a slave society or a society of institutionalized group repression like contemporary South Africa. Such a society will, if Hume is right, have a common standard of justice that applies to all its members.

The arguments presented in this paper up to now are not designed to show that Hume is wrong about this. What I have called the doctrine of the circumstances of justice and attacked is the doctrine put forward by Hume that in the absence of the circumstances of justice the concept of justice can have no applicability. We could concede that the presence of the circumstances of justice constitutes a *sufficient* condition for a society to have uniform rules of justice without allowing that the circumstances of justice are *necessary* conditions for the application of the concept of justice.

It should be noticed that, if the circumstances of justice are not necessary conditions for the application of the concept of justice, Hume's arguments in favor of the absence of external and independent criteria of justice collapse. For they depended on the notion that justice is a device for reaching agreement among approximate equals and that justice has no place where agreement does not have to be reached. But, at the same time, the view that the circumstances of justice are sufficient conditions for the application of the concept of justice is quite consistent with the truth of the view that there are no independent and external criteria of justice.

Of course, when we take standards of justice that would be agreed on by equals and apply them to condemn a society pervaded by systematic group discrimination we are in a sense making use of independent and external criteria. But they need not be independent and external in the sense in which Hume denied such criteria of justice exist. They need not invoke abstract relations of fitness and right, which is what Hume was attacking. All we need be doing is taking principles whose claim to count as principles of justice is no more than that they would be agreed upon in a society of a certain kind (one in which the circumstances of justice obtain) and applying these principles in another kind of society (one in which the circumstances of justice do not obtain).

We have so far postulated that we are dealing with a society in which the circumstances of justice hold. Although I am inclined to think that it is empirically questionable, I shall accept the Humean view that the members of a society will exhibit a common sense of justice, in other words that they will apply common standards in judging justice or injustice. We can now add the psychological datum that Hubin introduces: people care about their offspring, to the extent of identifying with their interests. According to Hubin, the principle that would be agreed upon "would require that we treat the interests of those in the next generation (at least) as if they were interests of persons in this generation–for in a real sense they are–except where doing so will cause severe hardship for this generation."[59] The proviso about hardship reflects the idea that one of the circumstances of justice is moderate scarcity. If things are so bad that it's us or them, the circumstances of justice do not apply.

The only part played in the argument by the original position is that it conceals from the parties whether or not they themselves are among those with an attachment to the interests of at least one person in the next generation. But we can get to much the same place by observing that very few people can be sure that they will not at some time get into a position in which they form such an attachment, even if they cannot or intend not to have children themselves. The argument then is simply that it is just to make savings for the benefit of the next generation because of the psychic benefit that those in the present generation gain from better prospects for those in the next.[60]

As it stands, this is clearly no argument at all. Unless we fill it out in certain ways it says that it is just to impose a collective decision to save on everybody because most people have psychic investment in the wellbeing of certain members of the next generation. (It must be borne in mind that we are supposing the motivation to arise from the fact that each person is likely to care about some member of the next generation, not that most people care about the collective welfare of the next generation.)

From the brute fact that most people care for certain members of the next generation, all we seem to be able to get out is that most people should (in order to get what they want to happen) be prepared to save for those they care about. In exactly the same way, anyone with a psychic investment in the wellbeing of a pet should (and it is exactly the same kind of "should") be prepared to spend time and money on looking after it. The notion is, in both cases, that a rational person's budget should reflect the concern he has for the interests of others (friends, children, pets).

To get beyond this and show why it is a matter of justice among the members of the current generation to provide for the next generation we have to add something. The most important thing we can add is that the welfare of individual members of the next generation is interdependent. Even if I do the best I can for those members of the next generation in whose welfare I have some psychic investment, the main determinant of their future prospects is the kind of world that they will live in, and that depends overwhelmingly on the decisions of *others*.

The welfare of the next generation is thus a public good. If I want my children to have a better public park, I have to be prepared to pay my share; and the same goes if I want them to have a better world. The anti-free-rider principle that Rawls places at the heart of the notion of justice as fairness, a principle that in my view derives from the more general principle of justice that one should make a fair return for services rendered, can be invoked now to underwrite a general duty of justice to contribute towards collective savings for the benefit of the next generation.

It should be clear, however, that this way of generating a relationship of justice is completely general and applies to any altruistic public good. Thus, it would underwrite a duty of justice among the members of a society if they wanted to prevent the extinction of the whale or if, out of sentiments of beneficence, they wanted to make another country more prosperous by transferring resources to it. Even dog allowances could be required by justice as requital for the provision of a public good if there is a general concern for the welfare of dogs.

The point here is that the prosperity of the other country, if it is a generally held objective, becomes a public good, so the "anti-free-rider" principle makes it legitimate to use taxation to raise the money. The argument often made (e.g. by Nozick) that individuals should be content to give charitably themselves and not to seek to coerce everyone into doing so overlooks the public good aspect. If someone's good is a litter-free environment (rather than a tiny bit less litter) it makes sense for him to support coercion to stop everyone littering, but not to pick up his own litter unless others do. Similarly, if someone's good is a certain kind of world it is not irrational to contribute to the cost of attaining it only if others do.

Of course, it is perfectly possible that someone may be so upset by litter that he picks up his own (or even other people's) in the absence of any similar action by others. Such a person is, in analytic terms, one who gets so much benefit from a public good that it pays him to provide some of it on his own. The same may be true of someone who wants to live in a world free of poverty: he may be willing to contribute if others do but not otherwise.

If this whole discussion seems peculiar and slightly repulsive, I agree but suggest that this is an inevitable result of assuming that the only reason for relieving poverty (or taking care of the interests of unborn children) is that it brings about a state of affairs that makes those who do it feel better. Justice is on this account parasitic upon the sentiments that people actually have. If people care for their children's welfare, and if the welfare of the next generation is a public good, it is unfair not to contribute to it. But it would not be unjust for people not to care about the interests of their children. The limits of caring are the limits of justice.

I conclude that some sort of a case can be made out for the proposition that members of the current generation have a duty of justice to contribute to the public good constituted by the welfare of the next generation—to the extent that the sentiments of the existing generation make the welfare of the next generation a public good. But the doctrine of the circumstances of justice, understood as the doctrine that justice applies only where these conditions obtain, still rules out any claims on behalf of the interests of future generations. If therefore we do not care about any generation after the next (or the one after that, say) we do not behave unjustly in totally neglecting their interests, as Hubin concedes.[61]

I hope that the importance of determining whether or not the doctrine of the circumstances of justice is true will now be apparent. If I am correct in arguing that the doctrine is false, the way is open to maintaining that there are criteria of justice relevant to the relations between different generations. The question is what they are.

## IX

I introduced the discussion of the circumstances of justice by citing Rawls, and it is worth asking how Rawls's own theory of justice is related to his endorsement of the doctrine of the circumstances of justice. Can Rawls somehow escape the limitations on the scope of the concept of justice that the doctrine of the circumstances of justice appears to pose? If so, can Rawls's theory be employed to suggest criteria for justice between generations?

One way of accounting for the complexity and difficulty of Rawls's theory of justice is to recognize that it is an attempt to incorporate both Hume and Kant in a single theoretical structure. Since Hume and Kant are commonly, and reasonably, regarded as occupying polar positions in moral philosophy it is hardly surprising if the result of Rawls's endeavors suffers from a certain lack of unity.

There are two tempting short-cuts open to us if we are looking for a way to characterize the relation between the Humean and Kantian elements in Rawls. Each has a grain of truth but is on balance more misleading than useful. One is to say that the premises are Hume and the conclusions are Kant. This suggestion fits in with the fact that the circumstances of justice, which are distinctively Humean, turn up in the premises, while the distinctively Kantian notion that justice has nothing to do with happiness turns up in the conclusions. But it falls on the fact that Rawls offers a "Kantian interpretation of the original position" and on the close relationship between the way in which Rawls derives the difference principle and the way in which Hume argues that everyone gains from the rules of justice.

The other short-cut is to posit a temporal sequence in Rawls's own thought: he started out with Hume and finished up with Kant. The difficulties in interpreting *A Theory of Justice* would then arise, on this view, from the fact that the process of transition was still incomplete at the time the book went to press. In support, it can be argued that articles written by Rawls subsequently to the publication of *A Theory of Justice* exhibit a greater stress on the Kantian elements and a further attenuation of the Humean ones.[62]

I do not see how anyone can doubt that Rawls's thought shows a process of development along these lines. But it is easy to overdo the contrasts between "Justice as Fairness" and *A Theory of Justice*. A lot of the apparent developments in a Kantian direction are better seen as moves to make explicit Kantian elements that were implicit in the early article than as fundamental reversals of perspective.[63]

The most illuminating way in which to think of Rawls's theory, I am inclined to believe, is to conceive of it as two parallel structures, one Humean and one Kantian, which overlap in their implications for a certain favored case—that of contemporaries in a modern Western society—and diverge elsewhere. The Humean structure is more apparent in the earlier work and the Kantian structure is emphasized more in the later, but they coexist throughout. Peter Danielson, who put forward this idea of a dual structure in a review article on Rawls, called the two theories "justice as rational co-operation" and "justice as universal hypothetical assent."[64] These are good names and I shall use them.

## *X*

The theory of justice as rational co-operation is, of course, the Humean one. Justice is, as Rawls says at the start of *A Theory of Justice*, to be defined for "the basic structure of society conceived of for the time being as a closed system isolated from other societies."[65] And "a society is a more or less self-sufficient association of persons who in their relations to one another recognize certain rules of conduct as binding and who for the most part act in accordance with them."[66]

As we have seen, Rawls endorses Hume's characterization of the circumstances of justice, and says that the people in the original position know that the circumstances of justice exist in their society. How can he say this? The other things that the people in the original position are said to know–various generalizations about psychology, sociology, and economics, for example–are claimed by Rawls to be genuinely true. But it is notorious that Hume's third circumstance of justice–approximate equality–does not hold universally. Hobbes thought that approximate equality of bodily strength and powers of mind were enough to guarantee that the "articles of peace" would have to recognize the fundamentally equal claims of all human beings. But Hume, as I observed above, admitted that gross inequalities of organized coercive power between different groups invalidated the third circumstance of justice. If, therefore, the people in the original position believe that the circumstances of justice obtain in their own society they are believing something that may not be the case.

I have a suggestion that I believe conforms with Rawls's intentions. Hume's doctrine of the circumstances of justice took the form, as we saw, of a theory to the effect that the three circumstances of justice constitute necessary conditions for the adoption and maintenance of rules of justice: if any of these conditions fails to hold, rules of justice are "perfectly useless" and therefore fail to come into being or (if they exist already) fall into disuse. But there is a weaker version of the doctrine, to which I alluded earlier, namely that the circumstances of justice are sufficient conditions for rules of justice to be created and sustained. It seems to me that Rawls's operations make sense if we interpret him as wishing to endorse this view of the role of the circumstances of justice.

What Rawls is then saying (in his Humean persona) is that we can find out what the principles of justice are by seeing what regulatory principles would be agreed on where the circumstances of justice obtain. That is why the people in the original position are to believe that the circumstances of justice obtain in their society: unless they believe that, their evidence is no help. The theory is after all one of "justice as fairness," and an elementary condition of fairness is that the parties should be equally matched.

But because the circumstances of justice are, on this view, a sufficient condition but not a necessary one, we do not now have to follow Hume in saying that the concept of justice has no application where the circumstances of justice fail to hold. For we can now say that a society of structured group oppression like contemporary South Africa is unjust because it embodies relationships that the disadvantaged members of the society would not have agreed upon if they were in a position of approximately equal power.

From here on, we can construct out of Rawls a coherent theory of justice as rational co-operation that adheres closely to its Humean antecedents. The vital common element is that Rawls accepts Hume's central claim that there are no independent or external criteria of justice. The principles of justice simply *are* the principles for regulating distribution that will be chosen by people in a society where the circumstances of justice hold. In other words, justice is, for Rawls as it was for Hume, a convention. Its basis is, for both men, an agreement founded in the mutual advantage of the parties.

This explains a feature of Rawls's theory that has led some to deny that he has put forward a theory of justice at all, namely the fact that his principle for the distribution of material benefits, the difference principle, is forward-looking rather than backward-looking. Thus, David Miller says that the two parts of Rawls's second principle of justice "are not distributive principles in the same strong sense as the ordinary principles of justice. They do not specify some property of the individual which will determine what his share of society's goods shall be. . . . [I]n this respect the contractual theory of justice resembles utilitarianism."[67] Rawls's theory is forward-looking, like utilitarianism, in that "the size of incomes and other rewards is not to be fixed in such a way that they fit the past, but in such a way that the greatest benefit is produced in the future for the least advantaged members of society. And although Rawls's theory is not strictly aggregative, because it does not allow the few to be deprived to obtain a greater balance of happiness for the many, it is not distributive either since it contains no principles directly prescribing an allocation of benefits and burdens to persons."[68]

I believe therefore that Hayek is right in recognizing a kindred spirit in Rawls—at any rate in the Rawls of justice as rational co-operation. Hayek writes that he has "no basic quarrel with an author who. . . acknowledges that the task of selecting specific systems or distributions of desired things as just must be 'abandoned as mistaken in principle' . . . ." He claims as "what I have been trying to argue" Rawls's statement that "the principles of justice define the crucial constraints which institutions and joint activities must satisfy if persons engaging in them are to have no complaints against them. If these constraints are satisfied, the resulting distribution, whatever it is, may be accepted as just (or at least not unjust)."[69]

The reason why Hayek embraces Rawls is precisely their common endorsement of Hume's rejection of independent and external criteria of justice. Where they differ is that Rawls sets tougher "constraints" than does Hayek. But the difference parallels a change in Hume's own thinking. Hayek is close to the Hume of the *Treatise*, arguing in effect that the important thing is that the rules should be fixed. In the *Enquiry*, Hume is prepared to argue for some rules against others in terms of their generally beneficial tendency, and his discussion of the reasons for not imposing equality, with their emphasis on the advantage to all of providing incentives, strongly foreshadows Rawls's own work.[70]

In order to make the parallel between Hume and Rawls quite clear, we need to take account of the fact that Hume talks about rules of justice and Rawls of principles of justice. We can restate their theories so that each has a view of the principles of justice and the rules of justice. The principles of justice are the criteria on the basis of which institutions are to be judged. Thus, for Rawls, one of the principles of justice is that economic institutions should be arranged so that the position of the worst-off representative man will be as good as possible. For Hume, the principle of justice is that the outcome of whatever institutions exist is to be mutually advantageous to the parties. (Obviously, this is fairly vague and is not inconsistent with Rawl's formulation). The rules of justice are, for Hume, the rules a society has for the acquisition, inheritance and transfer of property. The details may differ because at the margins different rules may equally satisfy the requirement of the principle of justice that the working out of the rules should be mutually advantageous.

Rawls speaks of institutions that are designed to satisfy the principles of justice. These play an equivalent role to the rules of justice in Hume. Rawls says that "to apply the notion of pure procedural justice to distributive shares it is necessary to set up and administer impartially a just system of institutions. . . . Suppose that law and government act effectively to keep markets competitive, resources fully employed, property and wealth (especially if private ownership of the means of production is allowed) widely distributed by the appropriate forms of taxation, or whatever, and to guarantee a reasonable social minimum. Assume also that there is fair equality of opportunity underwritten by education for all; and that the other equal liberties are secured. Then it would appear that the resulting distribution of income and pattern of expectations will tend to satisfy the difference principle."[71] Needless to say, this calls for a more active interventionist state than Hume (or Hayek) envisages. But the underlying idea is the same: once institutions satisfying the principle of justice have been set up nobody can properly use the concept of justice to criticize the particular pattern of distribution that arises.

Hume and Rawls both maintain that their theories can explain actual beliefs about justice. But they differ in precisely what they offer to explain. Hume claims that he can explain the rules (if not in detail then in broad outline) that determine property rights in societies where the circumstances of justice obtain. His view about the principles of justice is, I think, that most people would acknowledge them if pressed (that is, they would say that the rules must conduce to mutual advantage) but do not normally reflect on them. Rawls, however, does not maintain that existing institutions are just. Following the passage quoted above, he says: "As these institutions presently exist they are riddled with grave injustices."[72] What he does maintain is that the principles of justice coincide, at the most salient points anyway, with "our" considered judgements. Who are "we"? Rawls does not say, but, if there is anything in the analysis presented here, Rawls ought to claim, in his Humean persona, that the principles of justice (or something like them) will be found in societies where the circumstances of justice obtain but not in others. Thus, we have no reason to expect settlers who are in the process of killing the native population, slave owning families or whites in South Africa to acknowledge the principles of justice, except among themselves.

## *XI*

In laying out the Humean structure within Rawls's theory of justice I deliberately played down the original position and the constraints on knowledge that are built into it. I hope to have suggested that there is a self-contained conception of justice without it. The significance of the veil of ignorance is not so much to ensure agreement as to rule out bases of agreement that would take account of particular advantages that people bring to the bargain. It therefore forms part of the theory of justice as universal hypothetical assent.

There is no need to say as much about this construction since it is discussed explicitly by Rawls himself. Moreover, the great bulk of the critical literature on Rawls analyses this aspect of the theory in a more or less pure form. However, it is worth comparing the two theories.

The essence of the Humean theory is that the principles of justice are constituted by agreement among approximately equal parties: the principles of justice are the terms on which rational people would consent to engage in co-operative activites. The essence of the Kantian theory is that the principles of justice are constituted by a hypothetical choice made by an individual under conditions that ensure that his choice has universal validity: the principles of justice and the choices made by a noumenal self, that is to say an individual stripped of all particular attributes. "My suggestion is that we think of the original position as the point of view from which noumenal selves see the world. . . . Thus men exhibit their freedom, their independence from the contingencies of nature and society, by acting in ways they would acknowledge in the original position."[73]

This dichotomy–agreement versus hypothetical choice–explains what has puzzled many of Rawls's readers. Why does Rawls insist that the principles of justice must be agreed on by all the members of a society when the presentation of the choice problem in the original position makes it plain that only one agent is required, since all the people are interchangable? The answer becomes apparent when we see that Rawls is running two distinct theories.

The circumstances of justice play a crucial role, as we have seen, in the theory of justice as rational co-operation, since they provide for agreement to be reached under conditions that do not permit some to impose their "lawless will" (in Hume's words) on the others and get away with it. But the circumstances of justice seem to be irrelevant to the theory of justice as universal hypothetical assent. If I am to choose principles that I wish to see adopted generally, and do not know what my own actual circumstances are, surely I do not need to know whether the circumstances of justice obtain or not in my society, since

I will in any case want to protect myself against potential oppression by choosing appropriate principles. It is of course true that, if I knew the world was a place where scarcity was unknown, I would not bother to choose principles of justice since there would be no room for raising distributive questions. But this is, as I pointed out above, an implication of justice as a distributive concept, and has no special connection with the doctrine of the circumstances of justice in its Humean (necessary condition) or Rawlsian (sufficient condition) form.

I may, of course, be less sanguine about the chances for the implementation of the principles of justice that I choose in a society where the third of the circumstances of justice is violated. For in such a society one motive for respecting the principles of justice—their function as "articles of peace" offering a promise of stability to all—is no longer operative. The question then becomes: to what extent are the appeals of a universalistic morality capable of motivating people to act in ways that are strongly contrary to their interests?

It cannot be said that Rawls found the question in very prosperous shape when he came to it. Kant said that the possibility of acting on universal maxims that run contrary to our natural sentiments is a metaphysical necessity but an empirical mystery. Bentham made it even more mysterious by simply asserting simultaneously universalistic utilitarianism and the doctrine that every man pursues his own happiness. The foremost contemporary exponent of universalistic morality, R. M. Hare, seems to take the view that we can act on universalistic premises if we decide to, which encapsulates the mystery in a tautology.

Against this unpromising background, Rawls's efforts command respect. The key section is the penultimate one in the book (86) and to some extent the preceding one (85). It is, incidentally, an indication of the difficulty of coming to terms with *A Theory of Justice* that such a crucial part of the argument should come almost at the end of the book when the reader is already exhausted. On the whole Rawls's premonitions, expressed in the Preface, of "a danger" that "without consideration of the argument of the last part, the theory of justice will be misunderstood"—and he here cites seven sections, including 85 and 86, of special significance—have been borne out by the book's reception.[74]

I cannot hope here to take up Rawls's subtle and ramified discussion in any detail. The crucial point is that "we should not rely on the doctrine of the pure conscientious act," nor should we assume that the desire to act justly is "a final desire like that to avoid pain, misery, or apathy, or the desire to fulfill the inclusive interest."[75] Given these constraints, it is hardly surprising that Rawls's answer is highly reminiscent (except for its higher moral tone) of Hume's reply to the "sensible knave." Admittedly, Rawls invokes one motive that would have been unintelligible to Hume, namely that "acting justly is something we want to do as free and equal rational beings."[76] The other three are, however, quite Humean. First, there is the "psychological cost" of practicing systematic deception, professing principles to which one does not adhere. Second, there is the fact that over a wide range the requirements of justice overlap with what our natural sentiments would call for. "But in a well-ordered society these bonds extend rather widely, and include ties to institutional forms. . . ."[77] And thirdly, "participating in the life of a well-ordered society is a great good. . . yet to share fully in this life we must acknowledge the principles of its regulative conception, and this means that we must affirm our sentiment of justice."[78]

The trouble is that each of these three seems to work only in relation to justice as rational co-operation. Professing one thing and doing another is uncomfortable if it has to be carried out among acquaintances, but is much easier when it is a matter of the people in one country admitting that they really ought to do something about world poverty but not doing anything. The confluence of justice and natural sentiments works only when we restrict the scope of justice to a society, and merely points up the strains imposed on the sense of justice by universalistic requirements. The third point quite explicitly confines itself to the level of a society.

Moreover, Rawls is agnostic about the strength of all these motives even in the favorable setting of a society. "Whether or not it is for a person's good that he have a regulative sense of justice depends upon what justice requires of him."[79] Utilitarianism is too demanding: "a rational person, in framing his plan, would hesitate to give precedence to so stringent a principle."[80] But surely the theory of justice as universal hypothetical assent could quite plausibly give rise to demands that would be as severe as those of the rival universalistic theory of utilitarianism. The demands might well indeed be more in conflict with self-interest. For example, worldwide redistribution to satisfy the difference principle would seem to leave less room for maneuver to the rich countries than would redistribution to satisfy the utilitarian criterion.

## *XII*

Justice as rational co-operation and justice as hypothetical universal assent diverge as we leave the self-contained society of contemporaries to which Rawls confines the application of his theory of justice. The strains become manifest when we look at the problem of justice between contemporaries in different societies, justice between different generations of members of the same society, and (compounding the two) justice between different generations on a worldwide basis.

Rawls's commitment to the theory of rational co-operation conditions the way in which he tackles the first and second (he does not consider the third) and explains an aspect of *A Theory of Justice* that those who approach it as if it were a pure theory of universal hypothetical assent are bound to find puzzling.

Rawls's discussion of international relations is perfunctory and occurs only as a by-product of his discussion of civil disobedience and conscientious refusal, in other words in the context of a domestic issue. Rawls suggests that we should ask what representatives of different states would agree on behind a veil of ignorance and endorses, on their behalf, the standard principles of traditional international law.[81]

From the standpoint of justice as rational co-operation this is not unreasonable. The circumstances of justice do not hold between states, which are much too unequal in organized power to be covered by the condition of approximate equality, as H. L. A. Hart emphasizes in his analysis of the circumstances of justice in *The Concept of Law*. Justice between unequals, from the standpoint of rational co-operation, amounts only to those rules that are of mutual advantage to states, and the standard usages of traditional international law (e.g. the rules about treatment of foreign ambassadors) are precisely of this form. Some redistribution can arise from the mutual advantage of the parties: an example would be one country helping an ally because it wants to keep it strong or wants to ensure that it does not fall under the influence of some other country. But redistribution not motivated in this way falls outside justice as rational co-operation.

From the standpoint of justice as universal hypothetical assent, however, it would seem bizarre to set such limits to international redistribution. The natural way to develop the theory is to ask what principles for worldwide distribution someone would choose who did not know what country he belonged to. And whatever in detail we may suppose somebody would choose in such a situation, it seems vastly implausible that any rational person would fail to call for very much more redistribution from rich countries to poor ones than would be in accordance with the mutual advantage of all states involved.[82]

As far as relations between members of the same society at different times are concerned, Rawls adopts the line that the people in the original position are, and know that they are, contemporaries. This can again be understood once we allow for Rawls's commitment to the theory of justice as rational co-operation, since there obviously cannot be relations of mutual benefit between people who are not alive at the same time. Those alive at a given time can benefit or harm their successors but the relation is not mutual.

The problem then, of course, arises for Rawls how there can be any relations of justice between generations. And the answer that he comes up with is in essentials very similar to that of Hubin, even though (as we saw above) Hubin sets himself up as being in opposition to Rawls. Both of them introduce the notion that we have sentiments of attachment to the interests of our immediate successors (perhaps to the extent of the third generation) and claim to derive relations of justice from that. Hubin, as we saw, claims (or should claim if his argument is to make any sense) that the welfare of our descendants is a public good and we should therefore be unjust in refusing to contribute our fair share to it. Rawls's argument is simpler. He says that, since the people in the original position know that they care for their immediate successors' interests, they will choose to have them respected, and what they choose in the original position constitutes justice. I have criticized this part of Rawls's theory elsewhere,[83] and I shall not repeat myself here. But it is, I hope, fairly clear that laundering a sentiment through the original position does not make it into a basis for asserting a relation of justice. The larger point, however, is that for both Rawls and Hubin the limits of caring are the limits of justice, so there is no injustice where there are no sentiments; and it is presumably not unjust to lack sentiments of concern for future generations.

The approach from the direction of justice as universal hypothetical assent is, as might be expected, entirely different. We would have the person who is to choose the principles not know what generation he belongs to. He will then have to try to do the best for himself, allowing for the fact that if he comes early in history he will regret having chosen principles that demand too much saving; but if he comes late in history he will regret not having been rougher on resource depletion and damage to the environment. And so on.

## *XIII*

The preceding four sections of this paper have been devoted to the question whether Rawls has somehow succeeded in incorporating the doctrine of the circumstances of justice into a universalistic theory of justice, as one might gather from the form of *A Theory of Justice*. The answer is a negative one. The appearance is misleading, I have argued; what Rawls really offers in *A Theory of Justice* is two incompatible theories of justice. The incompatibility is muted in the book by Rawls's concentration on the case of justice between contemporaries in a single society. It becomes clear when we move outside those constraints.

Where does this leave justice between generations? The major effort of this paper has been to refute Hume's theory of the circumstances of justice. If I am correct, there is no reason to accept that the circumstances of justice set out by Hume are a necessary condition for the application of the concepts of justice or injustice to social arrangements. I regard the Humean doctrine as worthy of careful refutation because it seems well on the way to becoming an unquestioned axiom. Assuming that it has been cleared out of the way successfully, we can allow that the circumstances of justice do not obtain between members of different generations at the same time we deny that that eliminates intergenerational justice or requires it to be dragged in through the back door in the way that Hubin and Rawls attempt to do it.

Although the vogue for Hume's doctrine of the circumstances of justice stems from Rawls's endorsement of it, I argued that Rawls cannot in fact, consistently with the integrity of his theory, accept that the Humean circumstances of justice are necessary conditions for justice. First, that would commit him to saying that a society of "natural" utilitarians would not be unjust. Although one of his objections to utilitarianism—that it is too difficult to gain compliance with its requirements—would not have any weight in such a society, he also wants to say that it is *unjust* for some people to make sacrifices purely on the basis of a net overall gain, and that objection would presumably still stand. Secondly, he would have to say that a society in which the condition of approximate equality of power did not hold could not be described as unjust, whatever its arrangements were. I take it that he would not wish to accept that conclusion.

I therefore suggested that we should understand Rawls's endorsement of the doctrine of the circumstances of justice in a different way: as the idea that the circumstances of justice are a sufficient condition for the application of rules of justice. We could then take the rules of justice that would be agreed upon where the circumstances of justice do hold and apply them to societies where the circumstances of justice do not hold, such as the society of "natural" utilitarians or organized unequals.

It might be asked whether we could not extend this line of analysis to relations between countries or relations between generations. Might we not ask what principles would be agreed on if countries *were* approximately equal in power or if later generations had the same ability to help or harm later ones? The idea is not wholly crazy and perhaps even merits the description "suggestive." But I am bound to say it seems to me a very cumbersome way of getting at the basic moral notion of "How would you like it if others behaved the way you're proposing to behave?" Surely if that is what we are after we can get there more directly by moving to the universal hypothetical assent theory of justice and avoid having to imagine what might be agreed on in a wildly counterfactual world.

There is, I have argued, a self-contained theory of justice as universal hypothetical assent in A Theory of Justice, and, if we dump Hume's theory that the circumstances of justice are necessary conditions for the application of justice, we are free to use it as a guide to justice between generations. But at this point we have to ask: why should we equate the product of universal hypothetical assent with *justice*?

We can, of course, also ask why we should equate with justice the terms on which co-operation would be agreed to. That is a good question, too. But I think the lines of an answer are tolerably clear. Rawls would say, as I understand him, that what is agreed to under fair conditions is just. That is by no means a self-evident proposition, but it is not beside the point. It should be noticed here that, although Hume and Rawls would both agree that "what is agreed on in the circumstances of justice constitutes justice" they would diverge on the interpretation of that slogan. Hume would take it to mean that outside the circumstances of justice there is no *need* for justice, whereas Rawls (on my understanding of his theory) would say that outside the circumstances of justice you don't *get* justice. Ultimately, Hume founds justice on mutual advantage while Rawls founds it on fairness.

The trouble is that this rationale for the derivation of principles of justice from the original position applies only when the theory is construed on the rational co-operation model. In the theory of justice as universal hypothetical assent, the argument for the results of such assent constituting justice has to come from the Kantian line of development. The argument must be to the effect that there are "constraints of right" that specify the range of the morally arbitrary contingent facts about people's attitudes, preferences, social positions, etc., that have to be excluded from any judgement of justice.

Having devoted the bulk of this long paper to the relatively neglected Humean theory I can hardly at this stage launch into a full-scale discussion of the Kantian one. I shall therefore simply say that it seems, to me anyway, that the realm of the "morally arbitrary" that is needed to make the Kantian argument go through is too wide. The point is made succinctly in this criticism: "The prerequisites of justice are that in an established society, men press and acknowledge claims, evaluate and compare one another, feel resentment for injury, gratitude for benefit, and compassion for the suffering of others. These activities and emotions are the necessary underpinning for principles of justice such as desert and need. Rawls's isolated men, concerned only with advancing their own interests, have no possible reason to estimate one another's deserts, and so no reason to adopt a desert-based conception of justice; the same is true of the criterion of need. This explains why Rawls's principles necessarily diverge from ordinary ideas of justice and why he is drawn inexorably toward utilitarianism. For utilitarianism, which has no direct concern with the relative levels of well-being enjoyed by different individuals, is par excellence the moral theory of an impartial spectator placed *outside* society (having no claims or emotional responses of his own) and Rawls, by the use of the veil of ignorance and his other assumptions, effectively puts his hypothetical choosers into the position of impartial spectators."[84]

## *XIV*

There is a form of paper in which, after everybody else's theories have been knocked down, the author's own theory comes in at the end on a white charger and saves the day. The present paper is not constructed on that plan. The difficulties in both of Rawls's theories seem to me to be real, but I do not have any fully worked out alternative to offer.

However, to avoid ending on an entirely negative note, let me say two things. First, it seems to me undeniable that a lot of what is counted as justice (everywhere that we have records of) fits somehow into the general framework of justice as rational co-operation. Any theory that tries to deny that is, in my opinion, doomed from the start.

Second, justice as rational co-operation cannot be the whole of justice for the simple reason that it cannot itself define a just starting point from which rational co-operation takes place. If Crusoe owns (controls access to) the banana trees and Friday owns (controls access to) the coconut trees, justice as rational co-operation can talk about fair exchange between Crusoe's bananas and Friday's coconuts. Or if Crusoe owns (controls access to) all the trees and Friday climbs them to get the fruit, justice as rational co-operation can talk about a fair return for Friday's labor. But justice as rational co-operation is silent when we ask whether it is just that the initial possessions should be what they are.

We could, of course, say that the only form of justice is indeed justice as rational co-operation and that justice therefore comes into operation only when initial holdings (e.g. control over natural resourses) are defined. But this would be strange, to say the least. The question how the initial holdings should be allocated is a central distributive question. The way it is settled (e.g. which country gains control of a massive oil-field by annexing the territory of the weak state under whose land the oil field lies) may be far more significant than the way in which gains from co-operation are divided. Surely the key words for assessing distributions–just and fair–must have a role to play here.

I believe that the positions from which people enter into co-operative arrangements can be subjected to appraisal in terms of justice, and I want to suggest that the relevant concept of justice is justice as equal opportunity. It seems to me that the concept of equality of opportunity is one that is clearly not derivable from that of justice as rational co-operation, since it comes in prior to the stage at which co-operation takes place. Yet its appeal as an independent criterion of justice seems undeniable.

Evidence for the power of its appeal is provided by Rawls's acknowledging it in a way that does not fit in with the rest of his theory. Rawls, as is well known, divides the second principle of justice into two parts and gives the first part, which specifies equal opportunity, lexical priority over the second part, which is the difference principle. Yet in terms of Rawls's own theory, equal opportunity should be a rule of justice, along with income tax and other palliative arrangements, forming part of the complex of institutions that together produce results in accordance with the difference principle. That he pulls it out and gives it a special place is, I think, most reasonably explained as an illustration of the way in which Rawls's instincts are at times better than his theory.

I want to be the first to admit that the concept of equal opportunity is replete with difficulties. Equality of opportunity at one point in time is equal opportunity to become unequal at a later point, but that inequality may itself constitute an unequal opportunity. And so on. Nevertheless, it seems to me that, like all other concepts of political morality, it has clear cases (especially negatively—we can easily enough identify some cases in which it is violated) as well as ones that cause trouble.

In the case of justice between generations, equality of opportunity has to be taken in sufficiently broad terms. What justice requires, I suggest, is that the overall range of opportunities open to successor generations should not be narrowed. If some openings are closed off by depletion or other irreversible damage to the environment, others should be created (if necessary at the cost of some sacrifice) to make up.

This conception of intergeneration justice has several attractive features. First, it is a global extension of a principle that families with possessions to pass on have traditionally espoused: "Keep the capital intact!" Second, it underwrites the asymmetry that many people (including myself) feel between making successors better off, which is a nice thing to do but not required by justice, and not making them worse off, which *is* required by justice. And third, it does not make the demands of justice to our successors depend on our knowing their tastes–still less on our approving of them.[85]

## *Notes*

1. For an elaboration of these rather cryptic remarks, see my "Rawls on Average and Total Utility: A Comment," *Philosophical Studies* 31 (1977) 317-325.

2. John Rawls, *A Theory of Justice* (Cambridge, Mass.: Harvard University Press, 1971) p. 3.

3. Rawls, *A Theory of Justice*, p. 512.

4. Erik P. Eckholm, *The Picture of Health: Environmental Sources of Disease* (sponsored by the UN Environment Program and the Worldwatch Institute, New York: Norton, 1977), report in *Chicago Sun-Times*, Nov. 20, 1977, p. 24.

5. For a review of these theories and comments on their resistance to verification, see the papers by Karl Deutsch, Andrew Mack and James Caporaso, in Steven J. Rosen and James R. Kurth (eds.), *Testing Theories of Economic Imperialism* (Lexington, Mass.: D. C. Heath and Co., 1974).

6. Section 22 of *A Theory of Justice* is entitled "The Circumstances of Justice."

7. Rawls, *A Theory of Justice*, pp. 127-128.

8. *An Enquiry Concerning the Principles of Morals*, Appendix III. H. D. Aiken (ed.), *Hume's Moral and Political Philosophy* (New York: Hafner, 1949), p. 277. I shall give page numbers to the *Enquiry* and to the *Treatise of Human Nature* to this edition.

9. *Enquiry*, p. 277.

10. *Enquiry*, pp. 278-279.

11. *Treatise*, p. 91.

12. *Treatise*, p. 93

13. F. A. Hayek, *Law, Legislation and Liberty*, Vol. 2: *The Mirage of Social Justice* (Chicago: University of Chicago Press, 1976).

14. *Enquiry*, pp. 193-194.

15. *Enquiry*, pp. 188-189.

16. *A Theory of Justice*, pp. 126-127.

17. *Enquiry*, p. 185. The South Sea Islands before the contact with whites probably came nearest to the Humean "golden age" conditions with their combination of limited wants and relatively easy means of satisfying them: "Traditionally, when a Micronesian was hungry he caught a fish in the reef or picked some fruit." Associated with this was the idea that "It's Micronesian to share, not sell." (Fox Butterfield, "The Improbable Welfare State," *New York Times Magazine*, Nov. 27, 1977, 55-74, p. 64.) Even if there is an element of mythology here, it is surely significant that sharing and ease of acquisition are thought of as going together.

18. David Miller, *Social Justice* (Oxford: Clarendon Press, 1976), p. 164.

19. *Enquiry*, pp. 187-188.

20. Miller, *Social Justice*, pp. 163-164.

21. *Enquiry*, p. 188, my italics.

22. See Jay Katz and Alexander Morgan Kapron, *Catastrophic Diseases: Who Decides What? A Psychosocial and Legal Analysis of the Problems Posed by Hemodialysis and Organ Transplantation* (New York: Russell Sage Foundation, 1975) for a general discussion.

23. Renée C. Fox and Judith P. Swazey, *The Courage to Fail: A Social View of Organ Transplants and Dialysis* (Chicago: University of Chicago Press, 1974), p. 246.

24. Fox and Swazey, *The Courage to Fail*, p. 247, quoting D. Sanders and J. Dukeminier "Medical Advance and Legal Lag: Hemodialysis and Kidney Transplantation," *UCLA Law Review* 15 (1968) 357-413, pp. 377-378, my italics.

25. *Enquiry*, p. 187.

26. Interview with Belding Scribner, in Fox and Swazey, *The Courage to Fail*, p. 328.

27. Cf. Miller, *Social Justice*, p. 124.

28. Cf. Onora Nell, "Lifeboat Earth," *Philosophy and Public Affairs* 4 (1975) 271-292, p. 278.

29. D. Clayton Hubin, "Justice and Future Generations," *Philosophy and Public Affairs* 6 (1976) 70-83, p. 73.

30. *Treatise*, p. 65.

31. *Treatise*, p. 57.

32. *Treatise*, p. 58.

33. *Treatise*, p. 61.

34. *Treatise*, p. 62.

35. In the formulation (which pays acknowledgement to Hobbes and Hume) of H. L. A. Hart, in Chapter 9 of *The Concept of Law*

(Oxford: Clarendon Press, 1961), the intermediate position of human nature is expressed by saying that men are neither angels nor devils. "With angels, never tempted to harm others, rules requiring forbearances would not be necessary. With devils prepared to destroy, reckless of the cost to themselves, they would be impossible" (p. 192). But that men are not "devils," in this sense, does not entail, as Hart implies, that "human altruism is limited in range and intermittent" (p. 192). All it entails is that, in their conception of self-interest, human beings place personal security at the cost of constraints on the ability to attack others above the possibility of attacking others at the cost of a constant danger of being attacked by them. For a sophisticated game-theoretical analysis of the theories of Hobbes and Hume, see Chapter 6 of Michael Taylor, *Anarchy and Co-operation* (London: Wiley, 1976).

36. *Aubrey's Brief Lives*, ed. Oliver Lawson Dick (Ann Arbor: The University of Michigan Press, 1962), pp. ciii-civ.

37. *Enquiry*, p. 260.

38. *Enquiry*, p. 261.

39. *Enquiry*, p. 261.

40. *Enquiry*, p. 261.

41. *Treatise*, p. 65, italics in original.

42. *Enquiry*, p. 186.

43. Enquiry, p. 186. There is a slight complication here. When Hume says, just below this passage, that "my heart" "Shares all [my neighbour's] joys and sorrows with the same force and vivacity as if originally my own," this might make it appear that Hume is positing some kind of psychological mechanism ("sympathy") which literally makes my happiness a function of the sum total of the happiness of the human race. But I take it Hume does not really intend to mean that each person's happiness moves up and down to an equal extent with every change in the happiness of every human being (including himself). In Appendix II of the *Enquiry* he decries attempts to reduce all wants to the more or less subtle pursuit of personal gratification and says that "the hypothesis of disinterested benevolence"–that "from the original frame of our temper, we may feel a desire of another's happiness or good" (*Enquiry*, pp. 274-275) has the merit of simplcity and intrinsic plausibility. I shall therefore take it that in the world imagined by Hume, everybody *desires* and *pursues* the general interest, without necessarily deriving personal psychic benefit from anything except what he himself experiences.

44. See Amartya Sen, *On Economic Inequality* (Oxford: Clarendon Press, 1973), pp. 16-18 for an elegant diagrammatic exposition.

45. "Saki" (H. H. Munro) and Patricia Highsmith have both fictiously depicted such retribution with relish.

46. *Enquiry*, pp. 190-191.

47. *Enquiry*, p. 191.

48. See Dee Brown, *Bury My Heart at Wounded Knee: An Indian History of the American West* (London: Barrie and Jenkins, 1971), *passim*.

49. Brown, *Bury My Heart at Wounded Knee*, p. 187.

50. Hart, *The Concept of Law*, pp. 190-191.

51. Hart, *The Concept of Law*, p. 196.

52. Hart, *The Concept of Law*, pp. 154-157.

53. *Enquiry*, p. 261.

54. *Treatise*, pp. 49-50.

55. See Morris Ginsberg, *On the Diversity of Morals* (London: Mercury Books, 1962), pp. 112-115 for a discussion of the development of ideas of justice that stresses the increasing tendency towards universality.

56. Hubin, "Justice and Future Generations," pp. 79-80.

57. Hubin, "Justice and Future Generations," p. 71, italics in original.

58. Hubin, "Justice and Future Generations," p. 81.

59. Hubin, "Justice and Future Generations," p. 82.

60. Hubin, "Justice and Future Generations," pp. 81-82.

61. Hubin, "Justice and Future Generations," p. 83.

62. Thus, the paper "Some Reasons for the Maximin Criterion," *American Economic Review* 64 (1974), pp. 141-161, plays down the derivation of the difference principle from the constrained pursuit of self-interest and asks us to look at the principle as a reasonable one that accords with our ethical intuitions; and the article "A Kantian Conception of Equality," *Cambridge Review* (February 1975), pp. 94-99, scarcely mentions the derivation of the principles of justice from the original position at all but emphasizes their consistency with fundamental requirements of right.

63. This argument is elaborated in opposition to Robert Paul Wolff's *Understanding Rawls* (Princeton: Princeton University Press, 1977) in a Critical Notice forthcoming in the *Canadian Journal of Philosophy*.

64. Peter Danielson, "Theories, Intuitions and the Problem of World-Wide Distributive Justice," in "Review Symposium on Rawls," *Philosophy of the Social Sciences* 3 (1973), pp. 331-340, p. 336.

65. Rawls, *A Theory of Justice*, p. 8.

66. Rawls, *A Theory of Justice*, p. 4.
67. Miller, *Social Justice*, pp. 42-43.
68. Miller, *Social Justice*, p. 50.
69. Hayek, *Law, Legislation and Liberty*, Vol. 2, p. 100; quotation from John Rawls, "Constitutional Liberty and the Concept of Justice," in J. W. Chapman and J. Roland Pennock (eds.), *Nomos IV: Justice* (New York: Atherton, 1963), p. 102. Hayek says (note 44, p. 183) that he is "not aware" of a similar statement in *A Theory of Justice*; in fact the relevant passage is on pp. 86-88—the discussion of "pure procedural justice" to which I shall refer below in the text.
70. The link can be seen especially closely in Rawls's paper, "Distributive Justice," in P. Laslett and W. G. Runciman (eds.), *Philosophy, Politics and Society*, 3rd Series (Oxford: Basil Blackwell, 1967), pp. 58-82.
71. Rawls, *A Theory of Justice*, pp. 86-87.
72. Rawls, *A Theory of Justice*, p. 87.
73. Rawls, *A Theory of Justice*, pp. 255-256. For a defence of the coherence of Rawls's "Kantian interpretation" against Robert Paul Wolff's attack in *Understanding Rawls*, see my "Critical Notice."
74. Rawls, *A Theory of Justice*, p. ix.
75. Rawls, *A Theory of Justice*, p. 569.
76. Rawls, *A Theory of Justice*, p. 572.
77. Rawls, *A Theory of Justice*, pp. 570-571.
78. Rawls, *A Theory of Justice*, p. 571.
79. Rawls, *A Theory of Justice*, p. 572.
80. Rawls, *A Theory of Justice*, p. 573.
81. Rawls, *A Theory of Justice*, pp. 377-379.
82. See my *The Liberal Theory of Justice* (Oxford: Clarendon Press, 1973), pp. 128-133.
83. "Justice between Generations," in P. M. S. Hacker and J. Raz (eds.), *Law, Morality and Society: Essays in Honour of H. L. A. Hart* (Oxford: Clarendon Press, 1977), pp. 268-284.
84. Russell Keat and David Miller, "Understanding Justice," *Political Theory* 2 (1974), pp. 3-31, p. 28.
85. Compare M. P. Golding in "Obligations to Future Generations," *Monist* 56 (1972), pp. 85-99.

# Contributors

*William Anglin* received his B.A. in philosophy from McGill University and his M.A. in philosophy from the University of British Columbia. He has published in ethics and his interests include logic and epistemology as well.

*Brian Barry* is Professor of Political Science at the University of Chicago. His books include: *Political Argument* (1965), *Sociologists, Economists and Democracy* (1970), *The Liberal Theory of Justice* (1973); and he has edited *Power and Political Theory* (1976).

*Jonathan Bennett* is, currently, Professor of Philosophy at the University of British Columbia; from September 1979, he will be at Syracuse University. He has published widely in the history of early modern philosophy, philosophy of language, and ethics. His more recent books are *Linguistic Behavior* (1976) and *Consequences* (forthcoming).

*Gregory S. Kavka* is Assistant Professor of Philosophy at UCLA. His principal interests are in ethics and political philosophy. He is currently working on the morality of nuclear deterrence and has published on this and other issues in ethics.

*Jan Narveson* is Professor of Philosophy at the University of Waterloo. He has published *Morality and Utility* (1967) and numerous articles, principally in ethics and social and political philosophy.

*Thomas Schwartz* is Associate Professor of Government at the University of Texas in Austin. He is primarily interested in social choice theory and related issues in economics and political science; also, in social and political philosophy and logic. He has published *Freedom and Authority* (1973) and is preparing a book on the logic of collective choice.

*Robert B. Scott, Jr.*, holds a joint appointment in philosophy and the Freshman Honors Program at the University of Delaware. His main interests are in ethics, epistemology, and the philosophy of mind. The paper included in this volume was funded by a grant from the National Science Foundations's Program in Ethics and Values in Science and Technology.

*R. I. Sikora* is Associate Professor of Philosophy at the University of British Columbia. His main interests are in ethics, philosophy of mind, and epistemology. His articles have appeared in *Analysis*, *American Philosophical Quarterly*, *Mind*, and *Philosophy*.

*Leonard Wayne Sumner* is Associate Professor of Philosophy at the University of Toronto. He is preparing a book tentatively titled *Abortion and Moral Theory* and has written widely in ethics.

*Mary Warren* is Assistant Professor of Philosophy at San Francisco State University and teaches also at California State College at Sonoma. Her article, "On the Moral and Legal Status of Abortion," has been widely reprinted.

*Mary B. Williams* holds a joint appointment in philosophy and the Freshman Honors Program at the University of Delaware. She originally worked in mathematical biology, particularly with axiomatizing Darwinian theory; currently, she works in the philosophy of biology and bioethics. She has published in mathematical biology, theoretical biology, philosophy of biology, and bioethics. The paper included in this volume was funded by a grant from the National Science Foundation's Program in Ethics and Values in Science and Technology.